LEARNING MENTORS IN SCHOOLS
POLICY AND PRACTICE

THE LUTHER
HARTWELL HODGES
SERIES ON BUSINESS,
SOCIETY, AND
THE STATE

WILLIAM H. BECKER,
EDITOR

The University of

North Carolina Press

Chapel Hill & London

THE

RISE OF A

GOVERNMENT

ENTREPRENEUR

MR. KAISER

GOES TO

WASHINGTON

STEPHEN B. ADAMS

Library of Congress Cataloging-
in-Publication Data
Adams, Stephen B., 1955–
Mr. Kaiser goes to Washington: the
rise of a government entrepreneur /
Stephen B. Adams.
p.   cm. —
(Business, society, and the state)
Includes bibliographical references
and index.
ISBN 0-8078-2358-9 (cloth: alk.
paper)
1. Kaiser, Henry J., 1882–
2. Businessmen—United States—
Biography. 3. Industrial policy—
United States—History. I. Title. II.
Series: Business, society & the state.
HC102.5.K3A43   1997
338.092—dc21
[B]   96-53391
                                    CIP

01 00 99 98 97   5 4 3 2 1

TO MADELEINE

CONTENTS

A section of illustrations follows p. 86.

ACKNOWLEDGMENTS

The assistance I received from so many generous people provides evidence that academics are no more self-made than entrepreneurs are. This book began as a doctoral dissertation at the Johns Hopkins University. My mentor, Louis Galambos, has written extensively about America's twentieth-century political economy, about corporate and presidential leadership, and about how things get done in public and private organizations. In so doing, he redefined the historical study of American institutions—including the two that are the focus of this study, business and government. He probed to make sure I was pursuing the power relationships behind this story and pushed me to frame it in the widest, most significant context. I am extremely fortunate to have worked with him. I am also grateful to Jack Fisher, Robert Kargon, Francis Rourke, and Ronald Walters, who as members of my dissertation committee offered excellent advice on an earlier version of this manuscript.

When I was an undergraduate at the University of California at Davis, Roland Marchand and Robert Keller introduced me to business history. Years later, they helped guide me toward graduate study and more recently offered helpful and encouraging comments on my Kaiser work.

Just as I was starting the project, the first two full-length biographies of Kaiser were published. That alone was fortuitous, but both authors—historian Mark Foster and retired Kaiser Steel executive Albert Heiner—were extraordinarily enthusiastic supporters all along. They both provided invaluable comments on drafts of my chapters.

I was fortunate to receive the advice and encouragement of legal historian Tony Freyer and business historians William Becker and Diana Olien. Felice Bonadio shared his insights on some of Kaiser's western connections, such as Marriner Eccles and the subject of Bonadio's biography, A. P. Giannini. Roosevelt biographer Michael Simpson led me to the FDR–Edward Macauley connection.

Gerard Piel, who profiled Kaiser for *Life* magazine in 1942, then served as Kaiser's executive assistant at the end of World War II, sent many long,

probing letters chock-full of anecdotes—about both Kaiser and Piel's previous boss, Henry Luce—and analysis. He was quick to enlighten me that Kaiser did not engage in lobbying in the classic sense. Instead, he led me to a host of relevant issues, from antitrust to regional economic development, on which Kaiser became an agent of government policy.

More than two decades after his death, Henry Kaiser's name still opened doors in Washington. Robert Nathan, a New Deal economist, patiently explained how the government's industrial policy was created and carried out and enthusiastically described what it was like working with Kaiser as a representative of wartime agencies. Nathan referred me to his gracious friends Lauchlin Currie and David Ginsburg, who as government officials also had worked with Kaiser, and the three of them helped place this particular industrialist's experiences in the context of broad government objectives.

Lloyd Cutler, who provided legal services to Kaiser in Washington, promptly responded to my queries and told some vivid stories. I am also grateful to the following government officials, lawyers, labor union officials, and journalists who helped me understand the Washington environment and Kaiser's role in it: Jack Conway, the late Charles Corddry, Northcutt Ely, Bertram Fox, Lincoln Gordon, the late Eliot Janeway, Edwin Martin, the late George Meader, the late Joseph Rauh, and Victor Reuther.

Among the ranks of Kaiser employees and retirees, Donald Duffy and Robert Sandberg were particularly helpful. Duffy referred me to many interview sources and provided comments and anecdotes to bolster chapters I sent him. Sandberg offered comments on what I wrote and explained to me how Kaiser's Washington organization grew, then contracted.

Other Kaiser people who generously helped me out were Atwood Austin, the late Clay Bedford, Donald Browne, Jack Carlson, Fred Drewes, the late Pete Fowler, William Freistat, Dr. Clifford Keene, Hal Lauth, the late Clarence Mayhew, James McCloud, Louis Oppenheim, Edward R. Ordway, the late Thomas Ready, Joe Reis, the late Eugene Trefethen, and Alex Troffey. The Reverend Eugene Sill also told me how he came into the orbit of the Kaiser organization.

I am grateful to William vanden Heuvel of the Franklin and Eleanor Roosevelt Institute for contacting the Henry J. Kaiser Family Foundation on my behalf and to the Kaiser Family Foundation for supporting my research at the Roosevelt Presidential Library. Director Verne Newton and his able staff made the Roosevelt Library a rewarding place for a researcher. Up the road at Wilderstein Preservation, Pat Weber and Linda

Watson graciously gave me permission to see a copy of Margaret Suckley's diary.

The Bancroft Library at the University of California at Berkeley reorganized the Kaiser papers and created a new finding aid just in time for my most important research. Mary Morganti, the Kaiser collection archivist, was an enormous help in locating crucial documents. David Rez offered enthusiastic assistance throughout my many visits to the Bancroft.

Robert Irelan of Kaiser Aluminum, Michael Marsh and Maja Larson of the Todd Shipyards Corporation, and Thomas G. Corcoran Jr. arranged for me to have access to restricted papers in the Thomas Corcoran Papers at the Library of Congress.

At the National Archives, I relied on the assistance of Bill Creech, Tab Lewis, and John Taylor. Marilyn Ghausi allowed me to examine documents at the Bank of America Archives for the Henry Kaiser–A. P. Giannini connection.

Robert Notson, retired publisher of the *Portland Oregonian*, provided me with information about the Kaiser–Palmer Hoyt relationship. Marge Apperson, former publisher of the *Mount Shasta Herald*, gave me the run of the paper's morgue, where I was able to track Henry Kaiser's road-building exploits in the early 1920s.

Allan Holtzman of the Milton S. Eisenhower Library at Johns Hopkins University helped me find archival sources from the outset to the conclusion of the project.

It has been a pleasure and a privilege to work with the University of North Carolina Press. Lewis Bateman saw possibilities in my book that I had not seen and helped turn them into reality. In Pam Upton I had a very patient and helpful editor. Trudie Calvert did an excellent copyediting job, and Phil King prepared a first-rate index.

For hospitable places to stay near valuable sources of archival material, I imposed on old friends Kate Karpilow and Steve Sanders and a new friend, Esther Bradley.

For a multiyear project, the most important support group is family. I received support for my decision to change careers from business to academia, encouragement when the project did not seem to be progressing, and an enthusiastic audience for whatever I wrote. In choosing Kaiser, a Bay Area subject, I was able to impose on my mother, Lucille Adams, and my in-laws, Robert and Doris Bergman. They not only provided pleasant spaces to work within range of important archives but led me to interview people I would not otherwise have found. My cousin Ralph Adams welcomed me to his home those many times when I needed "just one last

glance" in the National Archives and the Library of Congress. My sister-in-law's parents, Milo and Mary Paul Lacy, welcomed me to their home and took me to visit what was once Kaiser's Fontana steel works.

Finally, my wife, Madeleine, read, critiqued, and edited the entire manuscript. She patiently weathered an onslaught of "Kaiser talk" and accompanied me to archives as part of vacations. Somehow she maintained enthusiasm for the subject from the beginning to the end of the project. Her suggestions and ideas enliven the book throughout. She is an inspiration, and I dedicate the book to her.

ABBREVIATIONS

ACC   American Construction Council
AFL   American Federation of Labor
AGC   Associated General Contractors of America
CEO   Chief executive officer
CIO   Congress of Industrial Organizations
CMR   Canadian Mineral Rubber Company
FDR   Franklin D. Roosevelt
FTC   Federal Trade Commission
HMO   Health maintenance organization
LBJ   Lyndon B. Johnson
M-K   Morrison-Knudsen Company
NAM   National Association of Manufacturers
NDAC   National Defense Advisory Commission
NRA   National Recovery Administration
OPA   Office of Price Administration
OPM   Office of Production Management
OWMR   Office of War Mobilization and Reconversion
PAC   Political action committee
RFC   Reconstruction Finance Corporation
TNEC   Temporary National Economic Committee
USGS   U.S. Geological Survey
USO   United Service Organizations
USS   United Seamen's Service
WPA   Works Progress Administration
WPB   War Production Board

MR. KAISER
GOES TO
WASHINGTON

Whenever the

others say something

or other can't be

done, Kaiser says:

"We'll attend to

that for you,"

and the others

have *to go along.*

Margaret Suckley,

1944

1 ——— INTRODUCTION TO A GOVERNMENT ENTREPRENEUR

In the summer of 1942, "fabulous" Henry J. Kaiser burst like a comet across the national sky. His West Coast shipyards had performed production miracles during the dark days of America's first six months in World War II, a time when merchant shipping across the Atlantic, a target of German submarines, was deemed the most crucial bottleneck to overcome for America's war effort.[1] He had made headlines for his magnesium enterprise and for the steel plant he was about to build, both of which provided the "arsenal of Democracy" with a West Coast alternative to sluggish East Coast producers.

Kaiser was introduced at the National Press Club in July as "the modern

Paul Bunyan," an appropriate description for an individualistic westerner. Kaiser, however, offered his listeners a different lesson than they may have expected to hear: "Every time I take anybody to a shipyard, they want to see the ways and they think that is the shipyard. Well, that isn't the shipyard at all, and when you go to an aircraft plant, you want to see the garage they keep the planes in or build them in. That isn't the aircraft plant. I will tell you where the aircraft plant is and where the shipyard is: it starts in Washington." Kaiser went on to describe a road to entrepreneurial success in terms that diverged from America's well-worn, self-made path, instead passing through the nation's capital along the way: "That is the first place you build it, and you keep steadily there all the time while you are making aircraft and while you are making ships, because you have got any number of people to see—people who control the things that you need. . . . You have got to help them get the things. Anybody can come in and say, 'Goodness, I need this. Don't you see how badly I need it?' Anybody can do that, but you have got to come to Washington and say, 'Here is a way. Now I know this is right, see if I am right,' and if he thinks you are right he is tickled to death you came."[2]

Washington was tickled that Kaiser came, and so was America. Henry Kaiser captured the public's imagination during World War II, receiving more attention from the press than any other businessman, even Henry Ford.[3] Yet Kaiser did not take the road to Washington only during World War II. As the federal government grew in the 1930s and 1940s he was a regular visitor to the nation's capital. Kaiser's organization provided his generation's most telling case study in the role of governmental relations in American entrepreneurial success. Henry Kaiser, then, looms as a significant figure in American business history because of the extent of his involvement with the federal government at a time when distinctions between the public and private economic sectors were rapidly diminishing.

This is the story of the relationship between the federal government and what I call a "government entrepreneur." The entrepreneur plays a key role in Joseph Schumpeter's theory of economic development, but the entrepreneur's relationship with government does not. I have, therefore, adapted Schumpeter's definition of entrepreneur to fit this mixed breed: a *government entrepreneur* carries out a new combination of materials and forces through the use of government capital for the government as customer or under the auspices of government regulation. Defined thus, the "creative destruction" (new combinations chasing out the old) accompanying Henry Kaiser's rise was almost exclusively governmental.[4] Even Henry J. Kaiser, the most powerful businessman in the West, could not

have achieved his success in shipbuilding, steel, dam building, or aluminum without a healthy relationship with the executive branch. The Kaiser story is just one example of how government entrepreneurship relies on both an activist government and venturesome entrepreneurs.

Most Americans do not associate the government with entrepreneurial opportunity any more than they did in 1934, when Will Rogers poked fun at the public's attitude. Rogers wrote in his newspaper column about a U.S. Chamber of Commerce dinner he attended with Jesse Jones, head of the federal government's Reconstruction Finance Corporation (RFC). A succession of industrialists and financiers spoke on the common theme of "keep government out of business." As each speaker stood up, Jones wrote something on the back of his menu. Finally, the last speaker rose, Jones scribbled on his menu one last time, and the speaker lobbied once more to keep the government out of business. Rogers wryly noted that Jones had been writing what each speaker had borrowed from the RFC.[5]

Businessmen are traditionally mute about opportunities government presents to them. At the same time, they loudly bemoan restrictions on their activities, such as those accompanying the federal government's rapid growth since the 1930s. This larger government could impinge on business in many ways—through regulation, taxation, and antitrust actions—and analyses of these restrictions have dominated the literature of business-government relations.

All the attention historians have paid to government's controlling aspects—and private sector complaints about them—has overshadowed the entrepreneurial opportunities presented by the growth of the administrative state. Even entrepreneurial tales usually follow the chamber of commerce model—focusing on the private sector, with only passing reference to the government (playing the role of setting roadblocks through obstructive regulations).[6]

There are three principal reasons why scholars have neglected government entrepreneurship. First, most government work is done by large organizations, which would seem to be beyond the entrepreneurial stage and well into the ranks of the bureaucratic organizations Alfred Chandler describes.[7] Second, in the latter half of the twentieth century, much of the work performed by government entrepreneurs has involved national defense and therefore has been veiled in secrecy (an extreme case being that of Howard Hughes). Third and most important, in the realm of American hopes and fears, the government tends to be a catch-all for fears and rarely embodies hopes. Tales of government entrepreneurship do not make their way into the American imagination as private sector better mouse-

trap (or personal computer) tales do. Stories of private-sector success tend to minimize or ignore the government's role.[8] Entrepreneurs such as David Sarnoff, Ross Perot, and Howard Hughes became legendary for the way they bucked the establishment, but each owed his greatest opportunity to changes in government regulation or to government loans or contracts. Yet each offered the public a "self-made" image.

Public knowledge of the government's role tends to deflate entrepreneurial reputations. Even the heroic achievements of Henry Kaiser during World War II are considerably qualified in *V Was for Victory*, John Morton Blum's account of life on the home front. Blum concludes (correctly) that Kaiser's exploits bear little relationship to the classic laissez-faire definition of "free enterprise" but fails to mention that our peacetime economy is—and long has been—a breed apart from such purity as well.[9] The entire country's economic landscape has undergone a revolutionary change since the 1920s. As Kim McQuaid puts it, "The federal government came of age in the United States."[10] Government spending as a percentage of gross national product rose from less than 5 percent in the 1920s to more than 30 percent today.[11] Such growth dramatically increased the opportunity for government entrepreneurship.

In assessing twentieth-century government entrepreneurship, it is fitting to focus on a westerner, and Henry Kaiser was based in Oakland, California. In many respects, dreams of the West preceded reality. During the nineteenth century, the West (however defined) was considered the place to go (a "safety valve") to achieve economic self-determination, whether as yeoman farmer or shopkeeper.[12] The people who settled on the West Coast, such as New Yorker Kaiser, often brought individualistic attitudes along with them.[13] While the world of the yeoman farmer and the shopkeeper was disappearing in the East, one transcendent quality the West appeared to offer newcomers was the promise of economic self-sufficiency.

In the first half of the twentieth century, however, regional economic self-sufficiency is just what the West lacked. Until the 1930s, western industry was characterized by a colonial dependence on the East. Westerners believed they lived in a "plundered province," and their subordinate relationship kept them decades behind the development of the East.[14] Typically, westerners would provide raw materials for eastern manufacture, then provide markets for eastern finished goods—much as colonial America did for England. On the eve of the Great Depression, eastbound raw material tonnage was three times as great as westbound.[15] As recently

as 1940, western steel consumption was nearly four times that of regional production.[16]

For much of the twentieth century, the political economy of the American West has been a great paradox. The two chief political goals have been to achieve economic independence from the East but also to secure money from the federal government, especially for water projects. Presumably, those projects and the industry they would attract would pave the way for regional economic independence.

Kaiser's enterprises offer a view of the changing opportunities in this environment for government entrepreneurs during the first half of the century. Kaiser was one of many successful road builders during the "good roads" movement of the 1920s, a major dam builder during the West's golden age of public works in the 1930s, and America's most widely publicized shipbuilder during the war years. Finally, he was the most prominent western industrialist in primary metals after World War II.

Kaiser's appetite for enterprise was legendary: he attempted ventures in any and all sectors of the economy. "Find a need and fill it" was his motto, and he launched more than a hundred businesses in a host of fields, ranging from construction to basic metals to health care to consumer products to broadcasting. Apparently, when Kaiser was in doubt, he started another company rather than wait for proper alignment of the economic heavens.

Kaiser did, of course, choose not to enter all industries, but such exceptions—some of which have become nuggets of corporate folklore—appear to prove the rule. In the 1920s, for example, Kaiser was offered half-ownership of a cemetery in Berkeley, California. An associate presented the idea as "a business that keeps growing." Kaiser would have none of it: "I don't want to wait until somebody dies to make a profit."[17] It is fitting that his greatest legacy was in helping pioneer the managed health care revolution in America with the Kaiser Permanente health maintenance organization (HMO), the focus of which is preventive care.

Kaiser became a symbol of a "can-do" age.[18] Americans have always been viewed as the world's optimists, but this was particularly true during the first half of what Henry Luce called the American Century. The "can-do" image has encompassed traits more commonly associated with Americans than with inhabitants of the Old World: individualism and innocence. Whereas Europeans had learned, through experiences with class systems, geographic limitations, and dashed hopes of revolutionary change, to limit their expectations of change, Americans had quite a different worldview, one less respectful of authority. Americans have tradi-

tionally preferred to view their country as the home of the individualistic, self-made man. Although this idea has meant many things to many people, a principal incarnation of the self-made man has been the entrepreneur. Shaped by their nineteenth-century experiences with seemingly limitless land, Americans applied the frontier ethos of possibilities to subsequent pursuits—including business enterprise. Warren Susman writes that "American business enterprise . . . appropriated the frontier past for itself and insisted that the pioneer spirit was being carried forward by modern industrialism," a spirit of "individuality, independence, and self-direction."[19]

Robert Bellah and his colleagues suggest that even in situations in which excessive individualism may have harmful effects, the language Americans speak is so imbued with individualistic phrasing that we have trouble verbalizing alternatives. They cite James Oliver Robertson's account of Gilded Age captains of industry, who could "ignore the clamor of public opinion" and rise "by economic means alone" (with little expression of social conscience) but whose entrepreneurial individualism was nonetheless attractive to the public whose interests they ignored.[20] Bellah and his colleagues do not dwell on modern attitudes toward entrepreneurship, but they could. America's ethos of individualism not only puts a premium on entrepreneurship but creates a tendency to cast entrepreneurs as shapers of their own world (the economic equivalent of "he was born in a log cabin he built with his own hands"). Individualistic entrepreneurs like Bill Gates and Ted Turner, who appear to make their own sets of rules, are still heroic figures in the American imagination.

Americans long to believe that the rules, natural or man-made, do not apply to America or its heroes, fictional or real. Huck Finn finally vows to escape the hypocritical rules of "civilizing" influences and light out for the territories. Jay Gatsby, however, discovers too late that only America's hereditary aristocracy can ignore the rules. Huck's message of radical freedom and self-determination plays better with ever-optimistic American business. Apple Computer captured the imagination of baby boomers by flying a pirate flag in the face of the corporate establishment. Merrill Lynch aired a television commercial celebrating the renegade bikers who made Harley-Davidson America's only successful motorcycle maker. Burger King ran a campaign based on the theme "sometimes you gotta break the rules."

With this antiauthoritarian spirit, the American public perceived Kaiser not as an organization in partnership with the government but as an

individual breaking the bureaucracy's rules on the public's behalf. The proper role for the government was to stay out of the way and let Kaiser take care of business. Kaiser fostered the belief that natural and engineering laws did not apply to his organization either. Some of the most often told Kaiser stories involve dicey work on dams where "the boys" triumphed not only over nature but over skeptical engineering "experts." Kaiser described much of his success as "we didn't know enough to know we were licked."[21] This was the success of an innocent. After all, if you do not know what the rules are, they cannot hold you back.

Both defiance of authority and innocence are quintessentially American traits, and Kaiser sustained both traditions. He institutionalized innocence into his organization in both practice and attitude. Kaiser would have been delighted to hear today's business consultants tell of the importance of a "forgetting curve" preceding a "learning curve."[22] He boasted of his shipbuilders' "learn-how" as being superior to the established producers' "know-how." Westerner Kaiser's organization had less to forget than Bethlehem Steel did so his people built ships faster, relying on new techniques.

Kaiser also established an experimental laboratory in 1943 to pursue ideas that came from both within and outside the organization. Kaiser was deluged with fan mail by this point, much of which included ideas for inventions. The role of the "hobby lobby" was to turn these dreams into reality. According to popular belief, only an innocent would invite the public to contribute; jaded eastern business was too set in its ways to listen to the common sense of the man in the street.

Just as Americans had long reveled in their position as innocents compared to Europeans, with their older and more corrupt institutions, so too did Californians when coming east. They brought stories with them that easterners were eager to hear and wanted to believe. Kaiser went to great lengths to foster such portrayals of innocence, but he probably did not need to do so. The eastern press took care of that, embellishing his tales of innocence. This projected image of the West was framed by the motives of the eastern viewers. The media also helped promote Kaiser's Washington agenda.

Thus Henry Kaiser became a national hero with the assistance of the media, particularly Henry Luce's empire. The media embraced "fabulous" Kaiser, portraying him as a figure of mythical stature, an appropriate symbol of what Luce's Time/Life later would call the "Fabulous Forties." Kaiser's enthusiastic cooperation with the media's and the public's insa-

tiable appetite for American heroes—he was, in Morris Udall's phrase, "unavoidable for comment"—helped forestall the need to develop an extensive public relations function within his organization.

At times it seemed as though Kaiser needed no public relations assistance because of his combination of charisma, conviction, and capability.[23] Reconstruction Finance Corporation head Jesse Jones, aware of Kaiser's gifts of persuasion, told him: "I don't want you to deal with anyone around here but me. You'd talk them out of their watches, and when I'd ask them about it, they'd say, 'See, he talked me out of my watch, isn't it wonderful?'"[24] If Kaiser wanted something, he would turn Washington upside down to get it, even if this meant personally carrying the requisite papers from office to office or "bombarding" the decision makers with telegrams.[25]

If Kaiser did not obtain a particular contract or job, he needed only to inform the press, and the resulting public outcry would take care of the rest.[26] In a time of great sacrifice, the public needed an avenue to vent its frustration closer than its overseas enemies. A seemingly sluggish federal government would do nicely. Kaiser was the people's industrialist who would cut the red tape of the "Arsenal of Bureaucracy."

Ironically, although a country impatient with bureaucracy and the alphabet agencies of the New Deal responded to Kaiser as a man of action, he has been accurately called the "principal extension into the industrial economy of the policies of the national administration."[27] In the 1930s, the government and the private sector had switched stereotypical roles, with the entrepreneurial impulse coming from the executive branch and resistance to change coming from Main Street "businesscrats." New Dealers were the "first movers" with a broad-gauged agenda of economic change for whom Kaiser's tremendous energy and vision were a godsend. New Dealer Thomas Corcoran remarked, "If we could find one financier who thought as Henry Kaiser does, we could show the world that our ideas work."[28] Kaiser demonstrated the dramatic success government entrepreneurs could achieve by being nimble enough to seize the opportunities presented by an activist government. His enterprises represented a confluence of administration policy and entrepreneurial zeal.

All along the way, Kaiser would become a symbol of New Deal industrial hopes as he changed course to align himself with the administration's direction. Kaiser's most dramatic reversal came in the late 1930s, encompassing two issues at the top of the New Deal agenda: labor and antitrust. Although Henry Kaiser built a reputation for treating his workers well early in his career, he adopted a conciliatory policy toward organized labor only after the Wagner Act became law in the late 1930s. Kaiser's relatively

liberal social attitudes were not new: corporate liberalism had been alive and well in Edward A. Filene, Owen D. Young, and Harry S. Dennison in the 1920s and 1930s.[29] But in Kaiser's case the liberalism was combined with a fine sense of entrepreneurship focused on new opportunities to garner government business. Kaiser was not just an opportunist, however: he would remain out front on the labor issue for the rest of his life.

At about the same time, Kaiser abandoned the uniform of trade association man and industry insider, donning instead the mantle of maverick and industry outsider. Yet Kaiser the maverick—who sponsored a television show by that name in the 1950s—appeared only when the administration pursued an antitrust agenda after blaming the recession of 1937 on industry's high prices and low output. With government support, Kaiser launched a cement company, the first of many Kaiser enterprises challenging entrenched oligopoly or monopoly. After the administration began to prepare for war in the wake of the Nazi invasion of the Low Countries in the spring of 1940, Kaiser quickly moved from domestic concerns to war production. Kaiser also offered the administration alternative entrants in industries that hesitated to increase production; his belief in production as the "Fifth Freedom" fit both prewar and wartime administration needs. By the time Kaiser and Franklin D. Roosevelt developed a personal relationship during the war, the president appeared sympathetic to Kaiser's goals for a simple reason: they coincided with Roosevelt's.

In late 1942, Kaiser shifted again, from contract seeker to industrial statesman, as an apostle of postwar economic prosperity. Kaiser spoke frequently of America's coming need for transportation, housing, and medical care, while implicitly promising to back up his words with enterprise. Finally, Kaiser became politically active in August 1944, heading an organization to get out the national vote when voter turnout was the key reelection strategy of the Democrats.

All this activity made Kaiser popular. A Roper poll conducted in the spring of 1945 found that the public believed Kaiser had done more to help the president win the war than any other civilian. Donald Nelson, chairman of the War Production Board, placed third, and James F. Byrnes, director of war mobilization, was fourth. A Gallup poll conducted less than a year later found that among nonpolitical figures "best qualified for the Presidency," only Douglas MacArthur and Dwight D. Eisenhower outpolled Kaiser.[30] Only Margaret Suckley knew that her cousin Franklin Roosevelt had earlier put Kaiser at the head of his list.

In May 1944, FDR told his cousin that he thought Kaiser would be the best man to succeed him.[31] The publication of her record of this conver-

sation in her diary fifty years later did not create even a ripple of reaction, although it represents the only time after 1940 that Roosevelt is on record as mentioning a possible successor. Such a revelation seems a non sequitur when viewed outside the context of the Kaiser-Roosevelt relationship. The president had no closer relationship with any businessman during the war: Henry Kaiser was Franklin Roosevelt's industrial alter ego.

Although the personalities of the sometimes abrasive Kaiser and usually smooth Roosevelt contrasted, their attitude and organizational temperament did not. Above all, they shared the classic American "can-do" attitude. The can-do president and the can-do entrepreneur shared a boundless optimism and personified the possibilities. And they were both nearly irresistible: few men in Washington have been more convincing in one-on-one situations than Roosevelt and Kaiser.

Margaret Mead expressed concern about both figures, warning: "If the war should ever come to seem a battle in which Roosevelt and MacArthur and Kaiser are supermen—father figures who do our fighting or our thinking for us while we simply watch the show—then there would be danger, for such an attitude would bring out not the strengths of the American character—but its weaknesses."[32] She was responding to the fact that, in an age of authoritarianism overseas, both Kaiser and Roosevelt created institutions at home characterized more by a cult of personality than by any dominant strategy or structure.

Kaiser embraced a style of business operation—"personal" capitalism—that preceded the modern bureaucratic organization. He was comfortable operating in organizations with permeable boundaries, allowing him to enlist anyone for any task. John Kenneth Galbraith writes that "in any large organization with varied and complex tasks, power passes down to those who are in daily touch with the action and have the resulting knowledge."[33] Kaiser's approach to government officials and to getting information from within his organization reflected that belief: instead of operating "through channels," Kaiser sought the person immediately involved in his subject of interest.[34] The willingness of this chief executive officer (CEO) to approach relatively junior members of government agencies surprised many, but most were favorably impressed.[35]

So Kaiser pursued entry into the metals industries and other defense work using a personal, idiosyncratic approach to government officials rather than an institutional and hierarchical one. At one point during the war, one of Kaiser's managers complained about "the Navy." Kaiser responded: "You know there is no such thing as the U.S. Navy! It's just

a bunch of guys down there in Washington. Now which one is your problem?"[36]

Roosevelt shared Kaiser's distaste for bureaucratic rules or structures that might get in his way. As Roosevelt biographer Frank Freidel puts it, he "dearly loved a semblance of insubordination." Reminiscing in 1920 about his years as assistant secretary of the navy (his final years as a public servant in Washington before his presidency), Roosevelt proudly recalled how well he bypassed bureaucratic red tape: "From Feb. 6 to March 4 [1917] we in the Navy committed acts for which we could be, and may be yet sent to jail for 999 years. We spent millions of dollars we did not have. . . . We went to those whom we had seen in advance and told them to enlarge their plants and send us their bills."[37] Although Roosevelt oversaw the takeoff of the modern bureaucratic state, he had little patience for many of its organizational features. As president, Roosevelt devised another way to circumvent a recalcitrant bureaucracy: he created new agencies to do what he wanted. While Roosevelt established agencies in the public sector, Kaiser created enterprises in the private sector.

Kaiser's saga reflected not just a change in opportunities available to entrepreneurs but an approach to obtaining government business at odds with many interpretations of American business-government relations. Despite the public image he cultivated during World War II, Kaiser certainly did not fit the Progressive model of businessmen fighting against government. Nor was Kaiser out to "capture" government agencies with which he dealt, as New Left history might suggest. Instead, Kaiser learned to compromise with the desires of executive branch officials at the same time he was attempting to influence them through skilled use of the media. The Kaiser story was of neither battle nor capture, but rather a process of continuous negotiation.

Kaiser's background building roads and dams provided excellent preparation for industrial government entrepreneurship. Kaiser had learned that government contracting was an organic process rather than a predictable series of discrete events. Just about everything was negotiable, especially after the acceptance of a bid. This necessitated political savvy, including a keen understanding of social process and influence. Such skills were particularly valuable to Kaiser because his experience in industrial government entrepreneurship would also involve an intricate series of negotiations.

Kaiser was not a one-man show in Washington; he had effective agents operating on his behalf, most notably his Washington representative, Charles F. ("Chad") Calhoun. In contrast with some other Washington

representatives, whose principal role was to arrange meetings for executives with government officials, Calhoun offered Kaiser advice on myriad policy and organizational decisions. While Kaiser seized the headlines, Calhoun assembled contacts, collected information, and reported on the prevailing mood in Washington. More than any other individual in the organization, Calhoun was the driving force behind Kaiser's entry into industries ranging from magnesium to aluminum.

Chad Calhoun also left behind a tremendous paper trail, describing both opportunities and ambiance in the nation's capital. Fortune 500 Washington offices subsequently became populated with lawyers, whose work would be hidden behind the protection of attorney-client privilege. Calhoun's memos to Oakland headquarters, then, offer a rare glimpse of the point of contact between business and government. Through them we are able to see how representatives of business and government sized each other up. Often they were trying to manipulate each other, fully aware of each other's not-so-hidden agenda.

A Washington corporate presence was of tremendous value to Kaiser. Only a handful of companies had Washington offices in 1940, the year Calhoun arrived. It is easy to see why the number soon increased. Repeatedly, an administration official would meet with Calhoun ostensibly about one industry or issue, then present him with an opportunity in another.

Calhoun's memos also demonstrate how the tensions between ideological stands and practical needs played themselves out. Because Henry Kaiser was a New Deal favorite, it was assumed in many circles that he was an ideologue. Kaiser and his associates were, however, above all practical men. In trying to obtain government support for a steel plant, for instance, Kaiser was perfectly willing to do business with the New Deal's nemesis, Tom Girdler, if he did not ruffle administration feathers in doing so. Kaiser and Calhoun had to learn how to balance the company's need to enlist experienced steel people (even Girdler) and the organization's ability to show that its labor relations policies were aligned with those of the administration.

To the extent that his enterprises promoted the interests of the administration, Kaiser was a beneficiary of legal expertise from the federal government, the "nation's law firm." Kaiser was also one of the first industrialists effectively to employ Washington's new breed of lawyer/lobbyist, who moved seemingly effortlessly from government service to law practices specializing in guiding businesspeople through Washington's red tape. Expansion of the federal government—especially the executive branch— provided an ever-increasing pool of attorneys experienced in federal bu-

reaucracy, including the first modern lawyer/lobbyist, Thomas Corcoran. Kaiser would retain Corcoran's services, as well as those of Lloyd Cutler and others. Thus, although Kaiser's organization was old-fashioned in its emphasis on one man, it was avant-garde in governmental relations.

I present the case of Henry Kaiser in the belief that his experiences can reveal much about government entrepreneurship. I will trace his experiences over time, as he graduated from local to state to federal relationships and as he moved from infrastructure government entrepreneurship to industrial government entrepreneurship. Henry Kaiser was by no means typical; he was more venturesome than the average entrepreneur. It is Kaiser's apparent uniqueness, his ability to push the edges of the envelope of possibilities, that makes him an ideal figure through which to trace the evolution of twentieth-century government entrepreneurship. Kaiser's experiences in relentless pursuit of enterprise provide a clear reflection of business-government relations. Yet his experiences were representative because there were many other entrepreneurs engaged in similar enterprises. Examining the experiences of this one man, therefore, is the beginning of a primer on twentieth-century government entrepreneurship in the United States.

*If the members of
the construction
industry are unable
to keep their own
house in order, an
exasperated public
will some day regulate
their house for them.*

*Franklin D.
Roosevelt, 1922*

2 ——— THE EDUCATION OF HENRY KAISER

When the national press discovered Henry J. Kaiser in 1941, he had toiled in obscurity for decades before becoming an overnight sensation. Before America could learn about this government entrepreneur, he had had to learn about government entrepreneurship at the local, state, and federal levels. Kaiser had gained political savvy by heading regional and national trade associations that promoted construction work and played big roles in determining who would perform it. Kaiser had made liberal use of lawyers for the necessary negotiations in this subjective business and had been a principal in the Industrial Indemnity Exchange, the West's second largest industrial insurance company.[1] This bold indi-

vidual had succeeded in part by enlisting help from experts and engaging in collective activity.

Risk reduction and the enlistment of experts were commonplace and necessary for any successful government entrepreneur, but the aggressiveness with which Kaiser employed them reflected his expansive personality. Kaiser employed these tactics as a means of matching his larger-than-life dreams. Henry Kaiser was a broad-gauged thinker with an infectious sense of mission. The world is filled with thinkers; what made Kaiser an American archetype was his ability to bring his ideas boldly to fruition. This is exemplified in the way Kaiser hired experts to mechanize construction work: instead of doing so to squeeze a little more profit out of small jobs, Kaiser did so as a means to tackle large jobs he otherwise would have been unable to perform. Therefore, a construction legend was born in large part through the way he used various means of risk reduction to enable him to climb higher mountains.

Today, bold action and government contracting seem mutually exclusive, but Henry Kaiser grew up in view of one of the boldest government endeavors of its day. It is probably no coincidence that Henry Kaiser, who would help build Hoover Dam, the greatest public works project of America's golden age of public works, grew up a few blocks from the Erie Canal, the greatest public works project of its day. Kaiser and his sisters spent considerable time watching the barges go by on the canal.[2] Kaiser therefore observed one of the symbolic centerpieces of the nineteenth century's most ambitious plan to involve the federal government in the economy—the Whig American System. Forty years before he worked with the New Deal, the twentieth century's most ambitious plan to involve the federal government in the economy, he had already seen firsthand the fruits of public-private partnership.

Born into a humble, although not poor, family, Kaiser left school at the age of twelve. He did not need to support his parents; he simply wanted to work. Kaiser's most evident gift was his promotional ability so most of his early jobs were in the field of sales—including working for a retailer of photography supplies, then a photography studio. Living only a few miles from where Kodak was based, Kaiser caught the bug and became a photographer by the time he was eighteen. In typically audacious manner, Kaiser promised Lake Placid's W. W. Brownell to work at his studio for no salary. Instead, if he could triple Brownell's sales, Kaiser would become full partner in the business. Kaiser succeeded and, as would become typical for him, his plans for growth exceeded his partner's ability to sleep at night so Kaiser bought out Brownell and proceeded alone. Kaiser the bud-

ding self-promoter posted a sign on his shop that read "Henry J. Kaiser: The Man With the Smile."[3]

One of his subjects, Bess Fosburgh, caught Kaiser's eye, and after a brief courtship, Kaiser asked Mr. Fosburgh for his daughter's hand. Fosburgh agreed, but with stiff conditions: Kaiser needed to go west, find a job that paid $125 a month, save $1,000, and build a home for his bride.[4] In 1906, Kaiser took the train across the northern plains to Spokane, Washington, where he landed a job as a hardware salesman, returned for his wife, and began a new career. Appropriately, to retrace Kaiser's trip today, one would ride a train called the Empire Builder.

Kaiser did not start an empire immediately, and when he did, his venture was modest and certainly not widely reported. In February 1914, Henry Kaiser wrote to a friend: "You probably were aware that the C.M.R. [Canadian Mineral Rubber] Co. and the Hill Co. finally decided to wind up their business after considerable friction between the Canadian and the American interests, with the result that some time ago I was thrown out on my own resources and, therefore, as I said before, I am now a real Contractor."[5] Kaiser had worked as a salesman for a couple of companies that sold material to construction firms in the Spokane area before joining the J. F. Hill Company in 1911. Two years later, Hill sent Kaiser to its northern subsidiary, the CMR. After CMR went bankrupt, although he had no contractual obligation to its customers, Kaiser completed work he had promised the company would perform. With a wife and young son to support, Kaiser was in a tenuous financial condition, but he built a reservoir of goodwill that helped his new business.

Yet even such a great self-promoter as Kaiser offered a subdued report on his early experience as a contractor: "I am completing [the job] well within my estimate, but of course I don't expect to retire on the profits."[6] The articles of incorporation for his new company hint, however, at how big the nascent entrepreneur's dreams were. Among lines of business he might pursue, Kaiser listed steel and cement production, home construction, and development of water and power resources. Kaiser had done nothing less than stake out an entire region's development as the possible purview of his organization.[7]

During his first year in business, Kaiser successfully bid on a paving job in Vancouver and sought capital for the performance bond. Contractors were required to provide a contingent payment of 10 percent of the contract value up front. Kaiser, with neither equipment nor workforce, approached a Vancouver branch of the Canadian Bank of Commerce for a $25,000 loan. The banker emphasized, the story goes, that "all you have

is a contract and an idea you think might work," but that was sufficient to convince the banker to get Kaiser started.[8] This story, like others in American corporate lore, makes it sound as if Kaiser's business owed its inception to the generosity of a banker from a Frank Capra movie. Kaiser had more going for him than that: a director of the Canadian Bank of Commerce had been connected with the Hill Company and no doubt was impressed when Kaiser completed Hill's contracts at his own expense.

Later, the Warren Brothers Company of Boston, which had patented the road surface Kaiser used on his jobs for the Hill Company, provided him with capital as well. Warren Brothers had first incorporated in 1899 to patent their "bitulithic all-weather" paving technique. As road builders, Warren Brothers competed with Kaiser's employers, most notably on the last 1913 contract CMR successfully bid before going bankrupt.[9] When Kaiser took over that job, Warren Brothers provided crucial financing. They offered similar help at other times and for a while were majority shareholders in Kaiser's company.

Contracting in the early twentieth century was a booming business. From the inception of Henry Kaiser's paving business in 1914 to the eve of the Depression in 1929, America's population increased by nearly 25 percent, while manufacturing output and new construction nearly doubled. During the same period, construction of highways, roads, and streets—Kaiser's segment of the business—tripled.[10] The growth of road building in California (Kaiser's future base) was fairly representative of this construction boom. As of November 1910, "there were 28 contracts and day labor jobs under way on the state highway system, involving 280 miles. On July 1, 1922, there were 152 contracts and day labor jobs with a total of 1,063 miles."[11]

Despite plentiful work, contractors were often only one mishap or disaster away from going under. Henry Kaiser was said to have once remarked: "Contractors are all alike. . . . They start out broke, with a wheelbarrow and a piece of hose. Then, suddenly, they find themselves in the money. Everything's fine. Ten years later they are back where they started from—with one wheelbarrow, a piece of hose, and broke." Kaiser later denied making the comment, but it was an apt description of the industry's early days.[12]

Future Kaiser partner Morrison-Knudsen (M-K) was a case in point. M-K preceded Kaiser in the contracting business by two years, beginning in 1912 in Idaho. After having graduated from the "wheelbarrow" stage to large projects, M-K lost $17,000 on a tunneling job. Ann Morrison, wife of one of the principals, wrote: "Two years of effort should have brought

a reward, but failure was close. Harry [Morrison] worried desperately. He laid off everybody but himself. He cut his salary to $100."[13]

The Texas firm Brown & Root had a similar experience. Herman Brown had entered the business about the same time as Kaiser and under similar circumstances. In 1914, Brown was foreman on a job when his boss went bankrupt. Instead of back wages, Brown accepted four mules and a fresno (a scraper) and was in business. In his early days on his own, Herman Brown was on the verge of bankruptcy when poor weather forced him to stop work on a key job. He was bailed out by a local merchant who offered him credit when Brown sought feed for his mules.[14] The harrowing experiences of Kaiser, Morrison, and Brown were not unusual. In 1921, for instance, U.S. Internal Revenue Service figures showed that 42 percent of construction companies filing tax returns showed no profit.[15]

The principal reason so many companies failed amid plentiful work was that the industry had low barriers to entry. The relatively quick transformations of Herman Brown and Henry Kaiser from employees to owners suggest how little equipment, workforce, and capital was required to get started. The result was an extremely competitive market with more newcomers all the time. Future Kaiser partner Warren A. "Dad" Bechtel, creator of the international construction firm that bears his name, would later make the issue of cutthroat competition a cornerstone of his participation in a national trade association, the Associated General Contractors of America (AGC). Bechtel was a midwesterner who had moved to the West Coast and garnered considerable business with the Southern Pacific Railroad. The phenomena he described—firms bidding at rates beneath a prudent estimate of the job's costs and taking enormous financial and physical risks to avoid idleness—were characteristic of an industry open to easy entry by newcomers. "We're killing each other off," he warned, referring not only to the number of bankruptcies but also to a high mortality rate among his peers.[16]

Indeed, construction could pose enormous physical dangers. It is little wonder that Ann Morrison reported in her diary that partner "Papa" Morris Knudsen told her "confidentially" that he wanted to get out of the business: "too hazardous and too many worries." Harry Morrison lost a job once by a mere $2,500. He tried unsuccessfully to buy his competitor out. Prices fell, causing Morrison to lament the lost contract even more until the successful bidder not only went broke on the job but lost his life in an accident.[17]

The mortality rate and chances of serious injury were greater still for construction workers, causing potentially great liabilities for contractors.

In late 1920, Warren Bechtel cofounded an industrial insurance company that became the largest private underwriter in California. Ordinary channels of private coverage in the state had become inadequate after passage of the 1913 California Workmen's Compensation Act, which led to soaring insurance costs. The Contractors Indemnity Exchange purchased workmen's compensation, property damage, and even life insurance at wholesale rates, then passed on the savings to members of Bechtel's Northern California Contractors. Henry Kaiser would become one of the three principals in the Exchange, which later became the Industrial Indemnity Exchange.[18]

After devoting his first couple of years to constructing streets in Vancouver, in 1916 Kaiser shifted his attention to work in the state of Washington. Kaiser had good reasons both to leave Canada and to return to the United States. The British Commonwealth was at war with Kaiser Wilhelm's Germany, and Canadians reacted more negatively to the Kaiser name than Americans did.[19] More important, the Federal Aid Roads Act, which Congress passed the year Kaiser shifted his operation to the United States, precipitated a nationwide boom in road construction. The act called for the federal government to pay half the cost of building roads in states that established highway departments to oversee planning, construction, and maintenance.[20]

Despite the federal government's involvement, road building remained a seat-of-the-pants business. It was very labor-intensive. For the general contractor, labor—at 40 to 45 percent of total expenses—represented a significantly greater proportion of cost than manufacturing's 25 to 30 percent.[21] A contractor not only would risk overruns by keeping labor on longer than necessary but would also forfeit possible bonuses for expeditious completion of projects. Many newcomers to a construction firm began their careers as timekeepers, and the discipline stuck with those who became successful. Time-saving devices were welcome in this business.

The industry's built-in sense of urgency was tailor-made for Henry Kaiser's temperament. One of the means to Kaiser's goal of big accomplishments was working fast. He drove his men—and himself—hard. To save valuable daylight hours, Kaiser drove his family from one work site to another at night. A. J. Hill wrote to Kaiser in early 1915, cautioning his onetime employee: "Now you mention about the speed you are developing. . . . Henry, you cannot keep up the gait you are going without taking some relaxation; all the business in the country cannot be done in one year." Kaiser was certainly going to try. When Kaiser was still in Canada, his right-hand man, A. B. Ordway, asked if Kaiser would give his men

the Canada Day holiday (July 1) off. Kaiser said no, there was no reason for Americans to observe a Canadian holiday. When Ordway asked if they could have the Fourth of July off, Kaiser said there was no reason to observe an American holiday in Canada.[22] Kaiser was going to squeeze every minute of labor he could from his men.

Little wonder that Kaiser was among those contractors who believed most strongly in the advantages of mechanization, which would revolutionize construction during the next two decades. When Kaiser started his business, construction work was performed by mules and men. By the time Kaiser graduated from road building to dam building in the early 1930s, much of the work had been mechanized, using power shovels and dump trucks. As early as 1919, Kaiser had established a shop to create experimental machinery for his jobs in King County, Washington.[23] Kaiser also went outside his company for an expert on mechanization, Robert LeTourneau, whose self-powered scraper was one of the three major advances in highway construction equipment in the 1920s.[24]

During this period, road builders owed much of their increased business to the proliferation of Henry Ford's automobiles. At the same time, contractors sought to apply Ford's assembly-line principles to road construction. By 1923, LeTourneau's scraper was helping to "transfer road-building into an assembly-line process."[25]

Henry Kaiser latched onto LeTourneau and bought not only his equipment but all his patents. Kaiser then hired LeTourneau to build what Kaiser termed "the ideal factory where we can really turn out your scrapers. Cranes, hoists, one of Henry Ford's assembly lines." LeTourneau's shop, located near Oakland, kept Kaiser on the cutting edge of earth-moving equipment. Later, LeTourneau established his own shop in Stockton and subcontracted for Kaiser.[26]

Kaiser's use of equipment and his relationship with LeTourneau reflected his vision of possibilities. As LeTourneau wrote, "[Kaiser] was the first contractor I had ever met who didn't look upon my machines as trick instruments to do small jobs faster. He saw them as instruments to make big jobs small."[27] LeTourneau was describing Kaiser's extraordinary skill at "job breakdown." Kaiser's ability to perceive the rhythms of labor and to organize materials enabled him to envision which jobs were fit to be split into simple, repetitive tasks or even mechanized—in short, applying assembly-line principles to road construction.

Kaiser's perception of the possibilities afforded by job breakdown transcended industrial boundaries. Kaiser applied assembly-line principles to road building, then to dam building. Later, as a shipbuilder, Kaiser suc-

cessfully executed others' ideas of breaking up shipbuilding crafts into multiple lower-skilled jobs. In so doing, Kaiser both opened wartime production to a large segment of the nation's workforce and employed a prefabrication strategy based on assembly-line principles. Kaiser followed a similar path in auto construction and, some would argue, in health care.

Even as the construction industry began to resemble modern manufacturing industries in some ways, it remained comparatively primitive in others. The twentieth-century construction industry remained relatively atomized while other industries consolidated, partly because of state regulations and partly because of small capital expenditure requirements. As a result, construction maintained an individualist aura. Many jobs were not publicized widely: such information often stayed within state borders. How the Washington-based Kaiser heard about his first California job is a good example.

In early 1921, A. B. Ordway took his first vacation since Kaiser hired him in 1912 (vacations, or the lack thereof, are a common theme in many Kaiser stories). Ordway took his wife to San Francisco, then returned by way of the Central Valley, stopping in Red Bluff. There he overheard two men talking about a local $500,000 job, for a road connecting Red Bluff and Redding. Ordway contacted Kaiser, and the two met in Portland. Small-time operators Kaiser and Ordway, accustomed to city and county jobs in the $100,000 to $200,000 range, saw the chance to move into a higher league. California was building more roads than any other state in the Union, and they might correspondingly expand the scale of their operation. According to Ordway and Kaiser, their train did not stop at Redding so the two jumped from the moving train. They ruined their suits but got the $500,000 contract—and established a new, more lucrative base of operations.[28]

Kaiser's first job in California gave him an opportunity to demonstrate some of his best promotional skills. Not content simply to build the road, he boasted that he was doing so, or would do so, in record time.[29] It is not clear how Kaiser knew what the old "record" was, but the challenge seemed to spur his men to greater achievement, and the "records" helped to establish relationships with state officials. Kaiser did naturally what many professional promoters did: announce a new record by virtue of being the first to keep track of milestones. The public, meanwhile, enjoyed the idea of a record-breaking performance.[30] This was a golden age of self-promotion in the United States. A trait commonly associated with the American character was being institutionalized in the new profession of public relations, as personified by Ivy Lee and Edward Bernays. At this

point, Kaiser did not need any professionals because he had a natural sense of public relations. Kaiser had made himself a builder, but he had been born a promoter.

Kaiser's abilities in self-promotion would later intertwine with an image of innocence. Part of this image came from the East Coast media, as a way of patronizing a westerner. Part of it had to do with the nature of the contracting business. Not all of the risks were immediately obvious even to an experienced contractor bidding on a job. The unforeseen seemed to be the rule rather than the exception, to the extent that unexpected risks resulted in one of the industry's rules of thumb, as related by a Kaiser associate: "It is an axiom among contractors that you never can get a second job next to the one you are doing. Another and a new man always wins. This is probably due to the original contractor knowing too much of the bad conditions of which the new man knows nothing."[31] The industry's self-image suggested, then, that many of the greatest construction feats were accomplished because the contractors did not know what they were up against. Most contractors—including Kaiser—had many stories of success in the face of stiff odds. It is not surprising that one of the principal characteristics associated with Kaiser the man, from his road-building days onward, was innocence—the idea that he succeeded because he never realized the odds against him.

In his new base of Oakland, Kaiser found that larger risks accompanied more lucrative contracts. Much of the risk involved the contract process itself and its subjective nature. In California, law required construction work to be advertised in local papers for four weeks. The state could then accept the "lowest responsible" bid. If none of the bids were considered "in the best interests of the state," the state could either readvertise or perform the work with "day labor" (work performed under the supervision of state engineers rather than private contractors).[32] The bidding process, then, was subjective enough to present both considerable risks and ample opportunities. In addition, once the winning bid was announced, the negotiating process had only begun, a process that favored not only the efficient and the swift but also the aggressive.

Potentially the most controversial aspect of the bidding process had to do with the state's interpretation of "lowest responsible" bid when it did not select the lowest bid. Such a decision could be made if the low bidder was deemed incapable of performing the work because of inexperience, poor financial condition, or inadequate equipment. An award to a contractor who was not the low bidder could raise cries of graft and become a headline story. Such a case occurred in Sacramento before Kaiser

arrived in California. Headlines ran: "Lowest bidder refused by super-visors," "Trustees resent charges of graft," and "Award was based on tech-nicality."[33] During Kaiser's first year in California, he bid $277,964, as opposed to his competitor's $205,689. Yet the state chose Kaiser because he would use concrete pavement, as opposed to his competitor's bitumi-nous macadam. The state's division engineer concluded that "[bituminous macadam] had been tried out and found wanting."[34]

Kaiser was also the beneficiary of a similar decision on a highway job in 1923. Bids ranged from a low of $395,432 to $553,964. Kaiser came in second lowest at $419,912. The low bidder, a Fresno outfit, was consid-ered too great a risk by the state because of its poor financial standing and inexperience. The state engineers believed Kaiser's competitor had insuf-ficient assets to tackle the job. More important, it had done only 4 miles of highway paving, as opposed to Kaiser's 106. Kaiser not only had done considerable work for the state by this point, but his self-promotion had clearly paid off. The state engineer noted: "The work done by this firm has *always been completed in record time*, and their . . . experience and ability to carry through the contract of the above nature is unquestioned."[35]

Kaiser, not content with a passive role, displayed some of the sales-manship that would later win federal contracts for his companies. Perhaps sensing he would not be the low bidder, Kaiser submitted a project plan to accompany his bid. The plan warned that "unless the job was carefully executed on a carefully estimated and preconceived plan, it could easily be disastrous to both the contractor and the public." Kaiser went on to list the equipment needed to complete the job successfully, noting that his organization already had such equipment. Kaiser closed by warning that "the problems on this job are of such a serious nature that there would be dire consequences unless the organization doing the work is thoroughly equipped and trained." Kaiser got the job.[36]

By the time Kaiser became a prominent California road builder, litiga-tion regarding state contracts had become commonplace. On a 1923 high-way job, Kaiser protested being asked by the division engineer to perform tasks not called for in the contract. Kaiser complained to the attorney for the State Highway Commission. The attorney's response is revealing: "Kaiser, for God's sake go ahead and finish that job up there, we have had trouble with every contract in that district, and let's try to make this one that we will not have to go to court over."[37] Even local jobs presented legal problems. On the paving of a street in the town of Mount Shasta, the local newspaper noted that "the contract was awarded to the Kaiser Paving Company, but some technicality was found by the bonding attorney. . . .

This will delay the whole work about six weeks." The paper concluded that "the history of the paving of Walnut Street would fill a large book."[38]

The importance of adequate legal representation was a concern shared by all government entrepreneurs and is captured by the experience of future Kaiser partner Morrison-Knudsen. The diary of Harry Morrison's wife, Ann, opens with M-K's first job. It involved a lawsuit, which M-K lost. The "moral," according to Ann Morrison, was "never depend on litigation to make a profit out of a contract." Yet the upshot of the case was that M-K hired the attorney of the winning side, who would be the firm's counsel for the next forty years.[39]

Contractors did not often acknowledge their reliance on legal help; instead, they spoke frequently of the value of their word, of verbal agreements as opposed to written contracts. Kaiser was no exception. One of his prized possessions was a silver goblet given to him for Christmas in 1932 by W. A. Bechtel, embossed: "To my dear friend Henry, whose word is as good as his bond." Kaiser strove to maintain a reputation for honesty and integrity, a quality most who knew him would acknowledge. Nevertheless, he aggressively pursued legal expertise as an organizational capability. Henry Kaiser was honest, but he was not naive.

Lawyers played key roles in contract interpretation, in the negotiating process, and in litigation. Lawyers also eased the contractor's navigation from business into politics. Some firms engaged lawyers not only to settle disputes but also to exercise influence. This was especially true in Texas, where "no matter how tight his finances . . . Herman Brown [of Brown & Root] always found enough for 'legal fees.'"[40]

Kaiser became accustomed to working with attorneys because of the litigious nature of contracting. He later secured the assistance of attorneys to help him first through Sacramento's bureaucratic thicket and then Washington's. It is not surprising that top-notch attorneys ultimately became part of the Kaiser team; they included Thomas Corcoran, Oscar Cox, Lloyd Cutler, and the San Francisco firm of Thelen, Marrin, Johnson and Bridges. His experience with the legal issues faced by all contractors helped position Kaiser well when Washington became a greater and greater source of work.

In an environment of negotiation, another factor in Kaiser's success was the ability to appeal successfully to higher authorities when thwarted at a lower level. In 1923, Kaiser complained to state-level officials regarding his financial award on a recently completed highway job. The resident engineer had offered to waive the state's charges to Kaiser for excessive cement use if Kaiser would accept the state's final estimate without argument.

Kaiser wrote a thirty-six-page letter to state officials, citing "absentee authority, inability, inexperience, and abuse" as obstacles to performing the work to his usual standards. He also noted the resident engineer's attempt at "intimidation." The "abuse" included the resident engineer calling one of Kaiser's Norwegian laborers a "Swede." Kaiser's appeal was upheld.[41]

Another episode from about the same time demonstrates Kaiser's understanding of the political process. Kaiser was performing a job just north of Los Angeles that required the construction of twenty miles of industrial railroad to transport materials to the job site. Stanley Abel, a member of the local board of supervisors (and local newspaper editor), objected, refusing to grant Kaiser permission to lay track. Kaiser appeared "several times" before the board, to no avail.[42] Kaiser successfully appealed to the state engineer, H. F. Morton, who intervened on Kaiser's behalf. Kaiser thanked Morton: "Your presence with Mr. Abel relieved a situation that has been tense for some time." Instinctively understanding not only how Sacramento worked but how Washington would work, Kaiser wrote: "I want you to feel free to ask me at any time to return the favor."[43]

From a political point of view, the Pacific Coast was the ideal place for Henry Kaiser to learn the ropes of construction. So much of West Coast construction was government-related that he learned valuable political lessons. The editor of America's leading engineering magazine noted: "In the Far West political considerations govern engineering. . . . This is a condition not peculiar to the West, but certainly it is more obvious there than in the older settled parts of the country. . . . The West has not progressed as far as the East in the separation of its engineering from political domination." This was because in the newly settled West most engineering was "public engineering," projects that "come close to the people, and are therefore subject to the people's whim through their elected representatives." Consequently, the West's engineering trade associations were more politically active than those elsewhere and proved a source of valuable political lessons for Kaiser.[44]

In the 1920s, a trade association movement galvanized a host of industries to establish standards of ethics, professionalism, and fair play in the marketplace. Inspired by the War Industries Board experience during World War I, which had encouraged industrywide planning and an easing of antitrust regulation, many businessmen sought to replicate the board in the Commerce Department. The movement found its leader in Commerce Secretary Herbert Hoover, who, beginning in 1921, encouraged industry self-government as a means of achieving economic stability. Hoover took particular interest in the construction industry's role in economic stability.

He saw the timing of public works as a possible "balance wheel" for the economy. Construction would be encouraged during periods of recession and cut back during boom times. The other major role for the government would be to assemble industry statistics, which would also assist industry planning.

The result was the rise of many industry-specific special interest groups that lobbied at the state and national levels. In addition, existing enterprises gained strength against potential competition from both the private and public sectors. In the private sector, the associations promulgated industry standards; in the public sector, the government eased antitrust prosecution. Ironically, Henry J. Kaiser, who would later build an industrial empire of new enterprises challenging established oligopoly and monopoly, did so after playing a leadership role in trade associations at both the state and national levels.

Kaiser joined the Northern California Contractors on the advice of Warren Bechtel at a time when they were engaged in a battle with the government. Entrepreneur and government often competed for the same business. When a state or federal department failed to receive a "reasonable" bid, it would often hire workers itself ("day labor"), who would be supervised by government engineers. Contractors perceived day labor as a threat to their livelihood. Certainly the trend was not positive for the contractors: in 1900, the Army Corps of Engineers did 12 percent of federal work by day labor and made the remaining 88 percent available to contractors. By 1924, 75 percent of the federal work was done by day laborers and only 25 percent by contractors.[45]

At the state level, the threat to contractors was not as great: as of 1922, California jobs done by day labor amounted to $4.7 million out of a total of $23.2 million. Nevertheless, California's contractors felt sufficiently threatened that in 1921 they supported a bill that would "require strict accounting on public work conducted by officials with their own forces." The bill resulted in a pocket veto. Two years later, a watered-down version passed, but it lacked sufficient provision for enforcement.[46]

This is when Kaiser got involved. As president of the Northern California Contractors, he addressed the Railroad Commission of the State of California on July 31, 1924: "It is evident that the [state] engineer's estimates of probable costs of construction of the various public utilities can be but an approximation at best. . . . It is our contention that . . . the only real definite way of determining the value of any piece of work is by taking the lowest responsible contractor's bid backed by a surety company's bond."[47] Kaiser argued that if all public utilities put their construction jobs out to

competitive bidding, the utilities, the public, and the contractors would all benefit "through greater efficiency."[48]

The campaign against day labor moved to the national stage. The 1924 platform of both the Democratic and Republican Parties provided hope for day labor opponents, including the Republicans' opposition to "attempts to put the Government into business" and the Democrats' opposition to the "extension of bureaucracy."[49] The Northern California Contractors, who had engaged this issue of national consequence, in 1926 became a chapter of the AGC, one of the nation's powerful trade associations. The AGC's 1925 convention represented a coming-out party. Speakers included President Calvin Coolidge, Commerce Secretary Herbert Hoover, Interior Secretary Hubert Work, and Budget Director H. M. Lord.[50] The AGC kept the issue of day labor very much alive until January 1928, when Hoover proposed an "independent investigation into the relative cost of public works departmentally as opposed to contract.... [He asserted,] as an engineer, that construction by contract work makes for natural economy."[51]

Those efforts finally bore fruit. In California, where contractors were known for their activism in Sacramento, the *Constructor* could report by March 1929 that day labor "has now been largely eliminated through the educational and legislative activities of the organized construction industry in the State." At the national level, the Campbell "day labor bill" passed, which made it "compulsory upon efforts to either award construction work to the lowest responsible bidder under the competitive contract system, or to account for every nickel [the state engineer] spends of public funds if he elects to depart from this system."[52]

Henry Kaiser was learning that in a risky business such as contracting, doing good work was a necessary but not sufficient condition for success. Nobody beat a path to an individual contractor's door, no matter how good the contractor was. Obtaining new work and sustaining it required vigilance, a sense of urgency, and good advocacy skills. For the contracting industry as a whole, an active presence in the political process was necessary for success, as Kaiser suggested when he spoke out on behalf of industry lobbying: "Don't be afraid of the old bugaboo that the public will say, 'Oh, it's just the contractors looking for work.' I am not afraid to tell the public that the contractors are looking for work. There is a record in Sacramento of the amount of money that is spent on proposed legislation, for and against, and investigation shows that the side which spent the most money was the side which won."[53]

Kaiser was referring to the efforts of California contractors through

the northern California chapter of the AGC to shape the environment in which they all operated through political action. The record he referred to was the campaign statement of receipts and expenditures, which showed individual and organizational contributions to each side for either a ballot initiative (task-oriented lobbying) or a legislative contest. The record shows that Kaiser was content to channel his money through his trade association.

The Northern California Contractors pursued a broad-gauged agenda in the state capital in 1925, Kaiser's second year as president. He enlisted attorney C. C. Carleton "to assist in the work at Sacramento during the legislative term." The results, as recorded in the Contractors' *Monthly Letter*, were impressive: "When the legislature reconvened following the constitutional recess there were 57 Senate bills and 51 assembly bills on the calendar which affected in various ways the construction industry." The *Monthly Letter* cited Carleton for "splendid services he rendered through the entire session. His construction in Sacramento and his splendid legal ability, coupled with unceasing activity, contributed a large percentage of the success attained."[54] Kaiser had found in Carleton an effective lawyer/lobbyist, the sort of expert he would call on with increased frequency when he pursued federal work.

State of California records indicate only one campaign to which Kaiser individually contributed in the 1920s: an effort to increase gasoline taxes to finance highway construction. The inaugural meeting of the Highway Promotion Organization was held in October 1925 with Kaiser as president. Kaiser's group organized behind California's 1926 gas tax initiative, calling for an additional one cent per gallon tax, to be used for highway construction. Kaiser contributed $1,000 to this cause.[55] The simultaneous appearance of a second gas tax highway initiative, sponsored by the Southern California Automobile Association, doomed both 1926 initiatives to defeat, but the following year a gas tax bill passed the state legislature.

Ultimately the California state legislature did what the contractors wanted, but only after the issue was presented to the voters. The entire gas tax episode demonstrated the possibilities of appealing directly to the electorate when elected officials were not immediately responsive. A few years later, Kaiser spoke to the AGC national convention about the value of promoting one of his pet projects: "Promotion and construction of transcontinental highway needs only the proper effort and national publicity. . . . If [the AGC] takes a well-prepared case to the public, they will win."[56] Kaiser would become a top practitioner of direct appeals to the American people when he was stalled by bureaucratic red tape during World War II.

There is no record of Kaiser contributing to campaigns of individual politicians.[57] This led many to refer to him as politically "naive" (which fit his image of innocence).[58] He was not. Rather, Kaiser would develop a task-oriented mode of lobbying, in which he would appeal personally to any number of government officials about a particular contract. Kaiser's approach contrasts with individual-oriented lobbying, in which a company or business executive forms a relationship with a politician (usually by making campaign contributions), who then becomes that company's advocate on a variety of issues—as Lyndon Johnson did for Brown & Root.

In tracing Johnson's power base, biographer Robert Caro asked Washington attorney and noted "fixer" Thomas ("Tommy the Cork") Corcoran for clues as to the Texan's fountainhead. "Money, kid, money," was Corcoran's response, and it led Caro to a tale of campaign contributions from oil and construction men.[59] Johnson, it turns out, had sponsors, including the Brown & Root construction firm. Kaiser's competitor from Texas contributed heavily to the campaigns of Lyndon Johnson and in return counted on a strong advocate in Congress.[60] At the outset of Johnson's congressional career, Brown & Root was a small, local firm; by the time of Johnson's presidency, Brown & Root had parlayed a series of government contracts into a position as one of the largest construction firms in the world.

Johnson's advocacy on behalf of Brown & Root brought his first contact with Kaiser. Kaiser had submitted the low bid—in competition with Brown & Root—on construction of an air base in Texas. Brown & Root appealed to then Congressman Johnson to intervene, and he convinced Kaiser to share part of the job with the Texans. When Brown & Root sought a larger share, Kaiser complained to LBJ, who convinced the Texans to accept Kaiser's offer.[61]

Although Kaiser, the trade association man, did not seek political relationships, one of his trade association brethren would become his greatest political benefactor. Shortly after being stricken with polio, Franklin D. Roosevelt became president of the American Construction Council (ACC), which acted as an umbrella organization for trade associations of architects, materials suppliers, contractors, and manufacturers. The ACC was a purely advisory body, which meant the interest group lobbying was left to individual trade associations. Roosevelt's appointment required neither much time (the council held meetings only twice a year, after which Roosevelt would issue a statement) nor travel (meetings were usually held at Roosevelt's New York City home) but provided him

with firsthand knowledge of how leaders in various sectors of the business world thought and acted: useful information for a future president.

The ACC's concerns were typical of the association movement: ethics and standards, stabilization of work flow. The ACC's creation in 1922 came on the heels of an investigation by the Lockwood Commission, which uncovered corruption in New York construction. As president, Roosevelt expressed his concern about seasonal fluctuation in construction: "Cessation of construction during the winter months is the result of psychological hallucination." Reflecting the association movement's nostalgia for the War Industries Board, in 1923 Roosevelt compared the current situation to the "most severe winter weather" of 1917, when "yards of concrete were poured while the tampers' gloves froze to the shovels. But the work went on. . . . The possibilities of a twelve month's construction year was revealed."[62]

Roosevelt's trade association experience proved to be a dress rehearsal for the First New Deal and the National Recovery Administration (NRA). The NRA hearkened back to the War Industries Board with its price-setting and barriers to new entry. When Roosevelt moved in an entirely different direction in the Second New Deal, conducting one of the most vigorous antitrust campaigns in history, he would use Henry J. Kaiser as a blunt instrument against concentrated economic power. If monopolies or oligopolies refused to cooperate with administration wishes regarding prices or output, the Roosevelt administration would assist Kaiser's efforts as a new industry entrant—in cement, magnesium, aluminum, and steel. Yet in the 1920s, Roosevelt and Kaiser were apparently quite comfortable as insiders in the old order which they would later attack.

Kaiser was an outsider, however, in his headquarters town of Oakland. Although Kaiser was one of California's premier road builders, in the city that boasts Henry Kaiser Auditorium, Kaiser Place, Kaiser Center, and Kaiser Hospital, he never paved an inch of road. He did work all over the Bay Area, from Palo Alto to San Mateo to neighboring Berkeley, but never in Oakland. The reason is that when Henry Kaiser moved to Oakland in 1921, a small clique of contractors had a stranglehold on the city's paving business.[63]

It was not until 1930 that the Oakland paving business became competitive again. Earl Warren, Alameda County's new district attorney, made a name for himself by prosecuting the Greater Oakland Construction Company, the deputy sheriff, two deputies, and the commissioner of streets. The charges, based on a complaint by another company, included various forms of bribery, discrimination against contractors not in the "ring," and conspiratorial regulations against use of certain materials.[64]

This was one of Kaiser's earliest experiences facing concentrated market power, and he chose not to fight. Like any good government entrepreneur, Kaiser was sensitive to the drift of government, which in the 1920s embraced neither antitrust prosecution nor the assistance of new entrants to an industry.[65] It probably would have hurt Kaiser's professional standing to blow the whistle on the competition. *Western Construction News*, the Pacific Coast's bible for general contractors like Kaiser, was initially defensive toward Warren's investigation. An editorial suggested that the inquiry "has the earmarks of an attempt to discredit the present political administration." Clearly protective of established contractors rather than supporting attempts to open the industry to new entrants, the editors summed up: "We have altogether too many of these political upheavals, which seldom uncover the true facts in the case, but result in the besmirching of many an innocent engineer and contractor."[66]

Another reason Kaiser did not make a complaint was that by the 1920s, street paving was a tiny segment of his business; he had graduated to state highway construction. Then, in 1927, Kaiser's old friends Warren Brothers offered him a subcontract for 200 miles of highway in Cuba. The Cuban project—750 miles in all—was one of the largest highway contracts ever granted. Warren Brothers chose Kaiser not only because of their ongoing relationship but because Kaiser had already demonstrated skill at assembling and handling sand and aggregates.[67] Warren Brothers was building in an area of Cuba (Camaguay) with no visible supply of rock, sand, or gravel. A Warren Brothers representative wrote that "the most urgent and immediate problems confronting the contractors were the investigation of sources of supplies of sand, stone, and gravel."[68]

Remote locations of jobs, far from urban centers (and from sites of earlier work), meant that western contractors could not count on local suppliers of key raw materials. Therefore, many contractors learned to provide their own. Consequently, America's largest vertically integrated construction outfits of the latter half of the twentieth century were typically western. Henry Kaiser integrated early, first providing his own sand and gravel rather than purchasing it in 1916, and established a reputation his brethren would later mention: "[Kaiser's] concern is noted for the effective manner in which it has produced its own sand and gravel and other materials for specific projects, a method of procedure frequently forced on contractors engaged in isolated projects in the West."[69] By the 1920s Kaiser had gone beyond filling the needs of his own jobs and had begun selling materials produced in his plants. Continuous vertical integration would be a standard mode of operation for the rest of his career.

In Cuba, Kaiser's people designed, constructed, and operated "semi-portable" rock-crushing plants because there were no rock quarries in the vicinity. By 1927, his people had already built numerous plants to crush rocks in the western United States. This ability was desperately needed on the Cuba project, an undertaking that vaulted Kaiser from a regional contractor into the ranks of international giants. At $20 million, it was more than twice the value of all Kaiser's previous work combined.[70]

Henry Kaiser received the education he needed in government entrepreneurship before coming to Washington in the 1930s. He learned how to counteract the risks endemic to contracting with government authorities (calling on attorneys when necessary) by vertically integrating his enterprises and by mechanizing as a means of speeding up his work. Above all, Henry Kaiser's education in the years 1914–32 involved a departure from the individualism for which contractors were once known. Kaiser learned the ropes of political process and influence as he became a leader in the trade association movement.

Upon his arrival in Washington in 1932, Kaiser was prepared to apply the lessons he had learned at the state and local levels to the federal government. In Washington, he would have ample opportunity further to develop his organization's governmental capabilities. Within a year, the New Deal revolution began, giving birth to a new set of opportunities for government entrepreneurs like Henry Kaiser.

The tax state is not altogether limited to derived revenues . . . but it can also create its own economic sphere within the world of capitalism and can become an entrepreneur itself.

Joseph A. Schumpeter

3 ——— GOVERNMENT ENTREPRENEURSHIP COMES OF AGE

In his 1955 classic, *The Age of Reform*, Richard Hofstadter echoed a popular conception of the New Deal: "With its pragmatic spirit and its relentless emphasis upon results, [it] seemed to have carried [Americans] farther than ever from the kind of society in which economic life was linked to character and to distinctively entrepreneurial freedoms and opportunities."[1] Such a view neglects one category of entrepreneurial opportunities that proliferated in that period.[2] As the federal government experienced rapid growth during the New Deal—which accelerated with the coming of World War II—the administrative state became an important source of entrepreneurial opportunity. Far from carrying American

society away from entrepreneurial opportunities, the New Deal offered expanded opportunities to a particular type of entrepreneur: the government entrepreneur.

Entrepreneurs did not have to shed their reputations for boldness and audacity to work with the New Deal. One of the organizing principles of the New Deal from its inception had been that the government should take risks on behalf of American society that the private sector might not. This could mean lending money when banks would not or offering assistance to industry newcomers who might not otherwise challenge entrenched market power. The risks New Dealers were willing to support accrued to the reputation of businessmen who were willing to work with them. Therefore, Henry Kaiser earned a greater and greater reputation as a risk-taker the closer his relationship with the federal government became.

Franklin Roosevelt's New Deal sustained a long-standing tradition of government entrepreneurship. In the nineteenth century the federal government had played a key role in the construction of public works projects such as canals and railroads. Such "infrastructure entrepreneurship" was typical of the projects undertaken by Henry J. Kaiser early in his career. By the time of the Great Depression, infrastructure entrepreneurship was common at the federal, state, and local levels.

For government entrepreneurs, the New Deal had three phases. The First New Deal (1933–35), included the planning period and the heyday of the original "brains trust" and was the time of the administration's healthiest relations with the business community. For government entrepreneurs, the most perceptible change was an increase in public construction's share of American construction activity. The Second New Deal (1936–39) was when the administration lost much of its business support, and the Keynesians and antitrusters were ascendant. The volume of public works projects dramatically increased during this phase. In the New Deal War (1939–41) the administration's economic goals dovetailed with mobilization needs, particularly in boosting production and decentralizing the nation's industrial base.[3]

During the 1920s there had been a stigma associated with performing government work. In 1928, the chief of the United States Veterans Bureau construction division acknowledged negative attitudes of contractors toward government contracting when he wrote that "such work has not been previously considered as a profitable field for exploitation." Introducing his article, the editors of the *Constructor* agreed: "The fact that government construction contracts, as a class, have not been regarded by gen-

eral contractors during recent years as especially desirable is well known." The editors noted that the Veterans Bureau chief's article was part of an effort to "make a government contract a prize to be desired rather than a thing to be avoided."[4]

Stagnation in the private sector changed that situation, boosting public construction from 20 to 30 percent of America's total in the 1920s to more than 50 percent during Roosevelt's first term.[5] By the time of FDR's inauguration, it was becoming increasingly difficult for businessmen to turn down government work. Opportunities for such work, however, would not proliferate quickly.

During its first thousand days, the New Deal did little to change the nature of government entrepreneurship or to expand opportunities for government entrepreneurs. The plums for government entrepreneurs, for instance, were along traditional lines: massive public works projects, some of which had been initiated during previous administrations. Federal spending for public construction actually declined during Roosevelt's first term compared to the Hoover administration.[6] Contemporaries criticized the New Deal's sluggish beginnings in the area of public works. The *Economist* noted in 1936, for instance, that "in the United States public works have not been increased; they have merely been prevented from fading altogether away."[7] Interior Secretary Harold Ickes was considered overly cautious, and the president showed no signs that he believed public works expansion could speed economic recovery.[8] Not until the Second New Deal (1936–39), when Keynesian ideas began to win converts in the administration, did the quantity of government work show an appreciable increase. During the Second New Deal an increase in opportunities, including public works projects, reinforced the increased popularity of government entrepreneurship.

The nature of government entrepreneurship changed when the mobilization for war began in 1940, and Henry Kaiser was part of the first wave of the "New Deal War." In contrast to earlier government entrepreneurs, the new breed was industrial and saw itself as playing a permanent role in the state. The new government entrepreneurs were more adept at lobbying the executive branch than business leaders had been in the past. Despite the Truman administration's sharp reductions in defense spending, many of the government entrepreneurs of the early 1940s survived to become principal players in the military-industrial complex of the 1950s and afterward. Government entrepreneurship had come of age.

Henry Kaiser's path in the 1930s shows in bold relief many of the op-

portunities for government entrepreneurs and how they changed. When the decade began, Kaiser's organization was in the midst of its final road-building project: a two-hundred-mile highway in Cuba. By 1940, Kaiser was poised to produce magnesium, steel, and aircraft as part of America's mobilization effort. Kaiser spent most of the intervening years constructing major dams in the West, the first of which was Boulder Dam.

No construction project of the 1930s had as much impact on public consciousness as Boulder Dam. The "great pyramid of the American desert" was built in Black Canyon, where the Colorado River marks the border between Nevada and Arizona.[9] Shortly after its completion, the dam was pictured in the *Christian Science Monitor* with the caption, "It Just about Rivals Yellowstone."[10] The project was designed to provide flood control for California's Imperial Valley and hydroelectric power, irrigation, and drinking water to an area including much of southern California. Boulder was America's greatest engineering endeavor since the construction of the Panama Canal; it was to be the largest man-made object in the Western world.

Boulder was more than just an engineering dream come true; it was a testament to federal involvement in regional economic development. Though public works projects and the concept of regional development are usually associated in the collective memory with the New Deal, Boulder was approved in the closing days of the Coolidge administration. Secretary of Commerce Herbert Hoover had actively pushed the project and helped shepherd the political forces necessary to gain congressional support.[11] In addition to his direct efforts to bring the project to life, Hoover also had an indirect impact on the contract process. The conception of Boulder Dam was a case study in Hoover's laboratory of industrial self-regulation through trade associations.[12]

Henry Kaiser's experience with the Boulder Dam project both shows the extraordinary value of trade association membership to a government entrepreneur at the time and offers a glimpse of the distinctive approach to government relations Kaiser later employed on his own. Before the bidding process on the dam began, Kaiser's Associated General Contractors of America had made its mark on the project. In October 1930, the Executive Board of the AGC passed a resolution regarding the suggested contract provisions in the upcoming project. Representatives of the AGC then discussed these principles with members of the Bureau of Reclamation. The chief issue—one at least partially aimed at discouraging newcomers to the process—was assuring that bidders provide "evidence of

their qualifications as to experience, organization, and financial resources" beforehand.[13] The negotiation process for this contract, then, began before any bids were made.

The huge contract was a jewel in the morass of the Depression years. Kaiser joined a consortium of western construction firms, which was established to perform this project. The consortium, called the Six Companies, was awarded the contract in April 1931 with a bid just under $50 million, the largest contract ever let by the U.S. government up to that time.[14] Each of the partners brought its own expertise to the table. Kaiser brought both experience in locating and assembling raw materials and the ability to deal effectively with government officials.[15] In the latter capacity, Kaiser would spend a good deal of time in Washington: he was guardian of the Six Companies' jewel.

Barely a year into the project, during the depths of the Depression, Kaiser's lobbying skills were tested. As part of a campaign to balance the federal budget, Congress refused to appropriate the money the Bureau of Reclamation requested to complete Boulder Dam.[16] When congressional hearings were held on whether to renew the appropriation, Kaiser testified on behalf of the Six Companies. He had help. Elwood Mead, head of the Bureau of Reclamation, testified on behalf of the appropriation. George B. Walbridge, past president of the AGC and now its "legislative affairs specialist" (lobbyist), testified immediately after Kaiser. Walbridge presented himself as a relative bystander, never having had any business ties with the Six Companies or any involvement with the Boulder Dam project.[17] The AGC was taking care of its own.

Kaiser and the Six Companies received help from another source: the White House. Herbert Hoover had been an early supporter of the project. He engineered the "Colorado Compact," a 1922 multistate agreement crucial to generating congressional support for the dam. Now Hoover intervened on behalf of the renewed appropriation. In July, Congress complied.[18]

In the Boulder Dam project, Kaiser was chiefly a federal government contractor. At the end of the 1920s, Kaiser had moved from highway construction for the state of California to highways in Cuba and to pipelines for Standard Oil of California, Texaco, and other private concerns. In 1932, for the first time, all of Kaiser's work was performed for the federal government.[19]

That year was also pivotal for Kaiser in gaining professional recognition and political contacts. In January, Kaiser was elected vice president

of the AGC. When the president-elect died in March, Kaiser replaced him. As president, Kaiser was one of two members of the AGC invited to the White House to exchange ideas on economic recovery with President Hoover.

Despite his professional advancement, Kaiser was relatively unknown to the public. The only mention of Kaiser in the *New York Times* in the 1930s came in the summer of 1932, when his son Edgar married the daughter of Bureau of Reclamation head Elwood Mead.[20] Kaiser was now moving in the circles of people who could help him promote the interests of the Six Companies. In 1934, Kaiser attached a letter from the superintendent of the Boulder Dam project along with one of his own to his son's new father-in-law. The superintendent had already approached the bureau's Denver office with a request, which had been denied. Kaiser wrote, "I know you will understand this is not an attempt to circumvent the Denver office . . . and therefore I take the liberty of addressing your office directly and furnishing you with the information."[21] Kaiser's denial notwithstanding, he was applying an important skill he had learned earlier: appealing to a higher authority.

Kaiser was also developing a reputation as one who could deliver in Washington on behalf of others. Earlier in 1934, the director of California's Department of Public Works wrote to Kaiser "to extend to you my very great appreciation for the help and assistance that you gave us in the financing of the Central Valley project when the cause seemed almost to be lost by reason of the lack of sufficient funds."[22]

The company Kaiser kept would have mattered little had he not been a superb salesman. Mead, Hoover, Walbridge, and others responded favorably to his initiatives. Years later, when Kaiser was the most famous alumnus of the Six Companies, he would refer to Boulder as "my dam." His partners, in turn, would refer to him as the "public relations guy."[23] They had good reason. Utah Construction's Marriner Eccles, who later became head of the Federal Reserve, recalled that Kaiser had pushed for building a visitor's cottage at Boulder. His partners saw it as a waste of money, a poorly timed extravagance in the midst of the Depression. Kaiser persevered, and the $25,000 cottage was built, complete with servants and a full-time chef.[24] The visitor's cottage was a precursor to the institutional television advertisements—aimed at members of Congress—aired in the Washington, D.C., area today by large corporations. Kaiser saw the entertainment of government officials as an investment in the sustained funding of the dam and as an opportunity to convince key government officials and opinion makers that the Six Companies was a professional outfit. This

was an approach contractors had not tried before, but Henry Kaiser realized the importance of marketing his organization to key individuals.

Kaiser also promoted himself. In late 1935, he told James Farley, chairman of the Democratic National Committee, "that he would raise a heavy contribution to the campaign fund." Aware of Kaiser's promise, a Roosevelt aide suggested that the president send Kaiser a telegram. Roosevelt did; he acknowledged the ailing Kaiser's regrets at not being able to attend the Boulder Dam dedication and sent "best wishes for your speedy recovery."[25] Kaiser never did make the contribution.[26]

Realizing that Boulder Dam was more than just a construction project, Kaiser strove to achieve the best possible political spin for the Six Companies. He hired a newspaper reporter to see "that the facts are truthfully presented to both magazines and newspapers."[27] The new publicist was also charged with "reception and conduct of prominent visitors." Construction mavens heretofore had not concerned themselves with public relations. The Six Companies produced a steady flow of news stories, reports, and briefings. Trade journals, science and engineering magazines, and even newsletters of companies not involved in the project were full of stories on the dam.[28]

Perhaps the greatest public relations challenge facing the Six Companies and Henry Kaiser involved working conditions at Boulder Dam. Kaiser's attitude toward labor relations would undergo a remarkable transformation in the 1930s, when he aligned himself with New Deal policies regarding collective bargaining. An examination of labor relations at Boulder Dam indicates how far Kaiser traveled on his road to a conciliatory labor policy.

When Henry Kaiser died in 1967, the principal accomplishment for which he was eulogized was neither the construction of Boulder and the other great dams in the West nor his shipbuilding feats during World War II. Instead, he was remembered for his conciliatory labor relations. He became the first industrialist ever to win the AFL-CIO's highest honor, the Philip Murray–William Green Award, in 1965. President Johnson saluted Kaiser as a "pioneer of the new breed of responsible businessmen."[29] Twenty-five years later, the U.S. Department of Labor selected Kaiser for its Hall of Fame.

Few who dealt with the Six Companies in the early 1930s would have predicted that one of its principals would receive such recognition for labor relations. These hard-nosed construction moguls were well known for their open-shop policies.[30] The Boulder Dam project offered some of the most miserable and hazardous working and living conditions encoun-

tered by the twentieth-century construction industry. When the dam was completed in 1935, the government installed a plaque to the memory of 110 men, women, and children who died in Black Canyon.

Just as the New Deal's embrace of collective bargaining would later shape Henry Kaiser's labor relations policies, Kaiser's Six Companies took some of their labor policy cues at Boulder Dam from the federal government. Ironically, the project's most miserable working conditions, those endured during the summer of 1931, came about in part because of the Hoover administration's humanitarian concerns. The original contract schedule called for work to begin in October 1931, but the national economic emergency was so severe that President Hoover and Interior Secretary Ray Lyman Wilbur prevailed upon Reclamation Director Mead to begin the work sooner so as to provide immediate jobs for the unemployed.[31]

Work began April first, months before the Six Companies could construct Boulder City and satisfy their contractual obligation to house 80 percent of the project's workers. The summer of 1931 brought temperatures as high as 140 degrees to Black Canyon, and daily highs averaged 119. Nighttime temperatures rarely fell below 90, and the men sweltered in barracks with no air conditioning. From June 25 to July 26, fourteen men died of heat prostration. Exhaustion and heat prostration also led to carelessness, accidents, and a generally restive workforce. In early August, a wage cut precipitated a strike by a thousand workers. The modesty of the strikers' demands suggests the egregious conditions under which they worked. Among their demands were pure water and flush toilets at the River Camp; a supply of ice water on and off the job; a "safety engineer" at each tunnel to give first aid to injured workers; and compliance with all Nevada and Arizona mining safety laws.[32]

The Six Companies announced that none of the deaths were job-related, then rejected the demands and fired the strikers. An abundant supply of cheap labor was available in Las Vegas to replace any strikers and to help convince the workers to accept conditions as they were. Sounding like a villain from *The Grapes of Wrath*, a Six Companies partner announced from San Francisco that "they will have to work under our conditions or not at all."[33]

The Six Companies' chief concern was speed. The contract required them to "turn the river"—divert the Colorado through tunnels, leaving the riverbed exposed for construction of the dam's foundation—by October 1, 1933. Failure to meet that deadline would cost the contractors substantial penalties. After having worked three shifts a day—with the gov-

ernment's approval—for months, the project's superintendent was in a position to announce that "we are six months ahead of schedule on the work now, and we can afford to refuse concessions that would cost $2,000 daily."[34] Cost won out over health and safety.

The Six Companies adopted an even more cold-blooded position on the issue of carbon monoxide poisoning. Although Nevada safety laws forbade the use of gas engines underground, the Six Companies used gas-powered muck-hauling trucks and caterpillar tractors. Many workers suffered respiratory problems. When some workers died from respiratory ailments, Six Companies doctors called it pneumonia, not carbon monoxide poisoning. Forty-two of Boulder Dam's deaths were attributed to pneumonia, more than any other single cause.[35]

In November 1931, a Nevada state mining inspector called for the Six Companies to stop using gasoline-powered trucks in the tunnels. Instead of abiding by the order, the Six Companies called on legal expertise, a necessary organizational capability for any successful contractor. They were advised to fight the state aggressively on this issue, then to contest any lawsuits from individual workers or their survivors.

In one respect, the strategy worked: the tunnels were completed during wrangling over restraining orders and case postponement. The Six Companies completed the dam more than two years ahead of schedule and cleared more than $10 million profit. Ultimately, after a circus trial in Las Vegas, the Six Companies settled forty-eight carbon monoxide lawsuits out of court. A careful historian of Hoover Dam concludes that the Six Companies "tried to cover up and evade responsibility" for a lethal safety hazard that they had knowingly sustained so as "to protect a $300,000 investment in gasoline-fueled trucks and avoid costly delay while electric motors were installed."[36]

The Six Companies would have done well to listen to the advice of a prominent industrialist, speaking in the nation's capital in 1942: "If you spent as much time and as much money keeping advised as to how your labor feels and thinks, and what it needs and wants . . . or if you spent as much time on your labor as your sales, you wouldn't have any problem."[37] The industrialist was Henry J. Kaiser.

Where was this labor relations wizard in the summer and fall of 1931? Where was the chairman of the Six Companies' executive committee, which oversaw the work of the superintendent and his crew? Henry Kaiser's lobbying responsibilities kept him away from the work site longer than any other member of the executive committee, but if the habits of a lifetime are any indication, he was in close touch by phone.

A man so willing to seize credit for the project's accomplishments must also bear responsibility for its worst moments. The closest Kaiser would come to acknowledging his mistakes at Boulder Dam came years later when he spoke of undergoing a "transformation" in his attitudes regarding labor relations and collective bargaining.

Transformed he was. The man who had battled the American Federation of Labor (AFL) during 1932 congressional hearings performed a 180-degree turnabout.[38] In 1937 he was a driving force in the establishment of an agreement between the AFL and Kaiser's Rock, Sand, and Gravel Producers Association of Northern California.[39] By January 1939, Kaiser had established a sufficient track record in collective bargaining to note—as part of his proposal to supply the cement for the government—that he had "faithfully followed the policies of this administration with reference to collective bargaining, both in letter and spirit, whether we were or not within the purview of the Wagner Act."[40] By 1940, Kaiser's ties with the AFL were close enough that he used an AFL official as a reference when trying to obtain defense work.[41]

Kaiser's rapprochement with organized labor in the late 1930s coincided with his evolution from a construction man to an industrialist. Although he had a loyal core group of workers—mainly supervisors—who followed him from one dam project to the next, many of the faces changed from site to site. When Kaiser began establishing large-scale industrial operations in cement, shipbuilding, and steel, his workforce was more stable and negotiating union agreements offered possible long-term benefits of loyalty and greater productivity. The construction industry, with its itinerant workforce, was resistant to collective bargaining. In the late 1930s, Kaiser was moving into an environment—heavy manufacturing—in which collective bargaining was more common.

In subsequent years, Kaiser would attribute his labor relations transformation to a personal epiphany. Yet his speech to the National Press Club in July 1942 reveals a key variable that changed in the 1930s: "I didn't believe in unions at all many years ago; I wouldn't hire union men on the job. When the Government decided that the men should be organized and that we should have collective bargaining I decided I should abide by what the Government wanted to do, whether I agreed with it or not."[42] Successful entrepreneurs like Kaiser follow Charles DeGaulle's advice: "Exploit the inevitable." In this case, the inevitable came from Washington: the New Deal's labor policy embodied in the 1935 Wagner Act and establishment of the National Labor Relations Board to protect collective bargaining.

A change in the law alone could never explain the lengths to which Kaiser went to help his workers. Kaiser went well beyond both the spirit and the letter of the law to take a leadership role in industrial labor relations. On subsequent dam projects in the late 1930s, he began to provide his employees with low-cost medical service, a plan that evolved into today's Kaiser Permanente HMO.[43] During World War II, the day care centers at his shipyards attracted national attention as a benefit to working mothers.[44] In 1946, Kaiser Steel began a pattern of breaking ranks with the competition to settle with the union in advance of industrywide agreements.[45]

These initiatives were the work of a man who had a change of heart in the 1930s. Kaiser had both the vision and the genuine interest in his workers' well-being necessary to anticipate and implement new possibilities in the workplace, some of which were decades ahead of their time. Yet as Kaiser noted, these innovations began as an entrepreneur's response to a great change—New Deal labor policy—in his environment.

Labor relations was not the only area of transformation for Henry Kaiser during the 1930s. The radical changes in government entrepreneurship provided great opportunities for those nimble enough to adapt. The biggest changes in the landscape were the increase in size of the federal government and a considerable shift in power from the legislative to the executive branch. Kaiser therefore shifted from a group lobbying approach focused on the legislative branch to a more individualistic approach focused on the executive branch.

The public Henry Kaiser of the 1940s—individualistic, maverick, headline-grabbing—is quite different from the Kaiser of the 1920s. The earlier Kaiser toed the trade association line, acting on behalf of an entire industry rather than one enterprise. It appears as though Kaiser simply shifted his allegiance from the group to himself and became utterly focused on his growing empire. To an extent that did happen, but it is far from a complete explanation.

From 1921 to 1932, Kaiser had allowed trade associations to speak for him as they lobbied Congress (and before that, the California state legislature). For years, he—along with his trade association—had lobbied state and federal governments regarding day labor, gasoline taxes, and public works policy. He gave numerous speeches in support of specific pieces of legislation. At the same time, he personally engaged government officials regarding specific contracts but saw the value of allowing the collective voice—and collective fund-raising ability—of the trade association to represent his views to legislators.

He also changed his approach in response to the new political climate in Washington. When the New Deal's experiment in industrial self-government, the National Recovery Administration, was declared unconstitutional, it marked the end of an era (1925–35) in which trade associations were engaged in "policy shaping."[46] A difficult period ensued for trade associations. They were no longer invited to join with the government to set industry prices, wages, and production levels. In addition, they saw their legislative lobbying function lose value as power shifted to the executive branch.

Henry Kaiser remained a trade association member but was no longer a trade association man. By the 1940s, Kaiser refused to take a public position on legislation. Instead, he directed his efforts toward a more individualistic, task-oriented effort to discover new opportunities in Washington. Kaiser abandoned traditional legislative lobbying; his Washington representatives were chartered to find work, not to change the law.

Which was the "real" Kaiser? He excelled as an insider, a trade association man, as any member of the AGC, the Rock, Sand, and Gravel Producers Association of Northern California, or the American Road Builders Association would testify. He had extraordinary leadership skills and was a gifted salesman given to Babbitt-like boosterism. Kaiser's involvement with trade associations helps explain why he devoted little energy early in his career to battling insiders. Kaiser had thrived in the trade association movement, the main impulse of which was to maintain the status quo and thereby protect the vested interests of established industry players.

This all changed in the late 1930s. Years of federal government cooperation with established industry leaders and their trade associations gave way to acrimony between big business and government. Now Kaiser proved he was also an excellent outsider. He seemed most comfortable and energized as a maverick attempting to challenge the big business establishment. Kaiser was above all an entrepreneur, and—as Joseph Schumpeter noted—entrepreneurs view the world as something to change rather than something to accept.[47]

Arthur Schlesinger Jr. described the First New Deal as a period when New Dealers "attached a high value to social cohesion and viewed the governmental process as an exercise in conversion and cooperation." During the Second New Deal, the administration "saw the governmental process as an exercise in litigation and combat."[48] Effective government entrepreneurship had always required both cooperation and combativeness. During the 1930s, cooperation with the federal government became more important than alignment with the industry establishment.

Much of Henry Kaiser's success as a government entrepreneur can be attributed to the fact that he—like Ross Perot more recently—was talented both as an insider and as an outsider. During World War II, Kaiser cultivated an extraordinary image as a maverick battler of bureaucracy at the same time he was building important relationships with key executive branch insiders. The publicity Kaiser received in 1941 was new to him, but his mixed role as insider/outsider was not. The anti–big business policies of the Second New Deal had already revealed Kaiser's gifts as a maverick at the same time that he began to assemble key administration allies.

Much has been written about the government's antitrust activities of the 1930s and big business's response. Unfortunately, little has been written from the point of view of potential new entrants. Henry Kaiser's saga reveals much about the resulting opportunities for newcomers. Although his reputation and enterprises grew as he tackled major dam projects in the 1930s, it was not until the antitrust crusade of the Second New Deal that the nature of his enterprises changed. Kaiser appeared as an attractive newcomer whose enterprises would help the government deal with both its budgetary and procurement concerns and its macroeconomic pricing issues.

Some of the fiercest battles Henry Kaiser waged were attempts to enter industries in which power was concentrated in a few hands. Kaiser launched his new cement venture in 1939 in response to the government's procurement complaints. The following year, his interest in helping the preparedness program dovetailed with the desires of New Dealers to inject "new blood" into the aircraft, magnesium, and steel industries. Kaiser became a symbol of the New Deal War, an attempt to assist Britain and France while simultaneously sustaining the policies of the Second New Deal. His attempts to become an alternative producer later attracted national attention when he entered the automobile and aluminum industries. His choice of established industries with such daunting barriers to entry made Kaiser appear bold to most, reckless to many. Yet he carefully chose his battles, usually going ahead only after performing extensive feasibility studies and when assured that he had the weight of the government behind him.

Cement is a great example. The popular press later portrayed Kaiser as blindly walking out on a limb, bidding the huge contract to supply cement for the Shasta Dam project in 1939 before constructing his plant. Yet before making a commitment, Kaiser learned that officials in the Treasury Department, the Interior Department, and the Reconstruction Finance Corporation wanted him to succeed. He had also done his homework, as

a letter to the Bureau of Reclamation nearly two months before bids were accepted on the Shasta job shows: "We have constructed a laboratory on the property [in Santa Clara Valley], opened quarries, initiated screening plants, built several miles of roads, have completed general plans for the most modern and low operating cost cement plant in the world. We have employed capable cement chemists and engineers." Kaiser also noted that he had spent nearly a million dollars on these preparations.[49]

Only when the New Deal began to pursue antitrust actions did Henry Kaiser became a symbol of those who felt they had been systematically barred from participation in the national economy. Kaiser's skill in choosing his battles and in aligning himself successfully with the powers that be is demonstrated in his approach to the cement industry, which was part of many antitrust skirmishes over the next decade.

A few weeks before Franklin Roosevelt's 1933 inaugural, Henry Kaiser already had fired a shot across the bow of California's cement combine. In a letter to five established producers, Kaiser warned: "You must be aware that this company has been considering the necessity of manufacturing cement."[50] As a prolific user of cement, Kaiser was concerned about excessive prices for raw materials.

Kaiser faced a system of "uniform delivered prices," under which prices of cement varied throughout the nation and the state of California but at any particular point all producers quoted the same prices. Like the steel industry, the other principal building materials industry singled out by the federal government, the cement industry was a notorious practitioner of the "basing point" system of price setting. This system required each producer to bid uniform prices and freight charges at each location based on production and shipment from an agreed-on basing point, usually the region's largest producer. A consumer—such as the government—"would get identical bids no matter whether the product was shipped ten miles or a thousand miles."[51] If buying from a nearby producer, a consumer would pay additional "phantom freight" as if the cement came from the basing point.

Even if customers were able to perform their own hauling, they would be charged as if the seller had shipped from the basing point. Therefore, there was little incentive to buy locally. Estimates of annual waste in "cross-hauling" ran above $40 million in the cement industry alone.[52]

A combination of product standardization—cement was a virtual commodity—and price collusion protected the cement industry from ruinous price competition. The cement producers were protective of their pricing system because of the industry's high capital costs and consequent need

for high volume to make any profit. For producers, the beauty of the basing point system was that when demand for local cement was insufficient to sustain their productive capacity, they could increase volume elsewhere without lowering the prices charged to their local customers.[53] A trustee of the Cement Institute, the president of a southern California cement producer, admitted in 1934 that "ours is an industry that cannot stand free competition, that must systematically restrain competition or be ruined."[54] In March 1938, when the administration was gearing up to battle the cement industry on the subject of administered prices, Treasury Secretary Henry Morgenthau Jr. showed President Roosevelt the cement producer's letter that included this quotation. Roosevelt gleefully accepted the ammunition and called it "an amazingly interesting letter."[55]

The federal government had sporadically complained, protested, and investigated cement industry pricing until the Roosevelt administration, when the complaints, protests, and investigations multiplied.[56] Individual states, including California in the late 1920s, had also periodically battled the cement companies over the pricing issue. In 1929, California state lawmakers had investigated the pricing policies of the state's cement industry. They discovered that for the year 1927, all northern California companies (the five to which Kaiser addressed his 1933 letter) had made identical bids for all contracts involving state institutions. Since 1921, all bids to the city of San Francisco had also been identical. Furthermore, although annoying to buyers, such behavior was legal as long as prices were not "unreasonable."[57]

From 1929 to 1931, the cement producers' solidarity on pricing was broken briefly in a spate of price competition. Prices of concrete ingredients fell nearly 15 percent during this period. From July 1932 to July 1933, they realigned and prices soared by more than 15 percent.[58] It was during this period of price increase that the issue of identical bidding escalated to the federal level.

In May 1933, barely two months into the New Deal, Interior Secretary Ickes rejected all the cement bids for the Boulder Dam project because they quoted identical prices. Ickes was outraged that the ten identical bids he received were nearly 20 percent higher than the government had received two months before on a different project. He asked the Federal Trade Commission (FTC) to investigate the "cement trust," which he believed endangered the social goals of public works programs: "Increasing the price of cement at a time like this, when the government is striving to alleviate unemployment by building public works, most of which require cement in their construction, must have a deterrent effect on the govern-

ment program." Ickes saw a direct relationship between the price increase and high unemployment rates: "It should be borne in mind that an increase in the price of materials will take just that much away from funds available for labor. The more we give to the cement trust, the less is left for wages."[59]

Ickes mentioned two possible courses of government action in response to the "trust": either the government could construct its own plant to supply Boulder Dam, or "it may be necessary for us to contract with one company, outside the cement trust, to furnish all the material we need at a fair market price."[60] The government would choose the latter option five years later at Shasta Dam, launching Henry Kaiser into the cement business.

Two days after the *New York Times* reported Ickes's tirade, Ickes noted in his diary that he had received "many telegrams and letters from manufacturers of cement uttering loud wails, and protesting their high virtues." Accompanying the complaints were telegrams and letters from those who saw an opportunity for government entrepreneurship, "persons willing to manufacture cement for the government if we will guarantee to but a quantity sufficient to justify the investment that will be involved."[61] One of those letters came from the general manager of the San Jose Cement Company, which sought government financing for a cement plant to be built "in Santa Clara County near San Jose," where Henry Kaiser ultimately built his plant. Nothing came of San Jose Cement's proposal or of Kaiser's threat earlier in the year, probably because America's cement producers were operating at about 30 percent capacity and northern California's were operating at only 25 percent capacity.[62] With the private sector market for cement so depressed, the only hope for a newcomer was to secure a large government contract. Therefore, the government's willingness to press the matter was the determining factor for new entrants.

The New Deal was not yet in antitrust mode in 1933. In fact, the business-government cooperation envisioned during the NRA (1933-35) led to suspension of antitrust laws and protection of the basing point system.[63] Harold Ickes fought alone.

Ickes's rejection of the bids was highly publicized but not particularly effective. The Interior Department's Bureau of Reclamation considered producing its own cement for the Boulder Dam project but finally chose to purchase.[64] Ickes ordered the Bureau of Reclamation to ask for competitive bids. He recalled later that "on one or two offers we did get such bids, but subsequently they refused to bid that way."[65] The practice of identical bids by the northern California cement producers, for instance, continued

for years afterward. Congress investigated "administered prices" of the steel and cement industries in 1936 but failed to pass any new legislation.[66] The hearings publicized the issue of unfair prices and helped raise the administration's consciousness about concentrations of economic power. Little changed in the cement industry until the Shasta Dam project.

At Shasta Dam, Henry Kaiser rebounded from one of his most bitter setbacks and scored one of his greatest triumphs. In 1938, Kaiser's Six Companies had tackled two large projects along the Pacific Northwest's Columbia River: they were finishing Bonneville Dam and had just begun work on the superstructure of the Grand Coulee Dam. In June of that year, Kaiser bid on the Shasta Dam, part of California's giant Central Valley project. He missed out by less than 1 percent. Kaiser surprised the cement producers and pleased the government by bidding to supply cement for Shasta, boldly invading the turf of northern California's cement "combine." Kaiser's was the low bid, and the government awarded him the contract although he did not yet have a cement plant.[67]

Reflecting on the cement battle years later, Kaiser's Washington representative, Chad Calhoun, noted that Kaiser's challenge to the cement combine "won many friends for Henry Kaiser on the national scene." Indeed, Ickes wrote that "on our Shasta dam job [Kaiser] broke the cement trust for us."[68] Yet Kaiser would not have acted had those powerful friends in the federal government not provided him with an opportunity. As Calhoun emphasized, "The battle that initiated Permanente Cement was fought right here in Washington, D.C."[69] When he acted in response to the government's initiatives, Kaiser became a visible symbol of the rising tide of New Deal resentment against concentrated market power. Following Henry Kaiser's actions is a good way to gauge shifts in administration policies that affected government entrepreneurship. Whereas Kaiser had hesitated to make such a move in 1933, by 1938 he sensed a healthier landscape for new entrants and seized the opportunity to align himself with administration policy, which had changed considerably in the intervening five years.

Kaiser's grievances paralleled those of the government in ways he did not always acknowledge. He was at least partly disingenuous when explaining that he embarked on his crusade against the combine because "it used to anger me to see the cement companies gouge the little contractor."[70] The cement companies did gouge the little contractor, but both Kaiser and the government were more upset that identical bidding would prevent quantity discounts. Indeed, in March 1938, a Kaiser associate summarized the reasons for his entry into the cement industry. First on the list

was "controversy with cement companies which showed a lack of proper interest in necessity for wet mix concrete paving having a preferential price in cement."[71]

In 1937 the Roosevelt administration was shifting toward an aggressive antitrust position and had the cement industry in its sights. Government officials believed they were being overcharged for building materials—including cement—and responded as concerned consumers. The government was a sufficiently valued customer—especially because private construction had virtually disappeared—that New Dealers believed they could make an example of the cement industry. In addition to their own budgetary concerns, many New Dealers believed the ability of cement and other industries to maintain their high prices while others fell might "impair the entire recovery effort."[72] In June 1937, Roosevelt asked the FTC chairman informally to look into cement prices. The cement industry was an excellent choice; for roughly the next two years, the cement industry offered more instances of identical bidding than any other.[73] In November, Roosevelt launched a formal investigation into prices of building materials. In March 1938 came the conclusion: prices for iron and steel, cement, and gypsum were too high.

Most of the planning for this battle went on in the Treasury Department, which was responsible for a majority of the government's procurement. On March 21, in response to a proposal by Treasury Secretary Morgenthau, President Roosevelt agreed to concentrate all cement purchases in the Treasury Department's Division of Procurement. Consolidating the purchases in one office would give the department maximum clout in the attempt to put pressure on the cement manufacturers. Roosevelt was enthusiastic about the upcoming battle. He told Morgenthau: "Now get plenty strong. . . . We're going into training for the heavyweight championship."[74]

Roosevelt had been in the ring before. As assistant secretary of the navy under Woodrow Wilson, Roosevelt had been involved in a similar dispute regarding steel prices charged for navy armor contracts. After three American steel companies submitted identical bids to supply armor plate for the construction of a battleship, Roosevelt obtained a bid from a British manufacturer sufficiently low that the American firms reduced their bids.[75]

The administration's position as consumer advocate on its own behalf resulted in a press release on March 31, 1938. Morgenthau announced "measures to protect legitimate bidders for Government contracts against unfair trade practices." The goal was to "insure free competition among contractors and suppliers of material for governmental construction or

other construction for which the government supplies all or part of the funds." President Roosevelt was in "hearty accord" with this resolution to sustain a competitive atmosphere for government entrepreneurship.[76]

For the government to challenge cement pricing, it would need to take a stand on a major dam project. After all, the Reclamation Bureau accounted for more than half of the government's cement purchases.[77] The most direct approach would be for the government to produce its own cement. Government plants already operated in South Dakota and Michigan. The chairman of the FTC advised Roosevelt against government production of cement, suggesting that a better solution would be "a restoration of competitive price conditions in the cement industry by strict enforcement of antitrust laws."[78] That is precisely the tack the administration took for the next two years.

Kaiser's people revisited the cement issue in early 1937. They searched Santa Clara County for deposits of limestone, a key ingredient for cement. They located a quarry but backed off from buying it in March.[79] If they were waiting for a sign from the government, their patience was soon rewarded. Changing administration attitudes toward antitrust and procurement left the door open to new entrants in the cement industry, and a major test would be the supply for Shasta Dam.

Perhaps sensing this opportunity, Kaiser had his people review the industry beginning in January 1938. One possibility they pursued the following month was buying out a member of northern California's cement "combine," the Henry Cowell Lime and Cement Company.[80] No deal resulted. Kaiser remained determined to enter the business and sustained an intensive investigation of cement industry entry well before the construction bids were opened in the summer of 1939. By March 1938, Kaiser's people had completed a "preliminary study of the possibilities, costs of production, market demand" of the northern California cement business.[81] Kaiser's intensified interest was no doubt spurred by government investigations and recriminations against cement makers over the previous year.

Kaiser's efforts were chiefly aimed at providing the cement for the Shasta Dam project, and his organization anticipated that Shasta would be a great opportunity for a nascent cement producer. The Treasury Department had rejected a recent set of identical cement bids by the northern California "combine." Kaiser's people found reason to expect "a general competitive break" soon, based on conversations with Treasury Department people in April regarding Shasta.[82]

In addition to the Treasury Department, Kaiser was encouraged by the Reconstruction Finance Corporation. The assistant manager of the RFC's

San Francisco office told Kaiser's treasurer that Shasta "could be the 'key' to accomplishing what the government was endeavoring to do," meaning to establish competitive pricing in cement. The San Francisco representative also volunteered that "this office would pull all the wires it could with Washington." He was "greasing" the Kaiser application because it was "unique" and "the very substantial basis behind this application really 'gave the Government a break.'"[83]

The extent of the government's determination that things would be different at Shasta is suggested by the Reclamation Bureau's response upon learning that a June 24, 1938, press release had not only indicated the bureau's intention to purchase cement but exactly how much at each destination point: "Invitations are to be issued calling for bids only at points of production or storage, and . . . under no circumstance shall the destination points be revealed to the prospective bidders. This is in line with the policy of the Administration to *prevent collusive bidding* and to break up the so-called basing-point pricing system under which uniform destination bids are quoted."[84]

Bold as Kaiser was, the challenges facing him—even backed by a sympathetic government—nearly made him lose his nerve. Would it be better to fight the combine or join it? One alternative his organization considered in May 1938 was a joint venture with the Calaveras Cement Company, another member of the northern California combine. Calaveras would handle the Central Valley business, Kaiser the San Francisco Bay Area. Such a venture would "be looked upon as a legitimate cement manufacturer . . . rather than be looked on as a threat and something to be avoided and driven from existence. . . . This might be made to look very much like nothing more than a Calaveras expansion."[85] Nevertheless, Kaiser chose to proceed alone.

After going back and forth with regional Reclamation Bureau officials, and in the face of heated opposition from the existing cement companies, Kaiser's bid—more than $1.5 million lower than the next lowest—was accepted.[86] The Treasury Department, in suggesting acceptance of Kaiser's bid, noted the Reclamation Bureau's experience on Boulder Dam: "When there were requirements for cement in sufficient quantities to justify the installment of a new mill, bid prices received at the beginning of the construction program [usually high and identical] were not maintained throughout the construction project." This meant that the construction of Kaiser's mill would "secure prices that result in a material saving to the Government."[87] Therefore, the comptroller general of the United States advised acceptance of Kaiser's bid. The Reconstruction Finance Corpo-

ration offered Kaiser a $3 million loan for the project at 5 percent interest. When Kaiser was unable to talk the RFC down to 4 percent, he elected to go ahead with private financing.[88]

Bringing together one of the era's most irrepressible entrepreneurs and a government determined to make an antitrust statement had a unique result for the cement industry. Very few ready-mix concrete producers ever consider integrating backward into cement manufacture, chiefly because of the high capital costs. Decades after the Shasta Dam bidding, an analysis of the industry noted that "the [American] cement industry is virtually free of vertical integration." The only exception was Henry Kaiser's Permanente Cement plant.[89]

Kaiser's experience in cement, then, was an intermediate step in the evolution of government entrepreneurship. During the Second New Deal, opportunities for government entrepreneurship expanded rapidly but were largely limited to infrastructure entrepreneurs. When the New Deal moved on the price issue, it found the path of least resistance to be an industry—cement—in which a substantial percentage of product went to government projects or to government-financed projects and a bold entrepreneur was already poised to make a move. The government's attempt to lower cement prices was part of a larger stirring of antitrust sentiment, and the cement battle was a catalyst in the establishment of the Temporary National Economic Committee (TNEC), which investigated economic concentration in America.

The aftermath of the 1936 presidential campaign, when much of the eastern business community deserted FDR, ushered in the most acrimonious business-government relations of the twentieth century. During FDR's second term, his administration further distanced itself from the policies of his predecessor with major consequences to government entrepreneurship.

The recession of 1937–38 and the resulting perception that the New Deal was failing led both to an expansion of opportunity and a revolutionary change for government entrepreneurs. Until then, annual government spending on public construction had exceeded that of the Hoover years only during the election year of 1936. Much of that spending had gone to the Works Progress Administration (WPA) in the form of small tasks directly funded by the government, not to opportunities for government entrepreneurs. No wonder Kaiser's AGC called the WPA the "Waste Propaganda Administration."[90]

That situation changed in 1938. The administration's two-pronged response to recession included increased spending on public construction

and a revival of government antitrust activity. The downturn in 1937-38 certainly catalyzed these events, but they were also the culmination of two more gradual developments in the New Deal: first, a deterioration of business-government cooperation that began even before the Supreme Court declared the NRA unconstitutional in 1935; and second, the president's assembling a new set of advisers by 1935. Gone were brain trusters Rexford Tugwell, Adolph Berle, and Raymond Moley and their ideas of national planning. In their place over the next four years appeared "a coalition between lawyers in the school of Brandeis and economists in the school of Keynes."[91]

The Brandeis crowd pursued an antitrust path, led by Thomas Corcoran and Ben Cohen (who together authored some of the New Deal's most significant legislation), Solicitor General Robert Jackson, and Interior Secretary Harold Ickes. The Keynesians included Marriner Eccles, head of the Federal Reserve, and Lauchlin Currie, Eccles's assistant and later economic adviser to the president. Two other economists rose to prominence whose beliefs did not fit neatly with those of either group: Leon Henderson, who had been economic adviser to the NRA, and Isador Lubin, economist for the Bureau of Labor Statistics. Their chief concerns were prices and wages, respectively. During the Second New Deal, pricing policy, in conjunction with an active antitrust program, became a central feature in attempts to stimulate the economy.

The ideas of Gardiner Means were important to this chapter of the New Deal. Means argued that administered prices led to fixed levels of profits, with employment and production falling variably with downturns in the business cycle. Henderson and Lubin would be the chief administration messengers of Means's ideas.[92]

Henderson's interpretation of Means's ideas was that the government needed to prime "bottleneck" industries. A bottleneck industry was one that either reached full production before the economy was at full employment or in which the major firms could garner a satisfactory profit well before achieving full production. The steel industry, for instance, achieved a break-even point at only 50 percent of capacity.[93] Henderson saw a "constant clash between the necessary drive for efficiency on the part of the individual enterprise and . . . the demand that we have full production." A 50 percent break-even point in a major industry such as steel meant a conscious choice not to "moderate its production and price policy," creating a "concomitant of unemployment."[94]

New Dealers concerned with high prices and their impact on the econ-

omy thought bottlenecks were the result of an excessive concentration of economic power. Administered prices, those reflecting "a price policy of management rather than being determined in exchange," were excessively high and offered the opportunity for profits at the expense of full employment.[95] Increased production—either by existing manufacturers or those established in the wake of antitrust proceedings—would lower prices and create more jobs. Here the antitrusters and spenders found common ground. Henderson and the other New Dealers, then, believed more in increasing capacity and production levels than in freezing prices.

The recession of 1937 was the pivotal event in the ascendance of pricing prophets Leon Henderson and Isador Lubin. In March, with the country apparently on the road to economic recovery, several industries—including steel—had raised prices.[96] The administration devoted particular attention to steel because it was considered a "bellwether" industry. Steel was used in such a wide variety of products that price changes could have a "ripple effect" throughout the economy.[97] Henderson, who had correctly forecast an economic upturn in 1934, wrote a memorandum in March 1937 predicting an economic downturn as a consequence of higher prices. Again his forecast was correct. The recession that began in August 1937 put the New Deal on trial. Though many businessmen had abandoned Roosevelt during the 1936 election, his mandate—the largest landslide in American history—was so great that most businessmen chose not to criticize the New Deal openly. The recession of 1937 helped them recover their collective voice as they blamed the New Deal for the downturn.

On November 8, 1937, Henderson, Currie, and Lubin met with Roosevelt and presented him with a five-page memo Currie had written, entitled "Causes of the Recession." Henderson and Currie had become familiar with each other's thinking when they served as economic consultants for the presidential campaign of 1936. Now Currie's memo listed a decline in government spending as one of the causes of the recession. Another issue Currie mentioned simultaneously provided both an explanation and a culprit for the recession: prices and the behavior of industry, most notably steel.[98]

Although the recession polarized the administration from the business community, it brought the New Dealers together: they circled the wagons against their critics. This defensive posture helped bring together the schools of Brandeis and Keynes. Concerns about a combination of limited output and high prices brought spenders Marriner Eccles and Lauchlin Currie into the orbit of antitrusters Bob Jackson, Harold Ickes, Ben

Cohen, and Tom Corcoran.[99] Henderson and Corcoran worked together to find common ground between the groups and concluded that pump priming and antitrust were complementary policies.[100]

In February 1938, a number of administration officials—including Federal Reserve head Marriner Eccles—proclaimed, "Those industries [including steel] that have maintained prices and curtailed output should seek the restoration of profits through increased rather than restricted output."[101] The president was convinced of the role administered prices played in the recession, elevating price control as an economic priority.

In the spring of 1938 the president acted in concert with the new Brandeisian-Keynesian coalition. He endorsed a large-scale spending package in an address to Congress shortly after he jumped on the antitrust bandwagon.[102] He appointed Thurman Arnold to head the Justice Department's antitrust division and urged a joint investigation by the executive and legislative branches into the "concentration of economic power" in America.

The resulting TNEC began hearings in December 1938, with Leon Henderson as executive secretary.[103] The economists who had recently attracted the president's attention helped frame the hearings of the TNEC. The "price hawks" played important roles: Henderson addressed prices, Lubin wages. Currie handled the "Keynesian phase."[104] Henderson's segment would be of greatest importance to government entrepreneurs like Henry Kaiser. Henderson and the liberal supporters of FDR's social programs argued for more competition in America's marketplace. Henderson sought "the real benefits of the competitive system," in which, as prices fell to a point approaching costs, "you have a pressure all the time for more production."[105]

In calling for more production, Henderson was voicing what would become Henry Kaiser's mantra. It is difficult to imagine a government ideology better suited to the personal style of a businessman. By 1942, Kaiser was giving speeches in which he called production "the Fifth Freedom."[106] Once Henderson's ideology gained Franklin Roosevelt as a convert in 1938, the New Deal was aligned to provide maximum opportunity for government entrepreneur Kaiser.

By the end of Roosevelt's second term, the administration had offered assistance to new entrants in many industries, including the bellwether, steel. Government assistance to newcomers was part of a macroeconomic policy toward recovery based on price stabilization. Newcomers were seen as providing a challenge to the artificially high prices created by the existence of excessive concentration of market power. The administration

must have been delighted to find Henry Kaiser, an entrepreneur willing to start new ventures to challenge monopolies or oligopolies. In late 1938, for instance, the Justice Department was so desperate to end Alcoa's monopoly that it asked U.S. Steel to enter the aluminum industry.[107] Now insiders from Marriner Eccles to Harold Ickes, Lauchlin Currie, and Leon Henderson to the president himself all contributed to the creation of industrial entrepreneurial opportunities and each would personally assist Henry Kaiser's pursuit of those opportunities. The most dramatic opportunity came in the steel industry.

Explanations of Henry Kaiser's entry into the steel industry in the West have usually presented the entrepreneur in the spotlight on center stage, the shaper of his own destiny. Such an "entrepreneurocentric" view usually limits the role of government, labor relations, or other factors over which the entrepreneur has less than total control.

The entrepreneurocentric view would describe Kaiser as the only one able to see the value in challenging Big Steel and as having succeeded despite the bungling of wartime bureaucrats. Indeed, the Kaiser folklore has it that once he began to build Liberty Ships for the U.S. Maritime Commission's wartime program, he realized before the bureaucrats (many of whom were on loan from Big Steel) that his success would be limited by the availability of steel. When the bureaucrats turned deaf ears to Kaiser, he resolved to build his own steel plant on the West Coast, near his Portland and San Francisco shipyards.

There is plenty of truth in that view, but it is far from the whole story. Kaiser had serious talks with government officials about steel production before he began building ships. His need for steel in shipbuilding finally proved the most effective argument in convincing bureaucrats to support his proposal but was discussed little during months of meetings in late 1940 and early 1941. More important, the idea of West Coast steel had been discussed in the halls of Washington well before Kaiser ever broached the subject. If certain key individuals in the government had not been predisposed to support Kaiser's project, it would never have happened. The most important individual pushing for West Coast steel was the president.

On October 31, 1939, President Roosevelt announced at a press conference that he would like to see "a steel plant or plants built on the Pacific Coast, using western ore, western electricity, and western labor."[108] The president vigorously followed up on this idea for the next two months. On November 15, Roosevelt wrote Frederick Delano, chairman of the National Resource Board: "This is the beginning of an effort on my part to develop steel making on the Pacific Coast."[109]

Roosevelt's announcement represented the merging of a variety of concerns he confronted during his second term: price control, economic concentration, regional development, the use of newly available power from the great hydroelectric projects of the 1930s, the need for a two-ocean navy, and industrial preparation for war. All these issues coalesced into administration support for an independent Pacific Coast steel plant. Even during his first term, FDR had explored the issue of steel prices. He wrote to Joseph Kennedy, head of the Securities and Exchange Commission: "A lot of businessmen feel that not the least important block to recovery lies in excessive steel prices. Do you want to do a little quiet looking into this for me?"[110] During the Halloween press conference, Roosevelt said that West Coast steel had been a "hobby" of his since 1913, when he was assistant secretary of the navy and concerned about departmental expenditures on armor plate.[111]

More recently, Roosevelt had become reengaged in the debate about the steel industry's administered prices and saw an independent West Coast plant as a means to achieve price relief. In addition, Roosevelt had spoken as early as 1932 of the Pacific Northwest as another laboratory in which to test ideas of regional economic independence. In a campaign speech that year, Roosevelt had argued that since most people were no longer farmers and free land had virtually disappeared, "there is no safety valve in the form of a Western prairie to which those thrown out of work by the Eastern economic machines can go for a new start." Furthermore, the concentration of power in six hundred corporations meant that "the independent businessman is running a losing race."[112]

During his first term, Roosevelt again trotted out ideas of regional self-sufficiency with respect to Muscle Shoals Dam in the Tennessee Valley: "Is it possible for us to develop small industries, where the people can produce what they use, where they can use what they produce, and where, without dislocating the industry of America, we can absorb a lot of this unemployment [allowing people to] live soundly and in a self-supporting way?"[113]

Now Roosevelt was suggesting that with government assistance, these trends could be arrested after all and people displaced by the Depression could be helped to their feet: "I hope the Government can lay down a definite policy that all lands will be open only to relief families or families which for many different reasons have abandoned their homes and fled to the coastal region or are now 'adrift' in various parts of the country." Noting that the Reclamation Bureau estimated that about one hundred thousand additional families could prosper in the Columbia River Basin

after development was completed, Roosevelt said, "I want to give first chance to the 'Grapes of Wrath' families of the nation."[114]

The final piece in the puzzle before Roosevelt announced his Pacific Coast steel initiative was Germany's invasion of Poland on September 1, 1939. Roosevelt declared a limited national emergency a week later.[115] Lauchlin Currie, who had become economic assistant to the president in May, gained even more influence at the outset of the emergency when Roosevelt approved his request to "act as a clearing house . . . to work on the problem of unused production capacities, potential bottlenecks. . . . I could insure that the right man is working on each aspect of the problem." Currie wrote to the president on September 19, seeking authorization for "a number of studies on potential bottlenecks" and warning that "the situation may become critical on railroads, the electric power industry, steel." FDR approved.[116]

Unable to prime industry with domestic defense orders, FDR had instead favored exporting the output of key industries. America's pledge of neutrality and an arms embargo of European belligerents prevented the steel industry from expanding its capacity as a direct response to war-related needs, but the Europeans' shortages in steel meant the United States could fill the breech in exports elsewhere. This meant a production increase from 61 percent of capacity in July to more than 93 percent in November by the steelmakers.[117]

By October, some steelmakers saw the skyrocketing demand as an opportunity to increase prices and announced their intention to do so. Leon Henderson, who could use persuasion and threats to keep industry in line, now appealed to the public. In mid-October, Currie wrote to Roosevelt, "After our discussion Friday I suggested to Leon that I thought the public interest would be served if he got an intimation through to the *Wall Street Journal* that there was some concern in Administration quarters over the advance in scrap prices and the possible advance in finished steel prices. As you will see from the attached clipping, he went to town on the suggestion."[118]

Henderson had "leaked" a story indicating that "the decision of the steel industry to retain or to increase its current price schedule for the first three months of 1940 was a decision which might well determine the entire course of New Deal price policy." The story went on to note that "government officials . . . [regarded] steel as not only the most important single price category, but also as the 'bell-wether' of industry."[119]

The next move, which was in line with Henderson's strategy of price

control through increased production, was Roosevelt's Halloween proposal for a Pacific Coast steel plant. What Roosevelt did not say was that the TNEC would begin its hearings on the steel industry the next day and that the issue of Pacific Coast steel would be discussed then. The president's intentions, however, were not yet accompanied by evidence of the feasibility of a Pacific Coast steel plant. Therefore, Roosevelt instructed Interior Secretary Ickes to have the Geological Survey and Bureau of Mines investigate iron ore deposits in the "far Northwest" (Washington, Idaho, and Oregon). They reported to Ickes that "the known occurrence of iron ores in these States are numerous but few have even potential commercial importance." Instead, their investigation pointed to expansion in the East: "By far the most extensive and richest iron ore deposits in the United States are in the eastern third of the country."[120]

Not content with the results from the Interior Department, Roosevelt wrote to his uncle Frederick Delano, suggesting that Delano's National Resources Board "do a little investigating to determine whether it is worthwhile to undertake a larger investigation." Roosevelt was clearly looking for a report that confirmed his beliefs about the possibilities on the West Coast: "I am not satisfied with this preliminary letter from the Geological Survey. I am still convinced that there are adequate iron deposits west of the Continental Divide to make steel making on the Coast profitable."[121]

By the next day, having discovered that he had misinterpreted the president's assignment in late October, Harold Ickes announced during a press conference the Interior Department's interest in the construction of additional western steel plants. He had directed the Bureau of Mines and the Geological Survey to reconsider their earlier conclusion with a more probing investigation.[122]

Frederick Delano immediately understood — as Ickes had not — that his charter was to provide support for a conclusion Roosevelt had already reached, rather than information to help him make a decision. By the end of November, Delano submitted a report entitled "Possibilities of Expanding Steel Production in the Pacific Coast Region." Among the report's conclusions were two sure to meet with the president's approval. Regarding steel production, "the present market for Steel in the Far West appears to justify an expansion of steel furnaces and rolling mills on the Pacific Coast." The electrical smelting of iron ore to produce pig iron not only might "be produced economically on the Pacific Coast" but promised a possible vindication of the New Deal's aggressive pursuit of water projects because now "low-cost hydroelectric power in the Pacific North-

west is a favorable factor." Therefore, electrical smelting "should be fully investigated, including further exploration of California."[123]

The president's Halloween announcement advanced toward self-fulfilling prophecy as it attracted additional support for his argument. In late November, Roosevelt received a letter from the director of Oregon's Department of Geology and Mineral Industries and a copy of a report titled "The Feasibility of a Steel Plant in the Lower Columbia River Area." The report, dated June 28, 1938, supported Roosevelt's belief in "the availability of all raw materials, including iron ores . . . [and] an available market to a lower Columbia steel plant very much in excess of the amount required for a steel plant of economic size." The report provided further ammunition for defense of New Deal reclamation policy: "The availability of cheap Bonneville power, although not a determining factor, presents a tangible incentive" for such a project.[124]

The successful use of power provided by the great Columbia River dam projects was much on the mind of the president as he directed the feasibility study of a steel plant in the Pacific Northwest. Roosevelt saw such projects as offering a proving ground for his theme of economic decentralization. In a December letter to Harold Ickes, the president urged that "the whole [Columbia River] Basin should be planned with the thought of making the Basin economically self-supporting as far as possible." Making sure that Ickes received the message loud and clear this time, Roosevelt emphasized: "I feel strongly on this subject."[125]

By this time, the media—especially steel industry trade journals—had seized the issue of Pacific Coast steel, and a flurry of articles appeared from November 1939 to April 1940. During this period, one of the administration's motives for the West Coast plant had temporarily evaporated: the pricing issue. After some acrimonious exchanges between U.S. Steel's Ben Fairless and Leon Henderson at the TNEC hearings in early November, the steel giant's Carnegie-Illinois subsidiary announced "reaffirmation of prices in virtually every steel product."[126] The administration's pressure was not entirely responsible for U.S. Steel's decision; overseas demand for steel had fallen in November, and a price increase would have been more than a softening market could bear.

So Roosevelt was left with regional independence as the main basis for a Pacific Coast plant just as his attention turned to events in Europe. The Pacific Coast plant moved to the administration's back burner in early 1940 and stayed there. The only new developments were continued sporadic responses to administration announcements of late 1939, including the actions of the Kaiser organization in September 1940.

Although the reports Roosevelt received in 1939 involved only the possibilities in the Pacific Northwest, Roosevelt's pronouncements expanded the possibilities to include the entire West Coast. In November articles about Roosevelt's plans, the *United States Daily* and *Iron Age* featured his reference to the West Coast. The articles brought an enthusiastic response from California. By September 1940, FDR had heard from the president of the Los Angeles Chamber of Commerce and from southern California congressman Leland Ford regarding Pacific Coast steel. The issue no longer had the executive branch's attention, and in response to Ford's letter, FDR's press secretary wrote Ickes, asking, "Is there anything being done . . . [on] the establishment of a steel industry on the Pacific Coast?"[127] There was, but it was mainly at the initiative of the Bonneville Power Administration, compiling reports and soliciting eastern and western interests for a possible steel plant in the Columbia River Valley.[128]

Many argue that the New Deal ended with the mobilization for war. Indeed, as the steel story shows, President Roosevelt's personal attention was directed to the war effort at the expense of his earlier domestic programs. Yet from May 1940 until December 1941, the principles of the Second New Deal and the imperatives of mobilization merged into the phenomenon of the New Deal War. Nobody symbolized this new combination of forces as well as Henry J. Kaiser. Kaiser was a newcomer in magnesium, steel, and aircraft, thus gaining support of the antitrusters. Kaiser's embrace of the principles of collective bargaining endeared him to the New Deal. Most of all, Kaiser's style—a sense of urgency and an irreverent disdain for the idea of "jurisdiction" or the channels of bureaucracy—was similar to that of the New Dealers. By the time of the New Deal War, Henry Kaiser and his organization were in Washington proposing industrial enterprises in steel, magnesium, and aircraft.

When Henry J. Kaiser, storming
Washington in 1940 for war
work, pounded into the office of
Leon Henderson, then in OPM,
the cornered Henderson picked
up the phone and called a Justice
Department lawyer who had been
jousting with the aluminum
and magnesium "monopoly."

"There's a man in my office
who says he can make fifty
million pounds of magnesium,
and if you don't hurry over,
he'll make it right here," he said.

Lester Velie, 1946

4 ——— A RENDEZVOUS WITH BUREAUCRACY

In the spring of 1940, Henry Kaiser and his associate Chad Calhoun went to Washington to promote a plan for a superhighway. Kaiser had not built roads for years and had established the beginnings of an industrial empire, but he had dreamed of such a system even before his dam projects established his national reputation as an infrastructure entrepreneur. Kaiser's plan called for a federal authority, similar to the Reconstruction Finance Corporation, that would loan money to states and municipalities for the program. Kaiser was hoping to assemble leaders of automotive, petroleum, steel, banking, cement, and insurance companies to lobby for the plan.[1]

Disturbing developments in Europe abruptly changed Kaiser's plans. In April, Hitler struck Denmark and Norway, and in May German forces attacked the Low Countries. Central Europe had already experienced Hitler's aggression, from his 1938 movement into Austria to his September 1939 invasion of Poland. The attack on Poland brought France and England into the conflict, but things had been sufficiently quiet in the early months of 1940 to prompt discussion of a "phony war." Now "Sitzkrieg" gave way to devastating warfare.

This was a watershed moment for Roosevelt and the nation. Roosevelt speechwriter Robert Sherwood wryly conveyed how monumental the change would be. He stopped keeping a diary in June 1940, "which is just when I should have started."[2] Not until the 1990s would a president's agenda again revolve principally around domestic issues.

Roosevelt's priorities changed virtually overnight. One of his major concerns after the September 1939 declarations of war had been planning for a postwar world (presumably after a war in which America would not fight). Now the European conflict had his undivided attention. He declared a limited national emergency, and in late May he created a new agency to deal with mobilization for world war: the National Defense Advisory Commission (NDAC).[3]

May and June 1940 proved to be a defining time for those who wished to have a close relationship with President Roosevelt. Roosevelt sought out individuals who had a sense of urgency about helping England. Symbolic of this shift was Roosevelt's relationship with his most trusted adviser, Harry Hopkins (which Sherwood later portrayed in *Roosevelt and Hopkins*). Hopkins had served on the front lines of Roosevelt's social welfare programs since the early days of the New Deal and now suddenly shifted his attention overseas (to the horror of his onetime ally, Eleanor Roosevelt, who believed the relief and reform work at home was not yet done). Hopkins served as Roosevelt's envoy to England and later to the Soviet Union. By contrast, Ambassador Joseph Kennedy's voiced doubts about England's ability to win created a conflict with Roosevelt that helped finish Kennedy's political career.

Henry Kaiser fared better than Joseph Kennedy. Indeed, Michael Beschloss argues that Kaiser replaced Kennedy as Roosevelt's favored businessman. Like Hopkins, Kaiser made a quick shift in the spring of 1940 from domestic to international affairs and modified his approach to government business. Kaiser had previously expanded his operations into industrial enterprise gradually to support his existing enterprises: sand and gravel for road building and cement for dam building. Kaiser quickly

changed gears, realizing that America needed to mobilize quickly, with airfields, ordnance, and other goods and services.[4] Kaiser seemed bent on entering as many industries as he could. He succeeded spectacularly. At the beginning of December 1940, Henry Kaiser had never produced ships, magnesium, steel, or aircraft. By 1942 he was a high-profile entrant in all four industries.

Kaiser had been making moves toward producing magnesium since January 1940, when his Permanente Corporation appropriated $25,000 for magnesium research. In May he redoubled his efforts.[5] He also began to pursue the construction of aircraft, and finally he followed up on the steel front. Initially, Kaiser and Calhoun sought to fill steel needs in ordnance (shells, for instance) and to provide tinplate for can companies. Ships entered the picture as an afterthought: "In order to *complete* our potential market survey of steel products . . . [consider] our own shipbuilding interests."[6]

As it turned out, Kaiser was able to secure an RFC loan for a steel plant only by convincing the government that he needed steel for his ships, but to get there he and Calhoun followed a very circuitous route. Kaiser applied pressure simultaneously on many fronts instead of proceeding on an industry-by-industry basis. The national emergency made Kaiser's choice of industry reflect less his beliefs about his organization's core competence than the specific market opportunities provided by the early wartime environment.

The president's appointments to the NDAC helped dictate how to pursue those opportunities. New Deal principles of antitrust (Leon Henderson—prices) and collective bargaining (Sidney Hillman—labor) were well represented. Yet the two most important posts on the commission went to individuals who were skeptical about certain facets of the New Deal. William Knudsen (industrial production) and Edward Stettinius (industrial materials) had been affiliated with General Motors and U.S. Steel, respectively.[7] Bringing big business executives into such prominent roles in the preparedness effort signaled the end of the New Deal to some, while to others it represented an opportunity to win over some of the New Deal's most powerful opponents.

Having Knudsen and Stettinius playing such important roles appeared to tip the scales in favor of established industrialists, as opposed to newcomers like Henry Kaiser. Though it had been a New Deal goal to decentralize America's concentration of economic power, Knudsen and Stettinius—as well as representatives of the armed services—preferred otherwise. They sought experienced operators to man the defense effort.

They were also slow to acknowledge the necessity of increasing industrial capacity in certain industries, regardless of whether newcomers or established businesses performed this task.

Henry Kaiser's experiences with the NDAC in 1940 suggest that the preparedness program was characterized by central stylistic aspects of the New Deal: intramural government battles over jurisdiction; an emphasis on access to the president as a means of resolving issues; the devaluation of titles and job descriptions. In Kaiser's case, this meant that a meeting with Edward Stettinius, who was in charge of industrial raw materials—including steel and magnesium—for the NDAC, might have less value than a meeting with Leon Henderson, who was in charge of prices. Kaiser was fortunate that his Washington representative, Chad Calhoun, understood the importance of access to the president and therefore embarked on a path that would lead him to insider Henderson in December.

In pursuit of defense-related enterprises, one of the first things Kaiser and Calhoun did was to set up shop in Washington's Shoreham Hotel. Kaiser and Calhoun were not alone. Various organizations representing private sector interests responded to the new environment for government contracts. Almost immediately, the Los Angeles Chamber of Commerce established an office in Washington designed to obtain government work for its members.[8] Kaiser's trade association, the Associated General Contractors of America, went to press in June 1940 with a series of tips on how to land navy contracts.[9] The following spring, Kaiser's friends at the Bank of America established an Office of Defense Information to assist the bank's California clients in participating in the defense effort.[10] Later, the National Association of Manufacturers and others published pamphlets on how to obtain government business.

Kaiser had become a familiar figure in Washington before 1940, but now he was spending a week a month there.[11] Although Kaiser was a frequent visitor, Chad Calhoun became a Washington fixture. Calhoun returned to the West Coast a couple of times for a few months, but for the most part he remained in Washington on Kaiser's behalf for the next quarter-century. In so doing, Calhoun developed what is now called an "inside-the-beltway" mentality. In the mid-1960s, he wrote: "People, primarily company executives, living beyond a thirty-mile radius of Washington are woefully parochial."[12] Government officials interviewed decades later remembered Kaiser well, but many remarked that the person they had most often dealt with was Chad Calhoun.[13]

Appropriately, Calhoun's background was in public sector engineering, which helps explain why he appeared more comfortable among gov-

ernment officials than among his Kaiser colleagues. Following his World War I military service, Calhoun worked for the Los Angeles surveyor and county sanitation district for five years. He then held positions in various construction firms, finally joining MacDonald-Kahn's southern California operation to tackle dam and viaduct jobs.[14]

Calhoun, as chief estimator, had represented the MacDonald-Kahn construction firm at one of Kaiser's great moments: the Six Companies' bidding on Hoover Dam in April 1931. Calhoun was chief engineer and general manager of MacDonald-Kahn's Los Angeles office when Henry Kaiser hired him away later that year. Calhoun was not immediately offered duty in Washington. That came later.

During the Depression years of the 1930s, the collapse of the private sector made federal government contracts seem more attractive plums than before. Contractors such as Henry Kaiser routinely traveled to Washington looking for work, and when Kaiser was on the West Coast, he relied on Washington attorney George C. Ober for news of impending requests for bids or of laws that might affect the construction business.[15] Ober's information was often little different from that presented in publications such as the *United States News*. Perhaps that was why the Kaiser people in Oakland quibbled with Ober about his fees.[16] An especially acrimonious example involved Kaiser's son Edgar's objections to Ober's expenditures in Washington. Young Kaiser wrote Ober that he was "against paying for boxes of candy sent to secretaries in various Government offices. You had no authority to make this expenditure in behalf of the company . . . and I am quite certain that [Henry Kaiser] would have disapproved of any such expenditure in accordance with his usual practice."[17]

Henry Kaiser had not always disapproved of such expenditures. A few months before Kaiser's death in 1967, his associate A. B. Ordway reminded him: "You probably recall that it was 46 years ago this month when you and I walked into the general offices of the Division of Highways [in Sacramento]. Possibly you recall that the receptionist the first time we called (who was also the switchboard operator) told us her feet were cold, so we promptly went out and bought an electric heater for her, which of course paid for itself many times over in later business."[18]

Even though Ober provided Kaiser with little information that was not in the public domain, California was a continent away from Washington and air travel was still not common for business executives. So the company decided that Ober provided a valuable service and continued to retain him.[19]

When Calhoun opened his office, the nature of the correspondence

from Washington changed. Kaiser's new man in Washington began to send him an astonishing flood of information. Because of his thoroughness and his desire to get everything in writing, Calhoun's letters provide an invaluable perspective on what went on behind the scenes in mid-century Washington. Some days three long (three-to-five-page) memos would arrive together at Oakland headquarters.[20] Upon his retirement in 1966, one of the tips Calhoun provided other Washington "reps" was: "Keep good records—written memoranda of all meetings, phone calls, etc. Company lawyers may disagree on this where antitrust or similar matters are concerned, but the overall value of meticulous record keeping is beyond dispute."[21]

Perhaps his engineering background explains why Calhoun did not have a lawyer's squeamishness about creating a massive paper trail; most other corporate representatives in Washington at this time were individuals who, according to John Kenneth Galbraith, "could best be spared at home"—either public relations people or lawyers.[22] Calhoun was not. His experience on major engineering enterprises made him particularly sensitive to how certain information might relate to a project's value. He was therefore prepared to pursue new enterprise more aggressively than the other Washington reps. While he of course sent Kaiser information about contracts to be let, he also reported extensively on the *atmosphere* in Washington. Calhoun advised his successors: "Keep close track of the prevailing mood in Washington. It sometimes changes frequently and sometimes quickly. The ideas or pressures guiding government officials and employees one week may be obsolete the next."[23] The presidential campaign of 1940 provides a good example. In late August, Calhoun commented on growing disillusionment with Republican nominee Wendell Willkie: "Consensus here seems to be that the Republican party leaders realize now that they have a New Dealer on their ticket. Just another fellow who wanted a job."[24]

Calhoun had an instinctive understanding of power relationships. He filled Kaiser in on newsworthy events and supplied him with accounts of the leanings and desires of key Washington power brokers. After meeting William Knudsen, head of the NDAC's Industrial Production Division, Calhoun noted: "Mr. Knudsen was somewhat skeptical and in fact cynical about contractors in general being motivated by any finer things."[25] Kaiser had a habit of reading information-filled memos from his executives and scrawling "so what?" in the margin. What he meant was "The information's fine, but what do you suggest we do about it?" Kaiser did not need to write such notes to Calhoun. Calhoun's memos were loaded with advice, news, or gossip. Sometimes the gossip would prove more useful than

the advice. Calhoun reported that in a December 1940 meeting, Kaiser's prospective steel partner, Tom Girdler, was "contemplating bringing suit for slander" against Interior Secretary Harold Ickes, a key administration supporter of Kaiser.[26]

Calhoun clearly viewed Kaiser as a historic figure, and he acted with a passion to match that conviction. Just as some of Roosevelt's staff felt more passionately about the various incarnations of the New Deal than the president did, Calhoun believed more fervently in Kaiser's roles as activist for western causes—particularly related to antitrust—than Henry Kaiser himself did.[27]

As his role matured, Calhoun's contribution to Kaiser's enterprises changed. He developed the ability to go beyond merely implementing Kaiser's agenda in Washington or following his boss's prescribed mode of governmental relations. Calhoun began to set the agenda. When Kaiser first explored a partnership with Republic Steel, Calhoun wrote: "It might be well worth while since we have now made this contact with Republic executives for us to make the utmost of it. In this connection I have thought that it might be well for me to make some sort of tours of inspection through the various plants. In the event that the present plan of combining our forces does not immediately materialize, the information which I could thus gain by such an inspection might prove to be invaluable aid to us later on."[28]

Nor did it take Calhoun months to get acclimated to the wartime environment, as it did Bank of America's Washington representative, Theodore Granik. Bank of America's executive vice president had to push Granik to provide more useful information: "The afternoon papers here carry complete information on the items covered in your wire of the same day. . . . In order for the information you obtain to be of value to us you must go quite a bit further back toward the source of those defense contracts and furnish us with really advance information."[29] By contrast, Calhoun had the "gift" in Washington from the start: beginning in May 1940 he became Kaiser's "political eyes and ears."[30]

Calhoun wrote to Assistant Secretary of War Louis Johnson in May 1940, offering Henry Kaiser's "phenomenal organizing ability and dynamic personality" as a means of achieving "quick results in your air defense expansion." Less than two weeks earlier, Hitler had invaded the Low Countries. A new sense of urgency gripped those sympathetic to England and France, and Calhoun played to this tension. Calhoun's telegram briefly summarized his organization's experience and emphasized Henry Kaiser's "excellent record of relationships with labor." Calhoun promised

"astounding results in the manufacture of airplanes." He concluded by providing a list of references, including Federal Reserve chairman Marriner Eccles.[31]

The reason a contractor used the head of the Federal Reserve as a reference regarding providing goods for the European war effort bears examination. This relationship tells much about the realities of wartime Washington. Marriner Eccles, a prominent banker from Utah, was also president of the Utah Construction Company, one of Kaiser's Six Companies partners in the construction of Hoover Dam, Bonneville Dam, and Grand Coulee Dam. Eccles had become chairman of the Federal Reserve Board in 1936. Sharing the suspicion many westerners harbored toward Wall Street, Eccles was instrumental in shifting the Fed's base of operations from New York to Washington.

After becoming head of the Fed, Eccles had been required by law to resign as president of both the First Security Corporation and First Security Bank of Utah and to dispose of his personal stock in them. Although he also gave up the presidency of the Utah Construction Company (becoming "chairman of the board on leave"), he still followed the firm's fortunes.[32]

During the fall of 1940 there would be plenty to follow. Utah Construction was part owner—along with Henry Kaiser and other veterans of the Six Companies partnership—of the Columbia Construction Company. Eccles unabashedly assisted Kaiser in pushing the right buttons so Columbia could obtain steel, magnesium, or aircraft contracts.[33] From a peacetime standpoint, this looks like a gross conflict of interest. Yet such dual allegiances were common during World War II. As Bank of America's Washington representative, for example, Theodore Granik was chartered with helping the bank's California clients obtain war-related business. At the same time, Granik worked for Donald Nelson at the War Production Board, securing loans for small businesses.[34]

Marriner Eccles's efforts on behalf of Columbia Construction were important to him beyond any gains to his company or partners. Eccles was a wealthy man, and Utah Construction's stake in Columbia Construction did not loom as a major factor in his well-being.[35] What he sought was a role in America's defense mobilization. He was frustrated with the Federal Reserve's relative exclusion from the growing defense effort. In May 1940 he met with the president and offered the services of the Fed's "underemployed" staff to investigate the long-term implications of the defense mobilization and reconversion on prices, employment, and availability of materials.[36] During this meeting and for the remainder of the year, Eccles's offer was rebuffed. Instead, the Treasury Department and RFC assumed

key financial responsibilities in the defense program. For Eccles, then, assisting Kaiser in an unofficial capacity substituted for greater official defense responsibilities.

Calhoun began a series of meetings in Washington with Marriner Eccles in May 1940. These sessions culminated in a July 9 discussion of the highway program. Although the attention of many (including contractors such as Kaiser) had turned quickly to defense mobilization, Eccles was convinced that the European war would be over by September. He feared that the subsequent contraction of defense preparations could represent a "serious blow to our economy." So a public works program of the sort Kaiser proposed interested Eccles as a means to "raise the national income." Eccles expressed interest in pursuing Kaiser's superhighway program so as to avoid the "complete collapse" of America's economic system.[37]

Eccles's subsequent realization that the war would last much beyond September did not reduce his interest in Kaiser. By September, Eccles was actively helping Kaiser's mobilization efforts.[38] Eccles enlisted the aid of Lawrence Clayton, his most trusted assistant.[39] Clayton had met Eccles before World War I and had worked for him at the First Security Corporation in Utah. In 1935 he followed Eccles to Washington to serve as his personal assistant at the Federal Reserve.[40]

Eccles was an important ally for Kaiser, but not just as a guide through the Washington maze. Eccles had friends in high places. Leon Henderson and Lauchlin Currie joined Eccles as principal administration proponents of Keynesian-style "pump priming": government spending—even when faced with a budget deficit—to stimulate the economy.[41] Eccles and his "unshaken allies" would become Kaiser boosters, and their support would be important in getting the ear of the president and in finding ways to get many things done in the nation's capital.[42]

In Eccles, Henderson, and Currie, government entrepreneur Henry Kaiser had an important group of allies whom many American businessmen did not trust. Eccles's assistance bolstered Kaiser's efforts throughout the fall of 1940. Eccles's role later diminished significantly, but by that time others in the administration were enthusiastically helping Kaiser. Eccles would continue to telephone Chad Calhoun periodically, but his greatest assistance came in the crucial months from May to December 1940, when Kaiser most needed help.

At first, it was not apparent that Kaiser would succeed, despite the support he had. During the summer months, Kaiser and Calhoun achieved little in Washington. They sought construction work, from airfields to

powder plants to bomb and shell plants.[43] They also discussed the manufacture of airplanes, magnesium, and steel in an all-out attempt to seek any defense-related work. The three agencies they approached during this period were the NDAC, the army, and the navy.

Summarizing their experiences later, Calhoun recalled the "runaround" they received. This was partly because the agencies tended to favor those who already were established in selected fields over new entrants. It was also because Kaiser had neither important contacts in any of these organizations nor expertise in several of the industries he wished to enter. Nor did he yet have the ear of the commander in chief.

Kaiser's organization had to walk a fine line. For instance, as a construction company, it sought to "avoid the stigma of the big company." But it also had to appear experienced and skilled to have a chance at manufacturing work. Similarly, Kaiser's interest in cost-plus manufacturing contracts could not be allowed to come into conflict with his efforts to land construction work.[44]

Forced to make difficult decisions, Kaiser quickly decided to pursue industrial work aggressively. But despite his acceptance of the industrial challenge and the perception that airplane production was a critical need —Congress had authorized production of eighteen thousand more planes in June and July, after Roosevelt had proposed fifty thousand in May— the organization was effectively rebuffed regarding airplanes.[45] Calhoun met with General H. H. "Hap" Arnold, chief of the army air corps, on September 7. It was an excruciating meeting. Arnold asked if Kaiser had a plant; Calhoun said no. Arnold asked if Kaiser had engineers; Calhoun said no. Arnold asked if Kaiser had a "plane of proven design"; Calhoun said no. Calhoun tried to recover by emphasizing Kaiser's achievements and personal qualifications, but it was clear that Arnold was not interested in experimenting with a novice.[46]

The meeting with Arnold devastated Kaiser's plans to enter the aircraft business, but he pressed forward on other fronts. Aircraft production was mentioned sporadically in meetings with government officials in the coming months, but Kaiser backed off in this area. In December, Calhoun voiced regrets about Kaiser's retreat: "I am beginning to feel that we made a mistake in not following through on aircraft during late September, October, and November, in spite of the opposition. . . . We laid down."[47] Calhoun's concerns arose because in late November the NDAC approved production of twelve thousand more airplanes.[48] It soon became clear that the established manufacturers could not handle the expanded demand, and companies in other industries, such as automobile manufac-

turers, would be forced to help out. Had Kaiser's organization more actively pursued aircraft production, its opportunity would have come in the brief period after the true extent of demand was recognized but before the help of other industries was sought. Once assistance from other industries was considered, Kaiser's enterprises might well be left out because "we are not industrialists."[49]

The disastrous meeting with Arnold would have implications for the Kaiser organization beyond its interest in aircraft production. Kaiser and Calhoun, chastened for their lack of industrial experience, would now be more willing than ever to team up with established producers. This need, more than anything else, explains why Kaiser, the New Deal's "darling," would rush into the arms of the New Deal's "devil," Tom Girdler.

With aircraft on hold, Kaiser spent much of 1940 pursuing the idea of production of the primary metals of steel and magnesium. Even before the Arnold meeting, Kaiser had received encouraging signals regarding steel. In late July, Calhoun informed Kaiser that "there is considerable talk in certain government circles regarding the need and necessity for a steel mill on the Pacific Coast." Such a mill would supply the steel required for "building up of heavy industry in the West" for national defense: tank and airplane engine factories and shipyards. Addressing a key barrier to entry in the steel industry—high initial capital requirements—Calhoun reported that "the Government will subsidize the required capital investment and probably some of the operating costs" of the mill. Best of all, "a new company might be favored or at least given favorable consideration."[50] The biggest piece of the puzzle missing from Calhoun's analysis was that the catalyst behind the idea for a West Coast steel plant was the president himself.

Kaiser and Calhoun began to explore the possibilities of going into steel production. They learned that even if a newcomer might be given "favorable consideration," experience in the industry was a crucial element sought by the NDAC and the armed services. Fortuitously, their efforts came to the attention of an individual who could help them out: Tom Girdler, president of Republic Steel—one of the industry's "big three," along with U.S. Steel and Bethlehem Steel. In late August, Girdler requested a meeting with Kaiser to discuss a joint venture to construct and operate a West Coast steel plant. A meeting between Kaiser and a Republic vice president got things rolling on August 29.[51]

Kaiser's plans for steel production gained considerable momentum in the first week of September. Calhoun learned that "as early as last November" the president had announced his intentions about Pacific Coast steel

and that "the idea appears to be definitely his and one in which he is personally interested."[52] The existing steel companies and other prospective entrants had shown little interest in the president's proposal—although from November to March it had received considerable attention in steel industry journals—because in April 1940 steelmakers were operating at only about 60 percent capacity. From the time of the president's proposal in October 1939 until the blitzkrieg in the spring, American steel producers launched no major expansion on the West Coast or anywhere else.[53]

By the time Chad Calhoun heard about the president's proposal, Roosevelt appeared ready to assist in financing the project. This was important because one of the greatest barriers to entry for a newcomer—especially in the capital-intensive steel industry—was the difficulty in obtaining start-up capital. Calhoun suggested that "the president would be agreeable to using funds from his recently appropriated special fund." He referred to a $750 million "emergency fund" Congress had appropriated to the president in June for "production, procurement, and storage of strategic materials and for the construction of emergency facilities."[54] Before the year was out, Calhoun would learn that "the president's advisors indicate he is quite miserly with these funds."[55]

Word of the president's plan had a direct impact on the Republic-Kaiser venture. Roosevelt had proposed a western steel industry on a sufficient scale to handle the requirements of a Pacific Coast navy, plus aircraft and ordnance needs. This was a much more ambitious undertaking than Kaiser and Girdler had planned. The two principals in the venture—the steel baron and the construction tycoon—now needed to reconsider their preliminary plans. A meeting was arranged for September 4 at Girdler's New York office.

The first item of business was the change in scope indicated by the president's plan. They agreed that although offering even greater opportunities, the new plan presented additional challenges in the area of financing. They agreed to pursue government financing for this project, realizing that it would be difficult to obtain the additional capital required in the private sector.[56]

The key question, however, was whether Girdler and the Roosevelt administration could work together. Tom Girdler was one of the great archenemies of the New Deal, particularly the administration's support of collective bargaining. In 1934, he had vowed, "Before I spend the rest of my life dealing with [labor leader] William Green, I'm going to raise apples and potatoes." Girdler had been spokesman of "Little Steel"—independents Republic, Inland, National, Bethlehem, and Youngstown Sheet and

Tube—in their 1937 showdown with labor leader John L. Lewis, which culminated in the "Memorial Day Massacre." Girdler promised, "I won't have a contract, verbal or written, with an irresponsible, racketeering, violent, communistic body like the CIO, and until they pass a law making me, I am not going to do it." "They" already had passed such a law in 1935: the Wagner Act.[57]

Girdler battled the administration not only over collective bargaining but also over mobilization for war. A few weeks after Germany invaded Poland in September 1939, Girdler expressed fears of "the vast powers for the regimentation and control of the nation's economic life" that war mobilization would provide the administration.[58]

The administration vilified Girdler both publicly and privately. During a June 5 press conference—just one week after Roosevelt appointed the NDAC to coordinate the emergency defense program—the president agreed with a reporter who compared administration foes Henry Ford and Tom Girdler to "fifth columnists" who would sabotage America's defense program: "Just exactly the same category . . . the Girdlers in life as well as people who try to put emery into the machinery."[59]

Aware of this history, in their September 4 meeting Kaiser asked Girdler whether he would have any difficulty working with the Roosevelt administration inasmuch as they intended to rely on government financing. Girdler said he had no problems unless the government tried to operate the plant. Continuing to test their partner's sensitivities, Kaiser and Calhoun asked Girdler about labor. They explained their intention to work with the American Federation of Labor on the project. Girdler claimed to have "no objections" to the AFL, but he did admit that he would continue to battle the Congress of Industrial Organizations (CIO). Calhoun's impression was that Girdler "expressed a conciliatory attitude toward labor in general, which was somewhat surprising because of a general impression which had been built up through the country."[60] Kaiser's own conversion to the cause of collective bargaining may have led him to believe there was genuine hope that Girdler would experience a change of heart. At any rate, Kaiser seems to have concluded that the acrimony between Girdler and the administration would not block their joint effort.

At this point, the Kaiser organization's energy in Washington was turning away from particular agencies and armed services and toward the president and his advisers. Calhoun advised Kaiser, "It appears to me to be best to take this matter directly to the president." And close to the president was Interior Secretary Harold Ickes, who had "some concurrence"; there was, as well, Under Secretary Alvin Wirtz, who was "extremely inter-

ested" in the "development of the Northwest."[61] Ickes had been one of the administration's earliest "all-outers" against fascism and also was one of the New Deal's most virulent opponents of entrenched market power.[62] As part of the defense mobilization, it would not be difficult for Ickes to support a newcomer—especially Kaiser, whose great dam projects had been built on Ickes's watch and whose challenge of the California cement combine at Shasta Dam in 1939 had appealed to Ickes's distrust of concentrations of economic power.

The steel venture gained an important administration ally when Calhoun met with Wirtz on September 19. Because Wirtz was "skeptical" of the NDAC, he suggested a strategy of appealing directly to the president. Though Roosevelt had appointed the NDAC, Wirtz believed that the commission was "not in sympathy with the president's wishes." Wirtz expressed a desire to speak to his boss, Interior Secretary Ickes, and to Roosevelt about Kaiser.[63]

This initial meeting with Wirtz demonstrates why Kaiser would sustain his partnership with Republic until December. While praising Kaiser's record, Wirtz indicated that Ickes or Roosevelt would be concerned that Kaiser was "a little weak on steel-making experience" (a polite way of saying that Kaiser had none). Only then did Calhoun tell Wirtz of Kaiser's prospective partner—Republic. Wirtz "was very much impressed."[64] To Kaiser it had become apparent that Girdler and Republic provided the necessary experience for a newcomer who wanted a serious hearing from the administration. Kaiser was still smarting from Calhoun's disastrous meeting with army air corps head Hap Arnold twelve days earlier. In his determination not to be embarrassed again by a lack of experience, Kaiser rushed to affiliate with Tom Girdler.

By the time Calhoun and Wirtz met again, on September 24, Wirtz had spoken to Ickes about Kaiser's steel proposal. Ickes was concerned about Girdler, however, and wanted assurance that Kaiser would "have a great deal to say about labor policy." Ickes had been hostile to Girdler for years. In 1937, Ickes suggested that monopoly posed a threat to democracy and "meant a fascist state with an end to our liberties." Ickes mentioned Tom Girdler and a couple of other tycoons by name in his "attack on great aggregations of capital."[65]

Perhaps Ickes's concerns about Girdler explain why Alvin Wirtz suddenly shifted his attention from steel to magnesium. Wirtz concluded the meeting by inquiring for the first time about Kaiser's intentions in magnesium, noting that he was "very anxious to see this industry established in the Pacific Northwest."[66] In magnesium, of course, Kaiser did not already

have a partner who was persona non grata to the New Deal. Meanwhile, Wirtz "seasoned" the steel issue by not following up on the venture for nearly three weeks.

Ickes's concerns about Kaiser's level of commitment to Girdler at this point were well founded. Kaiser was serious enough about Girdler to enlist the support of his East Coast partner, the Todd Shipbuilding Company, in the steel venture. On October 4, Kaiser wrote Todd president John D. Reilly: "In view of our association with Republic in this matter, you may decide that you may accord them a share in your plate business as it may result in mutual benefits."[67] Despite the administration's concerns about Girdler, Kaiser was doing all he could to make the relationship with Republic work.

Magnesium was another matter. Wirtz and Ickes were not the first administration officials interested in Kaiser's plans regarding magnesium. In September, Kaiser had met with Marriner Eccles to discuss the prospects for magnesium. Because Eccles was already a supporter in magnesium, the expression of interest from Interior Under Secretary Wirtz lit a fire in the Kaiser organization: two days later, Calhoun had prepared a "comprehensive outline" on magnesium. The first step was to send letters of proposal to Eccles and Ickes.[68]

The two letters, more than any correspondence to this point, reflected the Kaiser organization's acknowledgment of the president's commitment to a New Deal War, which would "harmonize the exigencies of mobilization for war" with his New Deal economic and social initiatives.[69] In late May, President Roosevelt had delivered a fireside chat in which he insisted "in all that we do, that there be no breakdown or cancellation of any of the great social gains we have made in the past years."[70] Roosevelt's subsequent fidelity to that pledge may have ebbed and flowed with campaign considerations later in the year, but those in his inner circle with whom Kaiser dealt were steadfast proponents of the New Deal labor and antitrust principles. Chad Calhoun's knowledge of the attitudes of his audience no doubt influenced the way he presented his organization's proposal.

Kaiser first wrote to Ickes on October 4 proposing that the principals of the Columbia Construction Company—Kaiser and his dam-building partners—form a new company to manufacture metallic magnesium. Kaiser emphasized three points sure to resonate with the "old curmudgeon." First, he noted the "limited production of this metal in the United States," a swipe at Dow Chemical's magnesium monopoly. Second, he argued the clear and present need for magnesium in America's aircraft program. Finally, he suggested that "the Pacific Northwest offers many opportuni-

ties to this industry," a good reason to choose a westerner—like Kaiser—to perform the job.[71]

Kaiser's letter to Eccles, dated October 14, was more personal and emphasized some additional points. It began with the three components of the Ickes proposal. Kaiser pressed the antitrust issue even further this time, noting that the "present production is limited to one producer and that present expansion may not meet even the secondary requirements of the expanded aircraft industry." Kaiser then made the same allusions to the Pacific Northwest and defense needs as he had to Ickes. Kaiser expressed frustration with the army and navy munitions boards for not classifying magnesium as a critical metal and attacked the NDAC for not pushing for additional magnesium production.[72]

The first response to Kaiser's letters came from Alvin Wirtz. He suggested that before approaching the RFC for financing, Kaiser "enter into discussion with those government agencies requiring your expected output." A little marketing was needed.[73]

Now Kaiser and Chad Calhoun not only were confident of the need for their services but had government officials in hand who eagerly awaited Kaiser's initiatives. What these individuals needed was someone—like Kaiser—aggressive enough to help the government officials do what they already felt needed doing.

Calhoun's reaction to the Wirtz recommendation formed the Kaiser organization's blueprint for dealing with the wartime government. Writing to Kaiser chief engineer George Havas, Calhoun noted: "Many agencies of the government from the President on down, have indicated that a steel and other allied industry in the Pacific Northwest would be highly desirable from a National Defense standpoint. However, neither of these in the absence of the other, or particularly in the absence of an already established steel industry, has been prepared to take the initial step." Calhoun noted that the relevant groups from the president to the Bonneville Power Administration, to the War Department and the Navy Department could benefit from an initiative launched by Kaiser's organization: "It will be necessary for us to bring all these agencies together and sell them on the idea of the possibility that would accrue to the Defense requirements if they would cooperate with us and the other Government agencies in bringing about the establishment of the steel industry in the Northwest."[74]

Calhoun had recognized that the primary service a government entrepreneur could offer the Roosevelt administration was to translate the president's vision for industrial development into specific proposals. That is why companies that merely expressed interest in helping the government

and left behind their calling cards made little headway. Private industry needed to provide details for the administration's industrial policy. Once the company made its proposal, the government officials would assist in obtaining contracts and loans. This symbiotic relationship between government and entrepreneur relied, then, on initiative and a venturesome attitude by both parties. This had certainly been true in the establishment of Kaiser's cement enterprise, and Kaiser would repeat the pattern again and again in other industries.

Calhoun and Kaiser had already been practicing what Calhoun preached, and they now received word that Eccles intended to speak with Ickes about the magnesium project. Kaiser had planted the seed by enclosing a copy of his October 4 letter to Ickes with his October 14 letter to Eccles. In his October 29 response to Kaiser's letter, Eccles informed Kaiser that Lawrence Clayton, his top assistant, had been paving the way for Kaiser: talking to representatives of the NDAC, the army, the navy, and others. The conclusion of Eccles's letter is very revealing about the divided allegiances many businessmen faced while working for the government during wartime. Eccles, as "board chairman on leave" of one of Columbia Construction's partners, expressed confidence that "*our* organization could do a real job in producing magnesium."[75] Though Eccles was head of a powerful federal agency, he was referring to Columbia Construction as "our organization."

Perhaps reflecting the urgency of the preparedness period, Eccles did nothing to hide his assistance to Kaiser: his October 29 letter was on Federal Reserve stationery. Meanwhile, Eccles's name still appeared on the letterhead of the Utah Construction Company as late as February 1941 (as both president and director). By June 1941, Utah Construction's letterhead no longer featured Eccles's name.[76] Although Eccles's principal goal was a general one—American military preparedness—it is doubtful Henry Kaiser would have received as much attention from the chairman of the Federal Reserve if they had not already developed a close business relationship.

Nevertheless, in the first week of November, Kaiser's steel project suffered a blow from one of its principal catalysts. In his final major speech of the 1940 campaign, President Roosevelt culminated a long-standing feud with Tom Girdler by using him as a symbol of disloyalty: "There are certain forces within our own national community, composed of men who call themselves American but who would destroy America. They are the forces of dictatorship in our own land—on one hand the Communists, and on the other the Girdlers." Roosevelt noted that such forces, whose purpose

was to "weaken democracy . . . are voting against the New Deal. You and I are proud of this opposition."[77] The rest of the year, when Kaiser and Calhoun discussed their proposed steel project with administration insiders, they heard deep grumblings about Tom Girdler's participation.

Despite this festering issue, in the second week of December Kaiser's Washington efforts fell into place. Chad Calhoun's understanding of the power relationships in Washington played no small role. Kaiser had told Calhoun to arrange a meeting with Edward Stettinius, who was in charge of raw materials for the NDAC. Stettinius had come to the government by way of U.S. Steel and had joined representatives of Big Steel in opposing rapid increases in America's steel capacity. Having already experienced the runaround from NDAC representatives, Calhoun decided to ignore Kaiser's directive. He chose instead to approach newspaperman Ernest K. Lindley.[78] On December 9, Lindley, a dyed-in-the-wool New Dealer (and author of an early FDR biography), had written a column in which he noted, "Government economists who are urging expansion begin with the fact that the present capacity [in steel] will be insufficient a year or so hence . . . [and that] arguments pro and con about the expansion may involve other industries."[79] Calhoun walked into Lindley's office the next day with the column, demanding to know who these "government economists" were. Calhoun complained that he had been "looking for weeks," while the members of the NDAC kept telling him they had no special needs. The upshot was that Lindley promised to make an appointment for Calhoun to meet Lauchlin Currie.[80]

In 1939, Currie had become economic adviser to the president—a solitary forerunner of today's Council of Economic Advisors. Currie brought along a number of his protégés from Harvard to key administration economic posts and had allies in the Bureau of the Budget, the Securities and Exchange Commission, the National Resources Planning Board, and the Departments of Commerce, Treasury, and Agriculture. He was a tireless proponent of Keynesian ideas regarding government spending. Currie's main concern was alleviating unemployment, and he favored breaking up concentrations in industry that set arbitrarily high prices and limited output—and jobs. One way to do so was to assist industry newcomers—such as Kaiser.

On December 11, after an introduction at Lindley's office, Currie and Calhoun attended a luncheon at the National Press Club, where they discussed Kaiser's proposed Pacific Coast steel plant. Currie expressed keen interest in the plan. He was especially supportive after Calhoun—responding to concerns about Tom Girdler—assured Currie that Kaiser would

dictate the proposed enterprise's labor policy. Currie then volunteered that Kaiser's project would require a different sort of contract "than any of the defense plant contracts heretofore granted."[81] Instead of using the unusual nature of Kaiser's project as an excuse to reject it, Currie suggested "between himself and some of the other of the President's advisors and ourselves that we could work out a satisfactory formula."[82]

The Currie connection was crucial. When he explained why Kaiser needed special attention, Currie probably was alluding to the roadblock to newcomers that Knudsen and Stettinius represented at the NDAC: "Kaiser was regarded in old-line industry circles as an upstart . . . [and] at some point he [would] need [Roosevelt's] intervention" in order to succeed.[83] In his position as the White House economic adviser, Currie could probably arrange that intervention. He met with the president regularly twice a week.[84] Calhoun had clearly reached the circle of people who could provide him the greatest assistance. Further evidence of Calhoun's favorable position came when Currie suggested that Calhoun approach Leon Henderson with the matter. Ernest Lindley had already arranged for Calhoun to meet Henderson the next day.[85]

Leon Henderson had made numerous enemies on Wall Street for his support of deficit spending and for his spirited attempts to break up concentrations of economic power in America. John Kenneth Galbraith, who worked for Henderson during the war, later wrote that as "the defender of the public and New Deal interest, Henderson saw himself in natural opposition to the businessmen."[86] Most businessmen, that is. Henry Kaiser's position as a challenger to entrenched market power in magnesium and steel made him an especially welcome figure to Leon Henderson.

On December 12, Calhoun visited Leon Henderson's office, where Henderson immediately announced his concerns about Republic Steel and Girdler. This was tricky for Calhoun because Kaiser and Girdler had met the week before: both were still dedicated to the deal.[87] But Henderson was adamant. He confessed that in the interests of national defense, he would "make a contract with the devil himself," but he dismissed Girdler as "beneath the devil." Calhoun, aware of the evangelical fervor of leading proponents of the New Deal, saw Girdler's transgressions as an opportunity. He suggested that "maybe through us [Henderson] would be able to bring about a modification of Girdler's views, and in turn make him at least acquiesce to New Deal policies." Whether or not Henderson believed Girdler's redemption was possible, he was willing to talk business with Kaiser. Henderson proposed a couple of options—a forging plant or an armor plate plant. He wanted to know whether Kaiser was abso-

lutely committed to the Pacific Northwest, since the Mid-Central states offered possibilities. Calhoun responded, presciently, that "there was no geographical limitation" to Kaiser's interests.[88]

The next day, December 13, Eccles aide Lawrence Clayton invited Calhoun to a Federal Reserve Board luncheon. Clayton regaled the board members with stories of Kaiser's accomplishments. Leon Henderson, who had spoken to Calhoun only about steel, interrupted to say that "these are the fellows we should get to build our airplanes."[89] Henderson met with Calhoun three days later to discuss airplane manufacture. In the course of a long meeting on December 16, Calhoun first raised the issue of magnesium to Henderson. Henderson produced a large file and commented that he had been working on the matter for years; he said he was very interested in helping someone put up a new plant. Henderson's reaction forms quite a contrast to the man portrayed in the myth as calling for help when Kaiser stormed into his office.

Exuberant over Kaiser's interest in magnesium, Henderson also wasted little time in pushing Kaiser's steel agenda in Washington. Because the key barrier to the project (as with magnesium) appeared to be financing, Henderson arranged for Calhoun to meet RFC vice chairman John Snyder. Calhoun received good and bad news. On the one hand, it would be necessary to obtain a certificate of necessity from either the army or the navy, plus the approval of the NDAC. On the other hand, Snyder suggested that the president might circumvent the NDAC and provide direct approval.[90]

There was one major obstacle at this point: Tom Girdler. The closer Kaiser and Calhoun got to Roosevelt's inner circle, the greater liability their partnership with Girdler appeared to be. Leon Henderson's comments regarding Girdler at the December 12 meeting prompted Kaiser and Calhoun to phone Girdler and inform him of administration concerns about him. Girdler promised to come to Washington with Kaiser and "meet Mr. Henderson or any of the other New Dealers" to convince them they could work together. Meeting again on the sixteenth, Henderson told Calhoun he was amenable to meeting with Girdler to discuss his concerns. Calhoun's thinking about Girdler now began to change. Calhoun wrote Kaiser that despite Henderson's stated interest in dealing with Girdler, "he is however not as wholly enthusiastic as he might be if we had some other arrangement."[91]

Calhoun's December 17 meeting with Lauchlin Currie finished Girdler as a potential partner. Currie revealed how close Kaiser was to his goal

when he told Calhoun that Marriner Eccles had "given both him and the President a big build up" concerning Kaiser, and Roosevelt was anxious to meet him. That, however, was not Currie's primary message. Calhoun reported, "The chief point which he discussed with me was the advisability of our entering into this project entirely alone as an independent group."[92]

Currie offered an alternative: a management contract with Republic, in which Kaiser retained both ownership and control. Republic's position as a major steel producer, it turns out, was as great a handicap as its labor relations reputation: "If Republic were identified directly with the ownership then the other major companies, particularly U.S. Steel, would bring so much pressure to bear that the whole deal would perhaps be blocked."[93]

Armed with this message from the administration, Calhoun wasted no time. He had breakfast the following morning with a Republic Steel vice president and Republic's chief metallurgist. Calhoun told them of Currie's concerns, and Republic's vice president agreed that a management contract appeared to be the best alternative. Less than an hour after the breakfast meeting, Currie called and, in the strongest language yet, stated that Kaiser could not "expect government cooperation" if Republic remained a partner.[94]

Later that day, Ernest Lindley told Chad Calhoun that Philip Murray, new head of the CIO (the labor union Tom Girdler had called "racketeers" and "communists") wanted to meet Girdler. This must have been heady stuff for Calhoun. Only eight days after he had first met Lindley, a principal intermediary to key New Dealers, the journalist was treating Calhoun as a trusted emissary to industry. Nevertheless, Calhoun told Lindley that he did not think it would be a good idea and "might easily be interpreted as interfering with Republic's business."[95] Actually, Calhoun's main concern was that if word got back to Roosevelt's inner circle that Kaiser was promoting Girdler's interests, it might interfere with *Kaiser's* business. Having been told numerous times in the past week by Lauchlin Currie and Leon Henderson that the administration would not deal with Girdler, Calhoun chose to play it safe. In meetings with Henderson and Currie just before Christmas, "nothing was said . . . about Republic Steel, or Mr. Girdler."[96]

Kaiser's connection with Girdler was far from over. Girdler inquired about employment for his son-in-law on a prospective dam project in Arizona. Kaiser's son responded in January 1941: "I shall keep your son-in-law's name in mind when and if we have any work in this area."[97] Meanwhile, engineers from Girdler's Republic Steel did provide assistance to

Kaiser's West Coast steel project, which began production in 1942. That same year, Kaiser briefly consulted Girdler—head of the newly merged Consolidated Vultee Aircraft Company—when he proposed to build huge cargo planes for the government.[98]

Having eliminated Girdler from ownership and control of the proposed steel venture, Currie followed up by suggesting two tax-saving ideas to improve the project's feasibility. One included accelerated amortization, and the other was to put the steel company beneath an existing profitable operation.[99] Currie also asked Kaiser to consider the aircraft business. Again bringing New Deal principles such as dispersal of economic power to the mobilization effort, Currie expressed interest in getting new "life and blood" into the aircraft industry.[100]

Kaiser spoke to Eccles on Christmas Eve and learned that Eccles had spoken to Leon Henderson twice on issues of concern to Kaiser: about steel at the Gridiron Dinner and about magnesium at the White House. Just a couple of days before, Eccles had discussed Kaiser's steel proposal with Currie. He reported to Kaiser and Calhoun that Henderson and Currie were both "favorably inclined toward us getting into the steel business." The big drawback was Republic. Both Henderson and Currie would be more comfortable if Kaiser hired steel technicians instead of dealing with Girdler. With that in mind, Eccles concluded that Kaiser's best shot was in magnesium, where he could sell himself as an "independent."[101]

The same day Kaiser and Calhoun spoke with Henderson again. As he had done with Eccles, Kaiser explained "the present plan," which would use Todd-California (Kaiser's new shipbuilding company) as owner for either the steel, magnesium, or aircraft operation. They would pledge profits of the company as collateral for the necessary RFC loan to build the plants. In essence, Kaiser had adopted the approach advocated by Wirtz and Currie.[102]

By Christmas it was clear that Henry Kaiser was on the verge of embarking on new enterprises in two industries that presented some of the most daunting barriers to entry in American business. Steel had long had "substantial" barriers to entry, including very high capital requirements.[103] Magnesium was a monopoly, controlled by Dow Chemical. Under prewar conditions, even the irrepressible Henry Kaiser would have faced nearly impossible odds.[104] Now the administration's distinctive New Deal response to war in Europe offered him an opportunity he was quick to exploit, and Kaiser realized he offered the New Deal more than just assistance in national defense. Calhoun reminded him, for instance, that a

Pacific Coast steel plant "will aid prices, break cartels and trade agreements, and benefit community in general."[105] This was a New Deal War.[106]

The literature of entrepreneurship describes entrepreneurs as initiators or creators of their own world. Government usually is either left out of the picture or is presented as a roadblock to progress. Certainly, liberal New Dealers developed an antibusiness reputation. Yet time and again, in the fall of 1940 Kaiser's actions came in response to the initiative of liberal government officials. Alvin Wirtz raised the subject of magnesium without prompting, causing Kaiser to undertake a serious study. Leon Henderson suggested that Kaiser extend his geographic sights to include the Midwest. Wirtz and Lauchlin Currie presented a strategy to secure a loan from the RFC. Eccles, Ickes, Henderson, and especially Currie talked Kaiser out of a partnership with Republic Steel. Finally, it had been President Roosevelt's personal interest in West Coast steel that galvanized Kaiser's Washington efforts in September 1940.

At the time, Roosevelt appeared to be most enthusiastic about the economic ideas of Bob Jackson, Henderson, Marriner Eccles, Lauchlin Currie, and Isador Lubin.[107] By December 1940, three of the five, Eccles, Henderson, and Currie—each representing different sectors of the government in different capacities—were enthusiastically telling the president about Henry J. Kaiser. As a member of the NDAC, only Henderson had a formal role in the defense mobilization effort. But Eccles was chairman of the Federal Reserve Board, and Currie was economic adviser to the president. Each man had access to considerable power. Kaiser made a big splash with these key people through a vigorous, all-out attempt to seek defense-related work.

In addition to showing that the preparedness program sustained the fluid, boundary-free organizational style of the New Deal, Kaiser's experience shows that to a great extent the government remained faithful to New Deal principles as well. The president and his key advisers were prepared not just to mobilize but to fight a New Deal War. Kaiser's enthusiasm for defense mobilization, his penchant for battling monopoly, and his embrace of collective bargaining qualified him to be a soldier in the New Deal War and were rewarded with a warm relationship with President Roosevelt. Of equal importance was the loyalty expressed to Kaiser by a core group of presidential advisers. They intervened on Kaiser's behalf when it was not expedient for the president to do so. The men who spoke enthusiastically to Roosevelt about Kaiser shared the president's opinions regarding pump

priming, antitrust, and collective bargaining. They saw the war not as the end of the New Deal but as an opportunity to expand the nation's productive capacity, thereby achieving lower prices, which would stimulate recovery. If monopolies like Dow Chemical or oligopolies like Big Steel chose to limit production, thereby keeping prices artificially high, offering a newcomer like Henry Kaiser entrée into the industry might bring them around.

Henry Kaiser now had a plan, he had the president's interest, and he had garnered the support of advisers close to the president. In late December, two additional events occurred that would help shape Henry Kaiser's contributions to the defense effort. On December 20, President Roosevelt announced his intention to establish the Office of Production Management, which would supersede the NDAC.[108] The same day, Henry Kaiser, who had until then built shipyards but not ships, signed an agreement to begin construction of thirty cargo ships for the British.[109] By the end of 1940, Henry Kaiser was poised to become the government entrepreneur who would symbolize the New Deal War.

Before Henry Kaiser (right) began borrowing from the federal government, his principal banker was A. P. Giannini (left). (Henry J. Kaiser Historical Collection, Bancroft Library, University of California, Berkeley)

Interior Secretary Harold Ickes and Washington lawyer extraordinaire Thomas Corcoran (shown here in 1938). Ickes promoted Kaiser's industrial ventures from within the government, while lawyer/lobbyist Corcoran did so from without. (Franklin D. Roosevelt Library, Hyde Park, N.Y.)

Kaiser testifies before a congressional hearing with his Washington representative, Chad Calhoun, at his side. (Henry J. Kaiser Historical Collection, Bancroft Library, University of California, Berkeley)

Federal Reserve Board Chairman Marriner Eccles shakes hands with Roosevelt at the 1937 dedication of the Federal Reserve Building. When Kaiser sought war work in the spring of 1940, his old partner, Eccles, helped out. Eccles saw a confluence, rather than conflict of interest, when assisting "our company" while working for the government. (E. L. Cooley, University of Utah)

New Deal economist Lauchlin Currie sought industrial newcomers to challenge entrenched economic power and found one in Henry J. Kaiser. (Library of Congress)

Leon Henderson was an example of the New Deal's freewheeling organization. As the National Defense Advisory Commission's pricing representative, Henderson assisted Kaiser and others who challenged industrial titans. (National Archives)

Shipbuilders Henry Kaiser and Andrew Jackson Higgins were linked in the minds of the public and of the president. Above, Roosevelt addresses workers at Kaiser's Portland, Oregon, shipyard. Below, Roosevelt strikes a similar pose while visiting Higgins in New Orleans. (Photographs by U.S. Navy; Franklin D. Roosevelt Library, Hyde Park, N.Y.)

Publisher Henry Luce (third from right) and Henry Kaiser at a 1943 launching. (Library of Congress)

When Howard Hughes (left) became Kaiser's partner, Jesse Jones (right) vouched for Hughes. (Library of Congress)

Sam Rosenman advised Kaiser on how to approach FDR. (Library of Congress)

In this Berryman cartoon, commander in chief Roosevelt becomes a political candidate, thanks to Dan Tobin and his Teamsters Union. (Library of Congress)

Kaiser with Henry Wallace, whom it was rumored he would replace on the 1944 Democratic ticket, and Eleanor Roosevelt, who invited Kaiser to chair the Nonpartisan Association for Franchise Education. (Henry J. Kaiser Historical Collection, Bancroft Library, University of California, Berkeley)

Kaiser speaks at the September 1944 inaugural of the Nonpartisan Association. At his side is George Fielding Eliot, just as a Democratic partisan had prescribed in April. (Henry J. Kaiser Historical Collection, Bancroft Library, University of California, Berkeley)

This photograph got Kaiser in trouble. On September 23, 1944, only days after the public launch of the Nonpartisan Association, Kaiser responds to Roosevelt's very partisan "Fala" speech to the Teamsters. (George Skadding, Life *magazine; © Time Inc.)*

OFFICE MEMORANDUM

UNITED STATES GOVERNMENT

SMALLER WAR PLANTS CORPORATION

PERSONAL AND CONFIDENTIAL

Date

September 26, 1944

Office of the
Chairman

Honorable Henry J. Kaiser
Waldorf-Astoria Hotel
New York, New York

Dear Mr. Kaiser:

Herewith $1.00--I wish I had $25,000--
and this is for you personally and to pay you for
the smile you had the other night at the Teamsters'
Union meeting.

In reply to your letter about the nonpartisan business, I want you to know that I am
with you 100% -- 1,000,000% -- and in the strictly
nonpartisan way that you are. Yes, sir! I am
nonpartisan, just like you.

Also, I am going to do everything I can
everywhere to get our people to vote--in the same
nonpartisan way as you are going to do.

Please do not waste this $1.00. This is
no time for waste, but if you will just continue
that nonpartisan smile, we can get a lot of people
to register and vote, and I hope to Christ they
will vote right.

Your non-partisan friend

Sincerely yours,

Maury Maverick
Chairman and General Manager

Enclosure

Maury Maverick's response to Kaiser's Teamsters appearance. (Henry J. Kaiser Collection, Bancroft Library, University of California, Berkeley)

[Washington is]

a frontier town

for lawyers.

Lloyd Cutler, *1971*

5 ——— GOOD OLD AMERICAN KNOW-WHO

Shortly after World War II, the secretaries of Henry Kaiser's Oakland and New York offices coordinated their phone lists. The individuals on the combined list could have been sorted into three groups, depending on the nature of their relationship to "H. J." First, of course, would be members of the Kaiser "family," including both relatives and company insiders. The other two groups were lawyers and members of the press.[1] That the latter two groups appeared so prominently on Kaiser's phone list leads to an explanation of how Kaiser achieved such success during the war: he enlisted outsiders to perform legal and public relations functions—two crucial capabilities of government entrepreneurs.

Having Ernest Lindley introduce him to administration insiders Lauchlin Currie and Leon Henderson was a necessary, but not sufficient, condition for Henry Kaiser to obtain industrial defense work. From early 1941 until mid-1942, Henry Kaiser sought an expanded role in America's defense effort with the benefit of two capabilities from beyond the walls of the organization: the legal talent of Washington lawyers and public relations support from the nation's media elite. By March 1941, Kaiser had one of Washington's first modern lawyer/lobbyists, Tom Corcoran, working for him and had been profiled for the first time by Time/Life. In this chapter, I describe the genesis of Kaiser's use of an external legal capability: the Washington lawyer/lobbyist. In the next chapter, I examine the role America's media played in Kaiser's public relations efforts.

Five decades later, one of the most compelling developments in corporate America is the art of reaching beyond the organization for expertise or services once performed by the organization itself. Functions peripheral to the heart of a company's business are contracted out, from janitorial, mail, and audiovisual, to cafeteria, security, and utilities services. At the same time, corporations call on lawyers or consultants to assist them in dealing with the government or with issues of workforce diversity, the environment, or overall corporate strategy.

The corporation of the 1990s bears little resemblance to the relatively all-encompassing giant enterprise many business historians have portrayed. Although the organizations themselves have indeed changed considerably in recent decades, the change has not been as stark as it appears. This is because, with a few exceptions, business historians have not yet investigated earlier corporate use of outside capabilities sufficiently to provide an adequate means of comparison.[2] Reaching beyond the walls of a business organization was by no means unusual in the 1940s; twentieth-century companies had begun to do so frequently in fields such as advertising, public relations, industrial design, and engineering. Indeed, Henry Kaiser had done so during his career as a contractor, calling on lawyers and inventors. What was new? World War II offered Kaiser and Chad Calhoun a brief opportunity to reap the benefits of outside expertise at little or no cost to his organization.

Whereas the efforts of Kaiser and Calhoun were ad hoc in nature, administration lawyers engaged in more structured efforts to engage American businessmen in the preparedness program. Kaiser would later become known as a battler of bureaucracy, but when he arrived in Washington in 1940, significant efforts were being made to attract government entrepreneurs to the preparedness program.

In May and June, administration lawyers were both drafting legislation and investigating ways to circumvent existing legislation to enable America to support the Allies in Europe. These lawyers operated, for the most part, behind the scenes, and their efforts were at first unknown to Kaiser and Calhoun. By the beginning of 1941, Kaiser had begun to reap the benefits of their work. Having worked principally with financial experts such as economists Lauchlin Currie and Leon Henderson, as well as banker Marriner Eccles, Kaiser began to rely on administration lawyers in 1941 and would count on them to help him for the remainder of the war—and after.

Enthusiastically offering his organization's services to the preparedness program was not the only thing that helped Kaiser's relations with the government. His organizational structure and operating style helped, too. Kaiser's outfit was a fluid collection of individuals, not bound by the rigidity of either organizational charts or detailed job descriptions. In this respect, he operated more like a nineteenth-century entrepreneur than a twentieth-century organization man. Kaiser would seek out the best person for a task, regardless of the individual's rank in the organization. Some executives kept their people away from the top floor at Oakland headquarters, fearing that they might lose a key person to Kaiser's clutches for weeks.[3] Dating from his days as a road builder, Kaiser had resisted a "multilayered managerial hierarchy."[4]

Such a fluid approach to organization was ideal for a government entrepreneur in the 1930s and 1940s. Distinctions between the public and private sectors were blurring, and the federal government under Franklin Roosevelt was adopting a style similar to Kaiser's. The New Deal encouraged extrajurisdictional behavior and disregard for organizational boundaries and job descriptions. Henry Kaiser's main customer, then, had the same attitude toward boundaries he did. When Kaiser dealt with the federal government, it was sometimes difficult to tell where the government ended and Kaiser's company began. One of the best ways to observe Kaiser's compatibility with the New Deal style is at his point of contact with the government, and in many cases that meant his relationships with New Deal lawyers.

One of the supreme ironies of the Kaiser story is that despite his reputation as a battler of bureaucracy—the old story of private enterprise coming to the rescue of the hapless government—Kaiser's guides through the government thicket in the 1940s were indigenous to Washington. Instead of the popular myth of a businessman, whether Henry Ford or Ross Perot, coming to Washington to straighten things out, the Kaiser story tells how

the federal government—and especially the "antibusiness" New Deal—provided the business world with a new corporate capability. Thomas Corcoran, Sam Rosenman, Oscar Cox, and other lawyers, most of whom spent their formative years in federal agencies, instructed America's "can-do" industrialist in how to get things done.

Kaiser's experience with New Deal lawyers was part of a growing trend in Washington. As government became synonymous with bureaucratic complexity, it also evolved a new species to cut through its complexity. The twentieth-century growth of the federal government combined with Franklin Roosevelt's expansion of the executive branch to spawn a pool of attorneys skilled in cutting through Washington's red tape. Concurrent with the arrival of modern government entrepreneurs—industrialists whose enterprises were largely dedicated to government work and who strove to sustain such enterprises in peacetime—was the emergence of the modern lawyer/lobbyist.

Before the New Deal revolution, government entrepreneurs had employed legal expertise, but they had normally done so to achieve specific, limited goals. Lawyers litigated disputes among contractors and between contractors and government agencies. They also provided services during the organic contracting process, especially after the contract was granted. This was the sort of legal representation Kaiser had until 1940. Before the coming of the New Deal, there were so few government entrepreneurs on the national stage that there was little need on Main Street for the skills attorneys had honed in Washington. Attorneys might shuttle back and forth between New York and Washington but most often between positions in Wall Street's investment banking houses and in the State Department, as did John Foster Dulles and Averell Harriman. This changed with the extended reach of government regulation in the 1930s, the growth of the executive branch—both in absolute terms and relative to the other branches of government—and the establishment of the federal government as a major source of business. The distinctive feature of the modern lawyer/lobbyists was that they had garnered experience in one of the new or expanded executive branch agencies and in private practice focused their lobbying attention predominantly on the executive branch. The first generation of lawyer/lobbyists to concentrate on the executive branch were, not surprisingly, veterans of the New Deal.

When Henry Kaiser expanded the scope of his relationship with the federal government in the spring of 1940, the proliferation of lawyers in Washington had been under way for some years. In the summer of 1933, for instance, Henry Fowler, who would later become secretary of the trea-

sury, joined Covington and Burling, the largest law firm in Washington. He was only the firm's eighteenth lawyer.[5] By 1940, some Washington firms had nearly thirty.[6] As he widened the range of his federal aspirations from construction and cement production to primary metals and aircraft production, Kaiser's organization tapped this supply of expertise as it set out to expand its capabilities in Washington. Kaiser began by establishing Chad Calhoun as his Washington representative in a suite at the Shoreham Hotel. The first new "capability" Kaiser brought in from outside the organization was the Washington lawyer. Individuals who worked in various government agencies during the New Deal—some also in wartime agencies—offered knowledge of how government worked and established relationships for Kaiser with people in government offices.

Kaiser also became accustomed to receiving advice from government lawyers and treating them as his own resource. In New Deal Washington, Kaiser discovered that the federal government had truly established itself as "the nation's law firm," and he became one of its regular clients.[7] Kaiser became accustomed to receiving advice and guidance from government attorneys for no fee. This was his tax dollars at work.

As he discovered, legal expertise in Washington was an amorphous resource, something that could come from inside or outside his organization. It seemed to know no organizational boundaries. This helps explain the chronology of Kaiser's relations with Washington law firms, a sequence that appears on the surface to make little sense. During World War II, Kaiser escalated his commitment to federal contracts and his reliance on federal loans. For all intents and purposes, the organization had two headquarters—one in Oakland and one in Washington. During the war, however, Kaiser had only marginal relations with Washington's law firms. Only when the war ended and Kaiser began to distance himself from government work as he engaged the needs of the burgeoning consumer society (automobiles, medicine, housing, and appliances) did he enlist the assistance of prominent Washington law firms.

The relations he established with New Deal lawyers followed a pattern. The lawyer would write legislation related to business opportunities and then, representing a particular government department, would help Kaiser find the optimal response to the new law or arrange for Kaiser to meet key people in the administration who would be responsible for implementing the measure. After Roosevelt's death and the end of the war, the lawyer would leave the federal government but not Washington: he would establish a private practice in the capital to take advantage of his knowledge and contacts. The next step was to establish a formal client relationship

with Kaiser, sometimes approaching on Kaiser's behalf the same agency at which the lawyer once worked.

V-J Day did not signal the end of opportunity in Washington. In one respect, World War II would actually end years later for government entrepreneurs. The government needed to dispose of its wartime plants, a process that launched Kaiser into the aluminum business. In addition, terms of contracts and loans agreed to during the war were scrutinized and renegotiated. Kaiser, for instance, sought better terms for his steel loan from the Reconstruction Finance Corporation. In another respect, V-J Day brought a clean break: it was followed by a round of congressional investigations that forced Kaiser and others to turn to Washington's new private law practices to defend themselves from charges of war profiteering.

Some lawyers did not wait for the end of the war to exploit this virgin territory filled with unusual opportunities for the well-connected. Lloyd Cutler called Washington a "frontier town for lawyers," and in 1941 Thomas "Tommy the Cork" Corcoran became one of the most publicized hired guns.[8] Congress had faced lobbyists for decades before Corcoran arrived in Washington, and countless lawyers honed their skills at government jobs, left the government, and profited handsomely from that experience in the private sector. Corcoran was one of the first group of lawyers who successfully applied that strategy to the executive branch.[9]

Lawyer/lobbyists often do not lobby in the classic sense, that is, by trying to influence legislation. Instead, they seek opportunities for their clients within the existing legal framework, opportunities for loans and contracts, for instance. Such skills have long met the needs of government entrepreneurs like Henry Kaiser. Kaiser did not personally endorse legislation on the national level until after World War II, and then only sparingly.[10] Nor did he ask for classic lobbying efforts from his lawyers. Tom Corcoran certainly was not a traditional lobbyist; he rarely found it necessary to register as such.[11] Corcoran himself disdained the label of lawyer/lobbyist. He called himself a "lawyer-entrepreneur."[12] Corcoran's gift was in arranging new combinations of individuals; he set up conferences and got his clients in to see the right people.[13] Corcoran's understanding of the law, although considerable, was overshadowed by what he had learned on Wall Street. He did not sell himself as a skilled specialist in any aspect of the law; he was a deal maker.[14]

Corcoran was a first mover in the new field, and he brought along a special cachet. He had been a presidential adviser, coauthor of crucial pieces of New Deal legislation, a man who could pull strings with key members of the executive branch and Congress. "This is Tom Corcoran, calling

from the White House," he introduced himself, even if calling from an agency office or a hotel lobby. The *United States News* credited him with selecting four Supreme Court justices.[15] That, however, was gilding the lily. According to New Dealer Charles Horsky, "Any Washington lawyer who is worth his salt and who has practiced in Washington for any length of time will have at least a speaking acquaintance with many of the staff in any agency where he may specialize."[16] This is where Corcoran achieved his real competitive advantage in private practice. Corcoran was the chief Washington recruiter for Louis Brandeis and Felix Frankfurter. FDR's relationships with Supreme Court justices Brandeis and Frankfurter were of major import to the New Deal. A careful scholar of "extrajurisdictional behavior" by Supreme Court justices concludes that two-thirds of all justices have engaged in such activity but that Brandeis and Frankfurter went well beyond the "norm."[17]

From his position as professor at the Harvard Law School, Frankfurter had acted as intermediary between Justice Brandeis and FDR and had recruited many talented attorneys for New Deal agencies. Frankfurter's protégés were steeped in the Brandeisian ideology, which lauded the virtues of small business and competition. Few knew the extent to which Justice Brandeis and Frankfurter—a justice himself by 1939—were involved in President Roosevelt's decision making. But they could not have been in Washington very long before they recognized that legal expertise was an essential (if amorphous) skill in the federal government—a skill that at times seemed to know no organizational bounds or even respect the constitutional separation of powers.

Corcoran brought recent law school graduates to Washington and put them on the payroll of the RFC, which operated as a "flexible emergency-legislation unit" when a new agency was created or a crisis arose.[18] At the RFC, he established the New Deal lawyers' equivalent to a steno pool. His recruits learned soon enough how little job descriptions and jurisdictions might mean in Washington. Corcoran ultimately had legions of apprentices and recruits scattered throughout government, from U.S. attorneys to prominent figures in various government agencies.

With the "active cooperation" of the RFC's general counsel, Stanley Reed, Corcoran recruited attorneys from top law schools—usually Harvard—and kept them in the RFC until an opportunity opened up for them in another agency. After Reed became solicitor general, Corcoran's "operating base" moved to the Justice Department. When a difficult legal task arose, Corcoran could quickly assemble the necessary task force, which would burn the midnight oil until the mission was accomplished. In addi-

tion, Corcoran's "pool" offered a means to circumvent the "benighted" (Republican) holdovers from prior administrations. This informal employment agency boasted sufficient talent either to reorganize old departments or to staff new agencies.[19]

In the 1930s, it was common to refer in Washington to the "Corcoran Gallery," the large collection of legal talent "the Cork" had brought to the city.[20] The resulting advantages to the clients of his private practice might be as pedestrian—but valuable—as the ability to "arrange a conference or to obtain a hearing for his client."[21] Corcoran also recalled benefiting from having his protégés keep him "informed of events in the offices where I'd placed them."[22] They provided entry for his clients and a sure knowledge of the talent they needed to hire.

Corcoran's style of operation would never have succeeded in Washington had the environment not been in his favor. Two things contributed: first, a sense of urgency, which invigorated certain phases of the New Deal and resurfaced during the war mobilization, and second, the attitude and style of the commander in chief. The fluid style of the New Deal was effective in quickly marshaling forces to confront emergencies. As his relationship with FDR developed, Corcoran's real responsibilities moved away from the RFC—although he was still on its payroll—toward doing whatever the president needed. His career was an excellent example of the New Deal's disregard for organization charts, job descriptions, and well-defined jurisdictions.[23] In keeping with that style, Corcoran worked for the president without written instructions because "if something were carefully written down . . . it became a rigid construct, losing the flexibility that allows an idea to take shape in the political world."[24]

The New Deal involved a process of experimentation and a degree of flexibility that reflected Roosevelt's own impatience with bureaucratic channels.[25] New Deal lawyers such as Corcoran were imbued with a resistance to established bureaucratic hierarchy; a sense of national emergency reinforced their belief in circumventing ordinary channels.[26] Many either participated in or observed the disregard for separation of powers demonstrated by Brandeis, Frankfurter, and Roosevelt. This style proved especially helpful in mobilizing the defense effort before Pearl Harbor. During the preparedness program, War Secretary Henry Stimson observed this tendency in Roosevelt: the president, he said, would be unable to employ "systematic relations, because that is rather entirely antithetical to his nature and temperament."[27]

Roosevelt's attempts to bypass Congress, for instance, were well known in Washington. Before Henry Kaiser had built any ships or produced

any magnesium, he was well aware of the president's attitude. Just before Christmas in 1940, Marriner Eccles told Chad Calhoun of his recent meeting with the president. The subject was aid to the British, and they discussed "the best means and methods of circumventing or repealing the Johnson Act or the Neutrality Act."[28] The Johnson Act of 1934 "prohibited government loans to nations in default of their World War I debts to the United States." Sending American ships full of cargo to England in the form of aid was prohibited by the Neutrality Act of 1939, which required "belligerents to buy munitions for cash and to carry them home in their own ships." Roosevelt was no doubt emboldened in his attitude toward the Neutrality Act by a letter from Felix Frankfurter in which the justice termed the act "fundamentally wrong in conception" and "in conflict with international law."[29] The barrier to helping England was doubly steep because that nation was both a defaulter and a belligerent.[30] The solution to this delicate problem was the Lend-Lease Act, which, as Walter Lippmann put it, moved America from "large promises carried out slyly and particularly by clever devices to substantial deeds openly and honestly avowed."[31] Lend-Lease would also provide Henry Kaiser with immense new shipbuilding opportunities.

Henry Kaiser's initial need for additional capabilities in Washington—that is, for something besides his skills and those of Chad Calhoun—arose out of his organization's efforts to enter the magnesium industry and out of the relationship between those efforts and Kaiser's shipbuilding concerns. Although his enterprise had not yet built any ships, Kaiser had been deeply involved in the shipbuilding business for more than a year. His entrée to shipbuilding came about in September 1939 through his connection with the Maine-based Todd Shipbuilding Corporation and its president, John Reilly. Todd's personnel constructed freighters for the U.S. Maritime Commission; the Six Companies constructed the shipyards and ways.[32]

After France fell in June 1940, Great Britain was in danger of strangulation as a result of Germany's submarine attacks on British shipping lines. The Neutrality Act prohibited the United States from sending its ships to the combat zone so the British Merchant Shipping Mission was dispatched to Washington in October in an effort to replenish the British cargo fleet through purchases from American firms.

John Reilly consulted his western partners—including Kaiser—and William S. Newell, president of Maine's Bath Iron Works. In agreement about this venture, they signed a contract on December 20, 1940, to build sixty cargo ships for the British. Newell was responsible for construction of thirty ships in South Portland, Maine, under the auspices of the

Todd-Bath Iron Shipbuilding Corporation, and Kaiser would build thirty at Richmond, California, at the Todd-California Shipbuilding Corporation.[33]

With these undertakings well under way as 1940 drew to a close, Kaiser's venture into shipbuilding and his exploration of primary metals—particularly magnesium—began to converge. Presidential adviser Lauchlin Currie suggested that Kaiser could improve his chances of obtaining a loan from the RFC to build a magnesium plant if he pledged his shipbuilding profits as collateral. Approval by the RFC, the U.S. Maritime Commission, and the British Purchasing Commission would be necessary. Currie and Leon Henderson informed Kaiser that the government could help by providing tax relief in the form of a five-year accelerated depreciation plan. The resulting reduction of taxable income would have little value to a business that would lose money for the first couple of years, as most start-ups do. Furthermore, the tax law prohibited the combination of financial results of separate corporations so Kaiser could not consolidate his losses from a second business (such as magnesium) with the gains from shipbuilding. But he could maximize the tax benefit by establishing a new venture as part of an existing, already profitable enterprise. That was where his connection with Todd came in. Todd-California, with its minimal initial investment, expected to be profitable immediately in shipbuilding, and a tax break would provide an instant benefit.

The depreciation privilege was part of the government's strategy of attracting private capital to the defense program, and it was one of several ways government initiative influenced the success of entrepreneurs like Kaiser. The five-year depreciation plan was developed in the NDAC by Henderson's price stabilization group, rather than in the NDAC industrial or raw material sections, demonstrating once again how little meaning areas of jurisdiction had in 1940.

David Ginsburg, chief counsel of Henderson's price group, composed the statute so Ginsburg's presence in meetings with Chad Calhoun in December 1940 and January 1941 provided some assurance that red tape would not derail Kaiser's projects.[34] Kaiser was sensitive to the red tape issue because of the runaround he and Calhoun had experienced from the armed services and William Knudsen's industrial and Edward Stettinius's raw materials sections of the NDAC in the summer of 1940. Ginsburg had worked for Leon Henderson at the Securities and Exchange Commission before becoming Henderson's legal adviser at the NDAC's price stabilization division. Ginsburg was as sensitive to the issue of red tape as Henderson and shared Henderson's tremendous sense of urgency about the mo-

bilization effort. They feared that the appearance of big businessmen such as Knudsen and Stettinius would slow the mobilization to a snail's pace.

With that problem in mind, the price stabilization group operated as "moles" in the government, as they attempted to push assistance for the Allies and to increase production so as to achieve full employment. If the industry leaders, such as Dow Chemical, Alcoa, and U.S. Steel, balked at building additional capacity, the solution was to approach operators like Henry Kaiser. In industries ranging from machine tools to copper to magnesium, they assisted newcomers.[35]

Dealing with Ginsburg and the price stabilization group provided Kaiser and Calhoun with their first glimpse of what effective New Deal lawyers could offer to government entrepreneurs involved in defense mobilization. Kaiser's next lesson involved lawyers in private practice, who had garnered rich experience in the ways government agencies worked. They, too, he discovered, could provide him important services in Washington.

New corporate capabilities such as these develop in response to new sets of business challenges and opportunities, and in January 1941 Henry Kaiser knew he had a series of special needs to fill if he was going to break into the magnesium business. He needed to obtain permission from the British Purchasing Commission to use its shipbuilding fees as collateral for the RFC loan; he needed to secure ownership of the patents for the manufacturing process; and he needed to obtain the personal services of the process's inventor. Most difficult of all, though, was that he needed to obtain a loan from the RFC for the construction of his plant. Breaking into an industry with steep barriers to entry like magnesium would be difficult even if these needs were satisfied. It would be impossible if they were not.

Kaiser looked to Washington, D.C., for help. By January 1941, however, Kaiser could no longer call on the economists who had assisted him in the fall of 1940. Lauchlin Currie would soon go to China as the president's emissary and would be gone until March.[36] Leon Henderson, convinced that the January creation of the Office of Production Management (OPM)—without a separate agency for price control—would yield too much power to big businessmen who did not embrace New Deal principles, registered his protest by taking a sabbatical from government until April, when Roosevelt selected him to head the newly created Office of Price Administration and Consumer Supply.[37] These developments set Kaiser on a course he would have had to chart eventually: reliance on Washington lawyers for assistance.

It is now commonplace for corporations to retain Washington attorneys, many of whom previously worked for the federal government, to advise

on responses to changes in the government environment. The use of such attorneys in the 1990s is considered an adaptive ("in the realm of existing practice") response. But Henry Kaiser's response in 1941 was creative ("outside that realm").[38] Kaiser had brought his own attorneys to Washington before, but he now complemented this expertise with that of New Deal veterans who could navigate in the complex environment of the new Washington.

Henry Kaiser secured Tom Corcoran's legal services as a consequence of Corcoran's political activities in the fall of 1940. After resigning from his position at the RFC, Corcoran spent September and October 1940 in New York with Fiorello La Guardia's Independent Voter's Committee for Roosevelt and Wallace. There he attempted to persuade Republicans to support FDR's bid for a third term.[39] Corcoran had to raise his own money for the project so he called on "old friends and friends of friends," including William Mahon and John Reilly.[40] Mahon, a principal in the firm Fitzgerald, Stapleton and Mahon, had been the legal counsel for the Todd Shipyards for twenty-five years. Corcoran had become acquainted with this old Tammany Hall operator while working on Wall Street in the 1920s.[41] When Corcoran first provided Washington services to Todd, he did so through his old friend. Therefore, although Corcoran worked directly with Kaiser, his contractual relationship was with Mahon, whose bills were paid by Reilly. This set of relationships would later cause problems.

When he met Corcoran, one of Kaiser's greatest needs was to obtain financing for his proposed magnesium plant. Corcoran, who had been one of the architects of the New Deal, had hired many attorneys in various government agencies, and had worked for the RFC, was the ideal person both to understand how to approach the RFC and to push the right buttons with old friends to help his clients obtain loans. Indeed, within two days of first meeting with Kaiser on magnesium, Corcoran had arranged a meeting for Kaiser and Calhoun with Clifford Durr, the chief counsel of the RFC.

Durr was known for being more amenable to making loans than the administrator of the Federal Loan Agency, Jesse Jones. Jones was notorious for treating the RFC like a private bank. Durr believed such an attitude was inappropriate at a time when war threatened: "Plants designed for military production were hardly 'sound' investments for the portfolio of an agency given to testing its operations by banking standards."[42] Kaiser and Calhoun met with Durr again on January 10 to discuss the magnesium plant and loan. After three more days of discussions, which included

Corcoran, Mahon, and the Kaiser people, Corcoran drafted a letter for the RFC. Kaiser's formal application to the RFC was not submitted until February 15, but RFC head Emil Schram immediately approved it. Schram also had a more aggressive attitude toward financing defense-related plants than his boss, Jesse Jones.[43] Despite the careful preparation, Jones still had the power to overrule Schram and deny Kaiser the loan. Corcoran moved quickly the next day to ensure that Jones would not block the deal. Though Corcoran no longer worked for the president, he still had influence in the White House. Corcoran called Roosevelt just before a cabinet meeting. Interior Secretary Harold Ickes noted in his diary: "Tom got the president on the telephone from my office just before Cabinet meeting. Apparently he did a good job because the president started in to crowd Jesse Jones on the issue. Jesse didn't like it any too well either, but the president, in effect, ordered him to take care of Kaiser."[44] It worked.[45] Three days later, Jones announced that the RFC was loaning money to Kaiser for the magnesium plant.[46]

Six weeks of work by Corcoran had yielded spectacular results. As Charles Horsky pointed out, "The Reconstruction Finance Corporation does not go seeking for people to make loans to."[47] Under ordinary conditions, it was fairly typical for such a deal to take three months to approve—if it was approved at all.[48]

Jones's announcement brought Kaiser to a significant moment in his career as a government entrepreneur: his first coverage beyond the respective locales of his enterprises. *Time*'s first story on Kaiser (March 3, 1941) set up a heroic conquest theme. It was about a serious problem. The defense mobilization effort was being crippled by bottlenecks in aluminum and magnesium, an issue that had received considerable attention since December 1940. "When last week began, the U.S. was worried about bottlenecks in magnesium," the story went—like those in many other magazines. *Time* concluded that because of the recent approval of Kaiser's proposed magnesium plant, "at week's end the bottleneck was smashed."[49] Apparently *Time* considered this true even though Kaiser had not yet produced an ounce of magnesium.

On March 2, 1941, just two weeks after Kaiser secured the magnesium contract, the *Washington Star* printed a piece by Theodore C. Alford called "New Genius Rises." Alford wrote that Kaiser "has enough romance surrounding him to fill a success magazine, some real and some fancied. . . . Those who know him . . . pronounce him one of the unsung geniuses in a period when a premium is placed on productive ability."

Alford acknowledged the government's initiative in bringing Kaiser

into the field of light metals, as the article's subtitle suggests: "Henry Kaiser Is Central Figure in Government's Effort to Break Aluminum Monopoly with Magnesium Club." Alford was unclear about how the relationship began: "whether the new deal was fortunate in discovering his business talents or he in selling his talents to influential new dealers will probably never be known."

Stories in *Business Week* at the time noted that despite the growing impression that "it's Kaiser this and Kaiser that, whether in ships, cement, dams or magnesium—he's still a mystery man." The source of some of that mystery was that he was "publicity-shy," but "part of the mystery revolves around his connections in Washington," such as Harold Ickes and Tom Corcoran. *Business Week* summarized Kaiser's debt to government initiative: "Kaiser is a man who realizes that sizable dough can be made by playing along with the economic and political objectives of the New Deal." Using Kaiser's cement and magnesium enterprises as examples, *Business Week* noted: "His approach is to find a field in which the Administration considers it is building a monopoly. Kaiser then goes into the field as an independent operator, and in so doing assures himself of government support."[50]

When Time/Life acknowledged the role of the government in the Kaiser saga, Kaiser wore the mantle of initiative. *Fortune*'s first reference to him, in July 1941, portrayed Kaiser as a catalyst in Washington, who "plays a canny game of political influence: he hires Tommy Corcoran to handle his Washington business, and he knows how to pull a useful string back home in Oakland."[51]

The stories about Kaiser and Corcoran left a lasting impression. When a picture of Kaiser with OPM head William Knudsen appeared in the *Washington Times-Herald*, Corcoran was identified as Kaiser's Washington representative. Other businessmen clearly understood the importance of the ties between Corcoran and Kaiser. When Theodore Granik was setting up Bank of America's Washington office in the spring of 1941, he received a note from a Bank of America executive vice president about Kaiser: "He has Mr. Thomas Corcoran representing him and gets along pretty well without any outside help, but if you or Earl Kelly found an opportunity to see him it would at least remind him that his bank is thinking of him."[52]

Kaiser's first industrial loan from the RFC brought him more than publicity—it positioned him to become a big-time war contractor. Kaiser was no longer one of a multitude of outsiders looking in for industrial war work (as had been so strikingly the case in Chad Calhoun's meeting with Hap Arnold the previous September). As a producer of primary metals, Kaiser's

name would now appear on select lists of industrial government contractors. Thus began a relationship that would provide Kaiser with $26.2 million in loans for his Permanente magnesium plant and $97.2 million in 1942 for his Fontana steel plant. In all, Kaiser's wartime enterprises would borrow about $300 million from the government to construct new plants.

Chad Calhoun's greatest fear in his early days in Washington, which had sent the Kaiser organization to ally with New Deal devil Tom Girdler, proved to be well founded. Not already being a "player" in steel, magnesium, aluminum, or aircraft would cause most newcomers to be left behind. Securing an RFC loan for magnesium meant that Kaiser had entered the "arsenal of democracy" just as its doors were closing to most small businessmen. World War II proved to be a time of great industrial concentration. From December 1939 to December 1944, firms employing more than ten thousand employees increased their share of manufacturing workers from 13 to 30 percent. From June 1940 until September 1944, 90 percent of prime contracts went to only 6 percent of America's industrial companies.[53]

Although Kaiser would end up among the top ten wartime borrowers from the RFC, his organization was the only one that would not have appeared on a prewar list of the RFC's major clients, including corporate giants such as General Motors, General Electric, U.S. Steel, Bethlehem Steel, and Dow Chemical.[54]

Two days after announcement of the RFC loan, Corcoran arranged a meeting for Calhoun and Kaiser with Ickes to discuss magnesium. Corcoran and Ickes were good friends; Ickes referred to Corcoran as part of the "usual crowd." In fact, they had partied together that week.[55] Ickes was impressed with Kaiser's track record with the Interior Department dam projects and his more recent enterprises. It was with Ickes's blessing that Kaiser had contacted the RFC about a cement loan in 1939, a loan the RFC approved but Kaiser turned down in favor of private financing. Ickes was now enthusiastic about Kaiser's entry into primary metals, and he had been supportive of Kaiser's bid throughout the latter months of 1940.

In a February 18 meeting, Ickes offered to supply Kaiser with government power for the proposed magnesium plant, and he directed his press secretary to release an announcement to that effect. Ickes then startled Kaiser and Calhoun by revealing his other plans: "As a complete surprise to us, Mr. Ickes asked us if we would be willing to operate an aluminum fabricating plant in the Bonneville region for the government. This came so suddenly and as such a surprise that Mr. Kaiser at first did not understand him and thought that he was referring to magnesium." Ickes "made

it clear" that he indeed wanted Kaiser to supply him with an *aluminum* proposal as soon as possible, to address national defense shortages. As if that was not enough, Ickes also said he wanted Kaiser to operate a second magnesium plant "in the Grand Coulee region." Ickes wanted Kaiser's proposals quickly regarding both Pacific Northwest plants so he could convince Navy Secretary Frank Knox to set aside funds for their construction.[56]

There was, in short, a New Deal brand of industrial policy at work. Government officials were attempting to mold industries and markets into the decentralized image they espoused, and they were using Kaiser as the conduit, just as he was using them to achieve his private objectives. In 1938, Kaiser had been encouraged by Interior Department, Treasury Department, and RFC officials to enter the cement industry. In 1939, the president had publicly sought new steel entrants, and in 1940, Interior Department, White House, and NDAC officials encouraged Kaiser to enter first the steel industry and then magnesium production. Now the secretary of the interior was inviting Kaiser to break Alcoa's aluminum monopoly. This exchange took place just weeks after the Justice Department indicted Alcoa for restraint of trade in violation of the antitrust statutes.[57]

Calhoun provided Ickes with the proposals. The secretary of the interior wrote Secretary Knox that, "looking about for some private manager who had demonstrated the courage to take on the Aluminum Company, I have had talks with Mr. H. J. Kaiser." Ickes was optimistic about the prospects for Kaiser's Permanente magnesium plant. He wrote that Kaiser "has already taken on and defeated the Aluminum Company interests in his fight to establish a new and cheaper process for making magnesium."[58] Ickes had already negotiated a contract for Reynolds to build an aluminum plant at Bonneville, but he had ordered it put on hold until he talked to Kaiser. As it turned out, Ickes ultimately went ahead with Reynolds, and Kaiser would not enter the aluminum business until several years later.[59]

Kaiser had been accustomed to finding an opportunity—in cement, steel, or magnesium—then approaching the government about it and having government officials act as agents on his behalf. The discussions regarding aluminum were the first in which the initiative came from the government before Kaiser had done any studies or even expressed interest. This pattern would be repeated later with an aircraft enterprise in 1943; after that, government officials began approaching Kaiser about problems of absenteeism, day care, and postwar economic reconversion.

The meeting with Ickes represented the high-water mark of the Kaiser-Corcoran relationship, although Corcoran's "know-who" provided Kaiser

with one more opportunity in April with respect to patented magnesium processes. Dow Chemical and the Justice Department were still in negotiations over the government's antitrust action against Dow. Ernest Cuneo, an old friend of Corcoran's, represented Dow. Cuneo wrote a letter informing Corcoran of the status of the negotiations. He commented on Corcoran's "general interest in the magnesium field," a reference to the fact that Corcoran represented Kaiser. The upshot was that fabricating patents would be "immediately available" and royalty-free. This news had no impact on the Permanente plant, where Kaiser was using a different production process, but it would have implications for any other Kaiser magnesium plans.[60] Corcoran had made good use of his contacts both inside and outside of government.

In late May, Corcoran pulled out of the project, demanding both a hefty fee and an equity stake in the magnesium enterprise. Henry Kaiser had become accustomed to having New Dealers offer him free advice so he may have resented having to pay anything at all, much less $100,000 plus 150 shares of Todd-California. Corcoran's bill launched an argument that lasted the rest of the year and resulted in some post hoc revaluation of his efforts. Six years later, Kaiser testified that Corcoran had done little for him and that he never paid Corcoran's fee.[61] Despite this outcome, there is no disputing the tremendous progress Kaiser made toward his goal to enter magnesium production while Corcoran worked for him. Corcoran gave Kaiser access to power in Washington, and although it was difficult to measure influence, it was impossible to ignore the results.

Personal reinterpretations aside, the controversy over Corcoran's role in these events continued to attract interest. For one thing, Corcoran was not modest about his contribution. In October 1941, he sent a clipping from the *Washington Daily News* about Kaiser's magnesium enterprise to Grace Tully, Roosevelt's secretary, for the president's edification. Corcoran noted, "I am sure he knows who was the 'catalytic agent' on this magnesium job—who held the deal together and fitted the pieces together until we got results."[62] Journalist Eliot Janeway was a friend of Corcoran's and a booster of Kaiser in the pages of *Fortune* at the time. Years later, he would argue Corcoran's case: "By far the greatest credit for Kaiser's remarkable achievements goes to his original lawyer; more precisely, lobbyist, as all Washington lawyers are. Tommy Corcoran, the powerhouse of the New Deal, sold Kaiser's idea to the Federal agencies involved. His reward was a royal screwing from Kaiser that was pretty chintzy. . . . No one earned more for Kaiser or got less from him."[63] Corcoran, it turned out, received $65,000 for his efforts from Todd, not Kaiser.[64]

Not all those who witnessed these developments saw them as a positive contribution to the war effort. Corcoran's activities in 1941 on behalf of Kaiser and other clients were investigated by the Truman Committee at the end of the year. Rumors of Corcoran's substantial fees, which were alleged to be indirectly paid by the taxpayers, led to widespread outrage and accusations of influence peddling. The committee could demonstrate no wrongdoing and appeared uncertain as to what to do about the information it acquired. Senator Carl A. Hatch of New Mexico decided to seek a legislative solution to the problem. He had earlier authored the law that forbids government employees from partisan political activities and now he unsuccessfully proposed another bill, which would have prohibited government employees from practicing before federal agencies within two years of leaving the government.[65]

Corcoran, in arguing against Hatch's proposed "restrictive statute," chose as a hypothetical case the committee counsel, Hugh Fulton, "who has no relationship to government departments, and yet he has been employed by the government." Because of his service, Fulton might be "practically unable to make a livelihood . . . for an indefinite period or even a long, fixed period after that service."[66] As it turned out, Fulton was a better example than Corcoran could have predicted. Fulton left government service in the summer of 1944 and by November of that year was providing counsel to Henry Kaiser.[67]

Senator Joseph Ball of Minnesota demonstrated the committee's ambivalence as he questioned Corcoran. First, Ball expressed reservations about the turn the federal government had taken: "It seems to me rather a reflection on our setup down here that any corporation or business that is organized to contribute to the defense program had to obtain the services of [Corcoran]." But then he took a different tack, framing his questions in terms of equal access to Corcoran—not to government. Ball went on to express the phenomenon as a corporate capability: "Doesn't it put the other concerns who may have just as much to offer to the defense program, if they can't possibly obtain the services of Tommy Corcoran at a little disadvantage?" Ball acknowledged Corcoran's considerable talents and advantages by virtue of his New Deal experience and contacts. He expressed more concern about the scarcity of this resource than about the nature of the services Corcoran offered and the demand for them: "You come down here and represent four clients and you cut through the red tape for them, but there is only one Tommy Corcoran. Who is going to do it for the others?"[68] Neither Ball, Hatch, nor Truman had an answer

to that question, but for Kaiser the question had long been mooted by his changed role in the war effort and in American business.

Kaiser's results in magnesium in 1941 contrast with his lack of progress in steel. The differences between the two show the importance of being aligned with presidential policy and also demonstrate the risks of being a subject of it.

Kaiser and Chad Calhoun had begun investigating possibilities in magnesium and steel during the fall of 1940. Aided by Tom Corcoran, Kaiser obtained a contract and a loan for magnesium production in short order. In steel, however, Kaiser not only did not have Corcoran's assistance, but he confronted numerous uncooperative representatives of Big Steel in government agencies. Before Pearl Harbor and his ascendance as a national figure, Kaiser had very little leverage. His best hope was the active involvement of the president, who warmed to the idea of a West Coast steel plant when it suited his current interests.

Utah senator Abe Murdock arranged to meet with President Roosevelt in April 1941 to discuss the establishment of a large-scale steel industry in the West and invited Kaiser to join them. A couple of months before the meeting, Gano Dunn, a consultant on loan from U.S. Steel to the Office of Production Management, had issued a report saying that America's existing steel facilities would be able to handle any potential wartime demand.[69] Roosevelt, influenced by Dunn's findings, gave Kaiser a vintage performance, as indicated by Kaiser's note of thanks for "your gracious reception during my recent interview with you, your parable of the Georgia cows and the Oregon apples."[70] As happened often when Roosevelt had not yet made up his mind concerning an issue, the topic of the meeting was probably barely touched upon.

This was the risk Kaiser assumed by relying on administration insiders as his power base in Washington. He succeeded only when his interests paralleled theirs. It was only when Kaiser enlisted the power of public opinion that he could hope to achieve goals about which the administration had doubts. Public interest in Kaiser was just beginning, however, in the spring of 1941, so things moved very slowly for him, especially in steel.

Six days after the meeting with Roosevelt, Kaiser applied for a certificate of necessity from the OPM for a West Coast steel plant.[71] In the interim between Kaiser's visit and his thank-you note, the statistical section of OPM had submitted a report that forecast steel shortages nationwide, particularly in the West. This is an example of how "all-outers" in the mobilization program were sometimes able to circumvent the sluggish

leadership of big business representatives. William Knudsen, the head of OPM and onetime head of General Motors, was known for his hesitation to expand production capacity. Therefore, it behooved the all-outers in the OPM statistical department, such as Robert Nathan, to provide evidence of their cause to presidential advisers. Instead of engaging in fruitless arguments with their superiors, Nathan and others took their chances on the ability of sympathetic advisers to make their case to the president.

Ironically, this statistical information, although supporting Kaiser's case for a new plant, was put to use in a way that *delayed* Kaiser's plans. Presidential adviser Lauchlin Currie, one of the sympathetic ears for "all-outers" in Roosevelt's inner circle, seized the opportunity to use Kaiser to bring recalcitrant steelmakers in line. Currie wrote to the president, recommending that "it might be desirable to take no action of any kind on the Kaiser application now as this would at least exert pressure on existing companies to expand."[72] Roosevelt heeded the advice. He ordered OPM to produce a plan that would call for production capacity increases of ten million tons in the East and five million in the West, which would go to a government-owned facility at Geneva, Utah, run by U.S. Steel.[73] Kaiser was not mentioned.

For the rest of the year, Kaiser made little progress in steel. In December 1941, of course, many things changed for government entrepreneurs. Though President Roosevelt had not yet given the press conference identifying himself as "Dr. Win the War," "Dr. New Deal" was one of Pearl Harbor's first casualties.[74] America's entry into the war, of course, expanded and accelerated opportunities for government entrepreneurs. This was particularly true for Henry Kaiser with respect to steel. Only after the emergency precipitated by the Pearl Harbor attack did he receive approval for his venture, nearly a year after meeting with the president.[75]

Before Kaiser became a household name, his Washington overtures faced the possibility of being turned down even if they furthered administration policy. He ran the risk that the administration could pursue its policy—in this case, western steel expansion—without Kaiser's help. But in 1942 the tables turned. Kaiser became a national hero and it became a matter of grave political risk for the administration to turn down his proposals.

When the legend

becomes fact,

print the legend.

The Man Who Shot

Liberty Valance, *1962*

6 ———— "FABULOUS" KAISER

In March 1945, White House aide Isador Lubin notified President Roosevelt that Dwight Eisenhower wanted Henry Kaiser to visit the troops in Europe. Lubin wrote that the GIs were eager "to see the guy who made so many ships." Lubin noted that "the Kaiser public relations machine has been very effective."[1] Lubin's reaction echoed results from a 1943 poll about Kaiser in which nearly 4 percent of respondents "volunteered comments which implied that Mr. Kaiser either has a well-organized publicity program or that he is adept in propaganda efforts on his own behalf."[2]

Effective or not, the public relations arm of the Kaiser organization was

still in embryonic form, at best. It consisted only of a couple of speechwriters and advertising experts, nothing comparable to that of most business organizations of similar size. One of Kaiser's people recognized his wartime position: "Our case is unlike any that I have known in the past, in that we are starting with complete public approval and all we need to do is set up the proper organization to maintain that approval."[3] Before such organizational growth, Kaiser's public relations "machine" lay outside the walls of the organization, in the mass media of national magazines and syndicated newspaper columnists. So eager had they been to create heroes that Kaiser had been able to construct a public image while expending little of his organization's resources toward that end.

Throughout his career after launching his own business, Henry Kaiser described himself first and foremost as a builder and wanted others to consider him one also. Even when he was an industrialist and national figure in 1947, he still described himself that way. Appearing before a Senate hearing, he began to recite his favorite poem, appropriately entitled "The Builder." Kaiser then told a questioner, "I am a builder"—then, pointing for emphasis into a newsreel camera—"not a promoter."[4] Actually, he was both.

Well before Kaiser was a household name, he vigorously promoted his interests in Washington. When Interior Secretary Harold Ickes was investigating violations of overtime laws in the construction of Hoover Dam, Kaiser launched a campaign to publicize the accomplishments—against formidable odds—of his construction consortium, the Six Companies. He also arranged to have a flattering account of the dam's construction, *So Hoover Dam Was Built*, distributed to key members of the press.[5]

Kaiser was well aware of his gifts as a promoter. In April 1941, just as the national media was discovering Kaiser, Stephen Bechtel, a longtime construction partner of Kaiser's and investor in his cement and magnesium enterprises, recommended an individual who could help Kaiser's new steel concern. Kaiser recognized that the man offered nothing that Kaiser did not already have: "Apparently he wants the same job I have of promoting the proposed development. He has no definite organization, engineering or otherwise for the development, merely ideas that it should be done. He has never operated a steel company." Acutely aware of his own weaknesses with respect to the steel venture, Kaiser chided Bechtel, "You know experienced organizations in a specific field are necessary and not promoters."[6] Years later, Bechtel would refer his old Six Companies partner as "that public relations guy."[7]

Yet Henry Kaiser, the born promoter, became a national figure as part of

someone else's promotion: a blitz by America's news media. Most significant to Kaiser's national image during this period was the support he received from Henry Luce and his publications.[8] Luce had at his disposal extraordinary means with which to shape public opinion. A Luce biographer estimated that during the war, "the Luce opinion, message, point of view, or slant promoted through all his outlets would be likely to reach at least a third and perhaps considerably more of the total literate population of the country."[9] From 1941 to 1943, 40 percent of the articles about Kaiser listed in the *Reader's Guide to Periodical Literature* were in Luce's *Time, Life,* or *Fortune.*[10] Time/Life also influenced other shapers of public opinion. A study done by sociologist Leo Rosten in the mid-1930s indicated that Washington correspondents read *Time* more than any other magazine.[11]

Luce's magazines described Kaiser as unusual or unique, but what was truly special to Time/Life about Kaiser was that he fit Henry Luce's model of an enlightened industrialist. At a time when the most successful business organizations were characterized by multilayered bureaucracies and relatively faceless leaders—compared to the charismatic captains of industry in the Gilded Age—Kaiser's personal approach was a godsend to Luce. From the early days of *Time* in the 1920s, Luce and cofounder Briton Hadden had personalized events that were becoming increasingly complex and abstract. In an age of bureaucratic, urban interdependence, Luce focused on charismatic leaders. As David Halberstam put it, Luce believed "men, not the great rhythms of history or economics, were the key to the past." Luce promulgated this ideology by featuring individuals on each week's cover of *Time* and by selecting a "Man of the Year" in December. Luce's goal in *Fortune* was to "seek out the handful of worthy businessmen and hold them up as examples."[12]

Ironically, in some ways Time/Life was better suited to describing how things worked in the Roosevelt administration—for which Luce had contempt—than in big business, which he supported. As we saw in Chapter 4, the executive branch under FDR did not always respect job descriptions and organization charts. The secretary of the treasury at times had more say about foreign policy than the secretary of state. The staff of the Reconstruction Finance Corporation might be involved in creating entirely new agencies. *Fortune's* 1941 organization chart depicting management of the U.S. defense effort was accompanied by a picture of federal loan administrator Jesse Jones and the explanation: "Jesse is not on the chart but he holds the purse strings."[13] The following year, *Time* ran its equivalent of an executive branch scorecard, called "The Roll of Honor," so that readers could identify key members of the administration.[14] Time/Life reveled in

showing its readers where the real locus of power was. Such an approach was required to understand the operations of the sometimes freewheeling Roosevelt administration.

By contrast, in many of America's giant corporations, personalities mattered less than relative positions on the organization chart. *Fortune* was not as concerned with such structured and formal relationships as were other business publications. Therefore, Henry Kaiser's personality-based organizational style was more amenable to profile using the Time/Life style than that of most business leaders. He was not only a regular subject of *Time* pieces beginning in 1941 but was a role model in the pages of *Fortune* for the next decade.

Even more important to Luce than promulgating the behavior of businessman role models was his vision of America in the world. An age of American isolationism was coming to a close as the 1940s dawned, and Luce did his best to stimulate interest in internationalism. He was among the media's most aggressive advocates of American intervention in the European war.[15] In May 1940, Luce had been in Brussels when the Germans unleashed their blitzkrieg. He cabled home that "the Germans have one weapon greater than all their army and that is the blindness and stultification of those in any country who are too fat to fight."[16] In October, when Henry Kaiser was sending letters to Harold Ickes and Marriner Eccles expressing his desire to produce magnesium for the government, Luce told a radio audience: "Today, we need the services of the ablest industrialists for the most efficient arming of America."[17]

Perhaps the best-remembered piece from any of his magazines at the time was an essay Luce himself wrote for *Life* in February 1941. Luce offered a view of America as a world power that highlighted free enterprise, American know-how, and "devotion to great American ideals," such as "love of freedom, a feeling for equality and opportunity, a tradition of self-reliance and independence and also of cooperation." Luce wrote that it was America's "time to be the powerhouse from whom the ideals spread throughout the world."[18] That meant entry into the war against Germany. This view also put Luce in the awkward position of supporting Roosevelt, who had just proposed the Lend-Lease Act in January. Luce's commitment to the war was further demonstrated in December 1941. After Pearl Harbor, Luce decided to substitute the hated Roosevelt for industrial icon Henry Ford as *Time*'s "Man of the Year."[19]

The Roosevelt administration could not have done better had it hired Luce to promote the nation's war effort—which it almost did. In early 1941, Roosevelt had considered creating an agency to battle "subversive"

propaganda, with Luce as director.[20] Instead, in June 1942, Roosevelt established a propaganda-creating machine: the Office of War Information. Assistant Director Archibald MacLeish saw his mission very clearly: "The principal battleground of this war is not the South Pacific. It is not the Middle East. It is not England, or Norway, or the Russian steppes. It is American opinion."[21] MacLeish had learned a thing or two about how American opinion could be influenced; he was an alumnus of Time/Life from the 1930s.

Henry Kaiser's involvement in the war brought him into Time/Life's sights. Kaiser's involvement at this perilous time reinforced his usefulness to Time/Life but also created a challenge for the organization: the issue of government entrepreneurship. The Luce mold called for an individualistic, self-made businessman, which was the antithesis of what the federal government in general—and the New Deal in particular—meant to Luce. Brain truster Rexford Tugwell, for instance, was described by *Time* as viewing "the New Deal [as] a grindstone to rub 'rugged individualism' down to a social if not a socialistic polish."[22]

In February 1940, *Fortune* had triumphantly reported the results of a survey that found that a majority of Americans would like to start their own businesses. This segment of the *Fortune* survey was titled "The American Is an Entrepreneur." Here a long-standing theme, which helps explain the attraction of Henry J. Kaiser as a subject, was repeated: "In the midst of vast concentrations of enterprise, the American stands as an individualist with an incurable desire to go into business for himself."[23] The problem with Kaiser was that many of his early opportunities—in cement, magnesium, and steel—were midwived, if not conceived, by New Dealers. So how could Time/Life present government entrepreneur Kaiser positively, that is, in the guise of an individualistic, self-made entrepreneur?

Time's approach to the government's assistance to Kaiser was to ignore it or assume it away. Such an attitude was foreshadowed by the magazine's 1922 prospectus. In a section entitled "Editorial Bias," Hadden and Luce had admitted to "certain prejudices which may in varying measures predetermine their opinions on the news." They offered three examples. First, the world was round. Second was "a general distrust of the present tendency toward increasing interference by government." Third was "a prejudice against the rising cost of government."[24] They were true to their word, even in chronicling the rise of the mid-century's most spectacular government entrepreneur. Kaiser's rise was explained with little or no reference to the roles of Harold Ickes, Leon Henderson, Lauchlin Currie, Marriner Eccles, and many others. What, then, did Kaiser's accomplish-

ments mean? *Time* argued that Kaiser's increased shipbuilding efficiency meant the ability to "maintain the U.S. standard of living and still compete with the world without government aid."[25]

The Time/Life stories on Kaiser had little to do with a personal relationship between Luce and Kaiser. The two rarely met, and their correspondence—when Kaiser was not complaining about what he believed were critical stories—was formal. Three years after first meeting Luce, Kaiser still wrote to him as "Dear Henry," rather than the preferred "Harry."[26] Those who wrote for Time/Life steadfastly argued that Luce did not meddle in their stories. By the 1940s, Luce ran too many publications for that sort of micromanagement. Besides, he did not have to intervene. One of his writers who covered Kaiser later noted that Luce's "shadow was a long and definite one so his conviction in the myth of the all-puissant entrepreneur . . . got strongly amplified in the pages of his magazines," even though Luce's personal involvement was minimal.[27]

In 1941, Luce's publications had not wandered from the tycoon-as-hero theme that *Time* had first propagated in the 1920s.[28] This meant two things: beginning with the premise of Kaiser as the nearly mythical initiator of all his enterprises, then having each story add to that legend—usually through presenting the resolution of a difficult problem—reinforcing the tycoon's position as a heroic figure. Any missteps by Kaiser were presented with hope for redemption.

Kaiser's fits and starts in magnesium gave *Time* ample opportunities to use another technique to shape the Kaiser story: cushioning any bad news regarding Kaiser within larger stories full of good news. Nearly a year and a half after Kaiser "smashed" the magnesium bottleneck, *Time* reported—in the midst of an enthusiastic article about Kaiser's cargo plane plan—that Permanente Magnesium had "proved a flop so far" but "was starting production at a new magnesium plant using the better, safer ferrosilicon process."[29]

The importance of a "safer" process was explained six months later; *Time* held off a story on some explosions at Permanente that killed workers in late 1941 until it could accompany that report with better news. In early 1943, a story appeared in *Time*: "From California's chaparral-cloaked San Jose Valley last week came good news to the whole U.S.: after many a delay, Henry J. Kaiser's $6,000,000 Permanente Magnesium plant is finally over the hump. . . . Although [production] is only one-third the production scheduled in 1941, the company expects to double output this month to the highest levels yet."[30] Indeed, Kaiser ironed out his magnesium problems in 1943. Late that year, Kaiser's people developed a new form of

magnesium-based incendiary bomb, nicknamed "goop," which the government ordered Kaiser to produce instead of magnesium.

The "over the hump" magnesium story, as well as the March 1941 story pronouncing the magnesium "bottleneck smashed," were examples of how Luce's magazines embodied his instinctive drive for resolution of an issue. He did not hesitate to seize a hint of good news or progress and see it through in his mind—and his publications—to its cheerful conclusion. Civil rights, for example, was an emotional issue for Luce, one that combined his sympathy for the oppressed with his passion for national consensus. (Indeed, Roosevelt's hesitation to promote the cause of African Americans in the 1930s so as to keep southern whites in the New Deal coalition contributed to Luce's antagonism toward the president.)[31] In 1954, upon hearing of the Supreme Court's decision against segregation, Luce said, "That takes care of that problem." To many, the decision meant that the civil rights battle was just beginning, but to Luce it was a signal to move on to the next issue.[32] Luce's tendency to premature resolution came across in his magazines and nowhere more so than in hagiographic stories on figures like Henry Kaiser.

Not surprisingly, Time/Life published the first feature-length Kaiser profile of which the industrialist approved. Yet the story was not a fait accompli. In January 1942, when Life reporter Gerard Piel had originally proposed writing an article on him, Kaiser was "reluctant to have this story come out at all." Kaiser was still upset over a feature called "Builder No. 1" by Frank J. Taylor in the June 7, 1941, Saturday Evening Post. Kaiser was an easy mark for Taylor, as he was for other reporters. Piel recalls: "Throughout the war he had no one between himself and the press; he was always utterly spontaneous and direct in dealing with reporters just as he was with me." Taylor interviewed Kaiser, then wrote a story depicting him as a man who claimed credit for all of the Six Companies' efforts. That caused some hard feelings with Kaiser's old partners. Chad Calhoun described the final result as "perfectly terrible."[33] The Saturday Evening Post story made Kaiser reluctant to cooperate with similar requests from other magazines.

Kaiser proceeded cautiously with Life: Piel could have access to him and his various enterprises, providing Kaiser could review anything Piel wrote and "might even request that nothing appear at all."[34] Kaiser made an immediate impression on Piel: "I was surely a complete patsy for his innocent enthusiasm and 'thrill of achievement' talk."[35] So Piel wrote Henry Kaiser in March 1942: "As I sit down to write your story, I find that my professional objectivity is hampered by my enthusiasm for your purposes and methods."[36]

While Kaiser was winning over Piel, Piel successfully overcame Kaiser's defenses. The result was a story in the June 29 issue of *Life*. Among the plethora of Kaiser stories in 1942, none proved more significant than Piel's "No. 1 Shipbuilder." Piel did *not* give all credit for the construction of Boulder Dam to Kaiser, instead emphasizing what might now be called the "core competence" of the Kaiser organization—its ability to handle raw materials on a large scale using innovative methods.[37] By June 1942, this meant, above all, shipbuilding.

Kaiser's West Coast shipyards set records for speed in constructing ships for the British Purchasing Commission, the U.S. Navy, and the U.S. Maritime Commission. They did so by applying assembly-line techniques to what had once been a craftsman's job. Kaiser certainly did not invent that approach; it had been in use before 1940 by the British and by some American yards on the East Coast.[38] In fact, Admiral Howard L. Vickery, head of production for the Maritime Commission, sent Kaiser photographs that indicated "that subassemblies are not necessarily a completely modern innovation."[39] Vickery always spurred Kaiser on to greater achievements by needling him about the accomplishments of rival shipyards. Now he had Kaiser in competition with his predecessors: the photos showed a shipbuilding subassembly operation in Camden, New Jersey, from 1912.

Kaiser's competitors—and predecessors—often lacked sufficient space for all the subassemblies. As designer and operator of newer yards, Kaiser had the luxury of building in adequate room to perform the job. Kaiser was also more willing to try new approaches than most established shipbuilders, particularly his future industrial competitor, Bethlehem Steel. Ironically, although Kaiser's lack of "know-how" kept him from competing with Bethlehem in steel for a year and a half, his "learn-how" vaulted him ahead of the more established Bethlehem in shipbuilding.

During America's early days in the war, Kaiser's shipyards rapidly improved their performance. At the outset, the Maritime Commission scheduled 140 days to build a "Liberty Ship"—the cargo ships America sent to England. As early as April 1942, the media had become caught up in Kaiser's assault on the record books. Broadcaster John B. Hughes reported Kaiser's goal to turn out freighters "as much faster than the present record of 37 days from keel to commission as it is possible to achieve. . . . The Kaiser men are after that old record and bid fair to break it considerably."[40] The record-breaking ship was no aberration; by June 1942, one of Kaiser's Richmond yards averaged 69 days and his Oregon yard 54 days

(against the national average of 118 days and Bethlehem Fairfield's average of about 100 days).[41]

Promoter Kaiser had made sure everyone knew when his yards set new records for speed, and he fostered competition between his yards. In an August 1942 speech to his Richmond workers, Kaiser said: "A Liberty Ship was launched [yesterday at the Oregon yard] in record time of 26 days. Today you have broken that record and have established a new one of 24 days. Today's record will be short-lived for I am told by our boys that tomorrow's record of less than 18 days will be established within the next few months." In the speech, Kaiser also pointed out a milestone: the Joshua Hendy Iron Works in Sunnyvale, California (partly owned by Kaiser), "just completed their one hundredth engine for Liberty Ships." Kaiser was conscious of Hendy's speed, too: "Still more amazing is the fact that the engine in the *John Fitch* was completely assembled at Sunnyvale in just thirty hours—and this is another record-breaking achievement."[42]

The following month, Kaiser's Oregon yard completed the *Joseph N. Teal* in ten days; in October, Richmond completed the *Robert E. Peary* in less than five.[43] Because "they were sensational achievements, aroused talk"—even though such performances were not sustainable—the *Teal* and the *Peary* were referred to as "stunt ships."[44] Henry Kaiser called them "incentive ships" because they helped motivate his workers.[45]

Kaiser showed that he recognized the power of positive "spin" and he was fortunate enough to have Time/Life's assistance in this area. Luce's publications had devoted lots of space to Kaiser, focusing on the positive aspects of his enterprises beneath positive-sounding titles. *Business Week* might run stories entitled "Kaiser's Problems," "Kaiser Plan Fails," and "Wonder Man Hit." More typical of *Time* were: "Winner: Kaiser," "Who Can't?," or "Kaiser's Circus: Production Miracle."[46]

Moreover, Time/Life's language helped shape the public discourse about him. Its articles popularized "fabulous" Kaiser and his "miracles" and compared him to Paul Bunyan. *Time*'s first Kaiser story in March 1941 described him as a "fabulously successful" engineer. By the following month, this was shortened to "fabulous" Henry J. Kaiser.[47] A July story, which mentioned the accomplishments of Edgar Kaiser, referred to his famous father as "Fabulous Senior."[48] This terminology caught on: even the staid *Wall Street Journal* began to call him "Fabulous Mr. Kaiser" and rave about his "fabulous contracts." "Everything Mr. Kaiser does is tremendous," the *Journal* gushed.[49] *Current Biography* of 1942 joined the crowd, calling him "Fabulous Henry J. Kaiser."[50]

"Fabulous" had special meaning for a publisher—Luce—who sought to make the achievements of certain businessmen the stuff of legend— or "fable." In 1929, sixteen businessmen had made the cover of *Time*, and Walter Chrysler, whose achievements *Time* called "fabulous," had been Man of the Year. According to *Time*, "the major part of [Chrysler's] fable was indeed fact."[51] The formula had been completed before the Great Depression and it did not change throughout the 1930s. The adjectives in the Chrysler piece could easily have come from a 1941 story on Henry Kaiser.

Time's reporting on Kaiser was also self-referential. On September 7, in another piece beginning "Fabulous Henry J. Kaiser," Kaiser's national headlines for the week were summarized. "There were fresh items in the saga of Henry Kaiser, around whom news and fables now collect as about a Paul Bunyan."[52] Nobody had collected or disseminated these fables more than Time/Life, and it was a *Life* piece in June that first compared Kaiser to Paul Bunyan.[53]

For Time/Life, the intense 1942 coverage of Kaiser was not just a public service. The corporation was in the business of selling magazines, and stories about Kaiser sold. Time/Life wanted more, however: a testimonial from Kaiser that *he* read their magazines. In September 1942, *Time* sent Kaiser a copy of "Appointment in Washington," its latest story on him. Accompanying the article was a note from *Time*'s Bureau of Special Services: "You must know from the frequent and friendly comments which have appeared in *Time* with what interest we have been following your work." The note closed with a request: "I would appreciate your telling us what you think of *Time* and the part it is playing today."[54]

The following month, Time/Life requested permission to use Kaiser's name "as an industrialist who finds *Time*, *Life*, and *Fortune* important sources of news." Kaiser granted the request.[55] (Kaiser's office, incidentally, had just begun a subscription to *Fortune* that month.)[56] Time/Life had, in effect, built up an industrialist into a national hero, then used him as an example of the sort of heroic figures who read its publications.

Kaiser had come a long way in the public eye from early 1941 until late 1942. On the eve of the war, Kaiser was an obscure figure called the "Mystery Man" by reporters because he appeared to avoid interviews and publicity.[57] In 1942, Kaiser's relationship with the media was changing: he began to play a more active role in shaping his public image. *Facts on File* in 1941 had no separate listing for Kaiser; in 1942 he was listed twenty-two times. Now Kaiser finished behind only Stalin and the archbishop of Canterbury for *Time*'s Man of the Year.[58] *Time*'s year-end wrap-up of

"Business in 1942" noted that "Henry J. Kaiser emerged as the most publicized businessman of 1942." This was true, thanks in no small part to *Time*.

To understand why Time/Life was able to translate Kaiser's can-do attitude and production performance into such popular acclaim, it is necessary to recall America's predicament after Pearl Harbor. During the next six months, things looked bleak for America's war effort. The country was eagerly seeking rays of hope, both in the war zones and on the home front. When good news arrived, it became a national sensation. Such was the case when Jimmy Doolittle flew a squadron of bombers from an aircraft carrier and raided Tokyo in April.[59] The raid did not inflict much damage, but according to the media, it lifted the nation's spirits.

In its eagerness to quench America's thirst for optimism, the media saw what initially appeared to be oases of production turn out to be mirages of promotion. One example was Henry Ford and aircraft. Ford, popularly credited with inventing mass production, proposed to apply the techniques that had worked so well for automobiles to the assembly of airplanes. Ford's new Willow Run plant—the world's largest manufacturing facility under one roof—was called "one of the seven wonders of the world" and "the mightiest wartime effort ever made by industry." *Time* called Willow Run "the most enormous room in the history of man" and summed up Ford's new venture as "a reenactment of the old American miracle of wheels and machinery, but on a new scale."[60] In May 1942, rumors—begun by the War Department, then encouraged by Ford publicists—circulated that the plant was producing planes at a staggering rate. The great enthusiasm with which this optimistic rumor was greeted is evidence of how hungry the American people were for good news and how eager the American media was to provide it. It took *Life* and the *March of Time* to puncture the Willow Run balloon. In mid-August, the two most popular branches of Luce's empire both reported that Willow Run had yet to complete one airplane.[61]

Kaiser's shipbuilding achievements, by contrast, were not illusory. In 1942, Kaiser was handling nearly one-third of the nation's merchant shipbuilding, and this performance would prove no flash in the pan.[62] The following year Admiral Vickery announced who the heroes of war production were: "I would say of all the yards and of the management in all the yards that the outstanding people who have done an outstanding job are Edgar Kaiser [head of Henry Kaiser's Portland, Oregon, yard] and Clay Bedford [head of Kaiser's Richmond, California, yard]." The official history of the wartime Maritime Commission noted that "the plum

of victory in the race set by the Maritime Commission was awarded by popular acclaim and by Admiral Vickery to the Kaiser yards."[63]

Shipbuilding was an ideal endeavor for a self-promoter like Kaiser. It was a photogenic activity, as Robert Herzstein explains: "Guns, ships, and battalions proved to be tailor-made subjects for *Life* and *Time*. Dramatic captions and striking photographs conveyed a sense of power, excitement, and national purpose."[64] There are also few better photo opportunities than a launching: erstwhile photographer Kaiser took advantage of this by inviting celebrities or spouses of celebrities to christen his Liberty Ships.[65] The president's daughter Anna christened the *Joseph Teal* in September 1942 when her father visited Kaiser's Oregon shipyard. Kaiser made sure the president was supplied with photos of the day's events.[66] The "man with a smile" arranged to have photo albums of the West Coast shipyards sent to the Washington office as a marketing device aimed at Kaiser's government "customers."[67]

Kaiser made sure his people realized the value of collateral publicity. When certain people visited the shipyards or plants, their hosts would send photos from the visit. John B. Hughes's visit was typical, as was his response: "Our public relations department here has seen [the photographs] and wonders if it would be possible to get either duplicate negatives or to borrow the negatives and use one or two of them for some public releases, tying in, of course, a mention of the blast furnace background and the Kaiser operations at Fontana." Eugene Trefethen reported to Kaiser: "I am attaching herewith a copy of a letter received from John B. Hughes, which is self-explanatory. I know you would be interested in the reaction."[68]

Such photogenic activity brought out the best in other self-promoters besides Kaiser, the most prominent of whom was New Orleans shipbuilder Andrew Jackson Higgins. During the war, Higgins built torpedo boats, patrol boats, and other small craft. Most important, though, were his various amphibious boats, which saw action in North Africa, Europe, and the South Pacific. More than fifteen hundred Higgins landing craft participated in the D-Day invasion of Normandy.

The most exciting of the boats was the Eureka, a shallow-craft vessel whose propeller and shaft were housed in a semitunnel to protect them from submerged obstacles. The boat was fast, durable, maneuverable, and could operate in less than a foot of water. Higgins adapted the Eureka into various forms of landing craft for wartime use, the most significant of which featured a ramp that replaced the rounded bow. This design allowed the craft to unload personnel or vehicles in shallow water. Higgins caught the attention of military brass in 1941, when the navy asked him to design

an experimental tank carrier. When Marine Corps and navy officials arrived a couple of days later, they were shown a completed forty-five-foot boat, rather than just the drawings they had expected to see. The boat had been designed, built, and launched in sixty-one hours. Higgins received an immediate contract for fifty of the tank carriers. With war raging in Europe and fears of possible conflict in the Pacific, Higgins soon found his steadiest customers in the armed forces.

Higgins Industries became one of America's most striking examples of war-related industrial growth. Sales rose from a 1937 value of $422,000 to a peak of $94 million in 1944; the number of workers Higgins employed rose from three hundred in 1939 to a wartime peak of more than twenty thousand. Higgins Industries ultimately built more than twenty thousand boats during World War II, more than any other American shipbuilder.

Higgins and Kaiser had much in common, which helped to connect their images in the national consciousness. Both applied mass-production techniques to shipbuilding in an innovative way; for Higgins this meant setting up an assembly line on Polymnia Street in downtown New Orleans.[69] While Kaiser built merchant ships for the U.S. Maritime Commission, Higgins built landing craft for the U.S. Navy. Higgins, like Kaiser, was a gifted self-promoter. Higgins and Kaiser shared more than success and national attention. Like Kaiser, Higgins had once resisted the idea of collective bargaining, then had seen the light and had established a reputation for conciliatory labor relations policies.[70] Indeed, in April 1943, the American Federation of Labor, which had unionized both Kaiser's and Higgins's yards, proposed that the two men handle *all* of the nation's shipbuilding needs. Like Kaiser, Higgins hired many African Americans (although Higgins followed local customs by creating separate assembly lines for blacks and whites, while Kaiser had them work together).[71] Like Kaiser, Higgins seemed not to fear a return to the Depression; he envisioned a postwar world of prosperity in which he would provide low-cost housing and transportation to millions.[72]

The most striking parallel between Kaiser and Higgins was the similar media coverage they received. Time/Life had been following and reporting the exploits of Higgins in much the same way it did Kaiser's. *Fortune* raved about "Andrew Jackson Higgins, fabulous New Orleans boat builder." *Fortune*'s 1943 article on Higgins began with a mythical allusion: "Andrew Jackson Higgins, like Henry Kaiser, sprang from the head of Mars with his arms full."[73] *Liberty* called him "today's Noah."[74] The *Saturday Evening Post* called him a shipyard Paul Bunyan, the same term that *Life* had applied to Kaiser the previous month.[75] If Kaiser had not

come along, Time/Life would have concentrated on Higgins because he fit the personalized mold: "Few big companies in U.S. history (save perhaps Henry Kaiser's) have been so much a single man."[76]

Although probably not mandated by Luce, the choice of a westerner (Kaiser) and a southerner (Higgins) to embody American wartime production success was congruent with one of the publisher's core convictions. Luce believed that nations otherwise divided by race and culture could achieve consensus forged by journalists. Although Time/Life may have been able to choose worthy production geniuses from its own backyard (the Northeast), using representatives of other regions was a better way for Luce's publications to be "instruments of national bonding."[77]

Kaiser and Higgins were also instruments of international bonding. Hilary St. George Saunders of the British Ministry of Information conducted a six-week tour of the United States in 1943, then wrote magazine articles and a book on his impressions. He visited with people from Wendell Willkie to Walt Disney and offered commentary on American taxi drivers, hotels, radio programs, and nightclubs. He also visited the yards of two shipbuilders: Henry Kaiser and Andrew Jackson Higgins. He witnessed a Liberty Ship launch and referred to Kaiser's operation as a "modern miracle." When he met Higgins, he concluded this was "the most outstanding figure I met in America [he did not meet Kaiser]. . . . I met many businessmen and not a few captains of industry in America. They all had drive, most of them vision, and a few genius. Mr. Higgins possesses all three."[78]

Even the official World War II history of the U.S. Maritime Commission was influenced by the media's description of Higgins: "a personality fabulous for his bounce . . . the faith which he aroused among his workers, and the gusto with which he and his four sons tackled whatever was presented to them as 'impossible.'"[79] It sounded just like media descriptions of Kaiser. Kaiser and Higgins, it seemed, were joined at the ship.

Until early 1942, Kaiser was the cargo ship builder and Higgins the landing craft builder. In late February, Roosevelt increased the Maritime Commission shipbuilding goals for 1942–43 by 33 percent.[80] At the time, Vice Admiral Vickery, commissioner in charge of production, was touring the South. Impressed by the Higgins boat factory, Vickery invited Higgins to join the Liberty Ship program, and Higgins agreed. In mid-March, Higgins was awarded a contract to build two hundred ships— the largest shipbuilding contract in history. Higgins sent one of his sons and his chief engineer to California to see Kaiser's Richmond yard, where superintendent Clay Bedford supplied Liberty Ship drawings.[81]

Higgins joined the cargo ship program at a perilous time. During early 1942, America's merchant fleet, including Kaiser's ships, were being sunk at an alarming rate by German submarines. More than eight million tons were sunk between December 1941 and October 1942.[82] Shipbuilding had become a Sisyphean task, as sinkings exceeded construction. The War Production Board (WPB) estimated that if trends from the first week of May continued throughout the year, the Allies would lose two tons of cargo for every ton produced.[83] Behind the scenes, government officials proposed a variety of solutions, from cargo-carrying dirigibles to cargo submarines.[84]

So serious was the situation that the WPB began discussions in May regarding the mass production of giant cargo planes, which would perform the same function as the merchant ships but at much less risk.[85] The idea of aircraft cargo convoys had been discussed for months, and the most persistent proponent of the idea had been aircraft engineer Grover Loening. Loening had been chief aeronautical engineer for the U.S. Army Air Corps before America's entry into World War I, started his own aircraft company, then consulted for Curtiss-Wright, Fairchild, and others. Loening gave high-profile speeches on air cargo transport in January and March.[86] Then he promoted the idea with an article in *Foreign Affairs* in April, titled "Ships Over the Sea: Possibilities and Limitations of Air Transport in War." The next month, addressing the Foreign Commerce Club, Loening had said: "It is not at all impossible, therefore, to envision the shipbuilding industry of the United States being turned over to ocean aircraft—ships that fly over the sea—not on it!"[87]

The public did not rally behind Loening, but the government paid attention. In May, the WPB began investigating the cargo plane issue and established an Air Cargo Committee with Loening as chair.[88] The *New York Times* first reported the cargo plane discussions in early June, on a day when it also reported that "the House devoted most of its session today to consideration of the problem of beating the U-Boats."[89] At the end of June, a congressional committee began to investigate such possibilities.

Meanwhile, Henry Kaiser began to have his engineers prepare reports about the feasibility of mass-producing cargo planes. The original idea was to have raw materials come from Kaiser's Permanente magnesium facility and to convert one of his shipyards to aircraft production.[90] Kaiser's plans were known in certain circles of the aircraft industry by mid-June.[91]

While Kaiser had his engineers working on a prospectus for presentation in Washington, Chad Calhoun held discussions with members of the Air Cargo Committee, which recommended waiting two weeks before submitting anything.[92] Kaiser could not wait that long. On July 9, he sub-

mitted a proposal to Vice Admiral Samuel Robinson of the navy and Philip Amran of the WPB's Air Cargo Committee. Kaiser proposed production of a two-hundred-ton flying boat of magnesium, stainless steel, and aluminum. Kaiser also sent a copy of the proposal to Marvin McIntyre, secretary to President Roosevelt.[93]

The next day, the Maritime Commission voted unanimously to cancel Andrew Jackson Higgins's Liberty Ship contract because of insufficient supplies of steel. The decision required the approval of the president, however, so it was not announced until July 18.[94] It quickly became the biggest story in the country.[95] By then, many Americans had seen the profile of Higgins in the July 11 *Saturday Evening Post*, which challenged: "Don't bet that Andrew Jackson Higgins can't convert a marsh into a shipyard and build 24 Liberty cargo ships all in eight months."[96] The cancellation caused a public outcry that resulted in a congressional investigation.

Higgins was stunned: "They have hung crepe on the biggest thing in Louisiana." He accused eastern industrialists of engineering the cancellation as a means of avoiding postwar competition. African American leaders argued that the cancellation destroyed "one of the biggest opportunities ever given to the Negro race": two of the four assembly lines were to employ all-black crews.[97] Perhaps the biggest factor in the cancellation, however, was the increased efficiency of existing shipyards: the president's production goals for 1943 could be achieved without using additional yards. In July 1942, however, that was a difficult scenario for the press and the public to imagine.

Public reaction to the Higgins cancellation, if anything, emboldened Henry Kaiser for his next move. Kaiser had just seen how, in the summer of 1942, successful and visible producers for the war effort could draw on a deep reservoir of media and public support. If he were ever to try something daring for the war effort, he could not choose a better time. Kaiser was scheduled to deliver a speech at a Liberty Ship launch in Portland on July 19. "Fabulous" Kaiser was about to launch a proposal that incited a nonstop discussion in Washington for the next two months.

Messrs. K. and H.

assure the public

Their production

will be second

to none.

John Lennon and

Paul McCartney,

1967

7 ———— TO MARS AND BACK

The man and the moment met on Sunday, July 19, 1942, when Kaiser delivered his first nationally publicized address. He spoke from Portland at the launch of the Liberty Ship *Harvey W. Scott*.[1] Kaiser began by lamenting the nearly four hundred Allied merchant ships that had been sunk by German U-boats in the western Atlantic since December 7. Sounding like the Wizard of Oz speaking to a crowd at the Emerald City, Kaiser said, "Our engineers have plans on the drafting boards for gigantic flying ships beyond anything Jules Verne could ever have imagined." Those dreams, however, would become reality later: the immediate need could be met by mass-producing an existing ship, Glenn

Martin's seventy-ton Mars flying boat, "five thousand of [which] could land 500,000 equipped men in England in a single day."[2]

Kaiser suggested converting shipyards nationwide—not just his—to produce the Mars. Then he promised, "We can have the assembly line functioning in six months or less." Finally, Kaiser vowed that this project would transcend the exigencies of war: "Not only will this war be terminated by sky ships, the postwar world will be won by them also. . . . Prosperity will be ours in the postwar period, for the reason that during the war, devastating as it is, we will have changed transportation."[3] Kaiser, dubbed "prosperity's prophet" by biographer Mark Foster, would champion his vision of an abundant postwar world for the next three years.[4]

This was a new and precarious position for the government entrepreneur. He was shifting from the role of instrument of administration policy to that of lobbyist trying to shape policy. When Kaiser had approached the government about cement, magnesium, and steel, he did so with the knowledge that key policy makers were already aligned in support of his proposals. The government had pursued Kaiser as vigorously as he had pursued new enterprise. Now Kaiser was submitting his proposal to the public *before* the government had asked the private sector for help.

Kaiser's approach to cargo planes also represented a departure from his organization's usual approach. Previously, he had conducted detailed studies and submitted formal proposals in advance of any publicity. This time, although Kaiser's people had done preliminary designs of huge cargo planes, the rest of the organization had not had time to lay the usual groundwork for entry into a new industry. Chad Calhoun had not had a chance, for instance, to line up powerful administration supporters in advance.[5] No wonder when Calhoun heard Kaiser's July 19 broadcast, "you could have knocked him over with a feather," a witness recalled.[6]

Things had never moved so quickly for Kaiser, not even in December 1940. Kaiser acknowledged as much in a telephone conversation with Washington radio broadcaster Fulton Lewis Jr.: "I don't ordinarily take a position like I have on this but I don't have the time to go through all the ordinary channels and get okays from everybody I would like to get."[7]

In addition to America's entry into the war, three relationships contributed to Kaiser's less patient approach in July 1942 than in December 1940: relationships with President Roosevelt, Andrew Jackson Higgins, and America's media. In June, Kaiser had approached the navy with a proposal to convert one hundred cargo ships into "baby flattop" aircraft carriers. One admiral after another turned Kaiser down until President Roosevelt personally intervened—awarding Kaiser a contract for fifty.[8]

That experience gave Kaiser confidence that he could gain administration approval without locating a powerful group of supporters in advance.

The appearance of Andrew Jackson Higgins on the national stage—and the inevitable comparisons with Kaiser—also changed the nature of opportunities for Kaiser. The uproar following cancellation of Higgins's Liberty Ship contract provided Kaiser with the timing he needed for his cargo plane proposal. The two shipbuilders would cross paths repeatedly for the remainder of the war.

Higgins phoned Kaiser the day of his Portland speech with a message of support and to offer Kaiser the use of Higgins's now vacant New Orleans shipyard. Higgins called for a "new pied piper" who would "drive [the bureaucrats] out [of Washington]." He saw Kaiser as "best qualified for the job," for which Higgins did "not believe he needs help, but if he does he can draft me."[9]

Mr. Kaiser and Mr. Higgins. At President Roosevelt's July 24 press conference, one reporter asked, "Are you going to discuss the cancellation of the Higgins contract with Mr. Higgins?" After the president said he did not know, the next question was, "Are you going to see Mr. Kaiser when he comes here next week, about the possibility of his plan?"[10] By now Higgins and Kaiser were so closely associated that if a government agency hamstrung the efforts of one, the other might expect more consideration to compensate. Higgins's enthusiasm was a mixed blessing for Kaiser. Before Kaiser had a chance to present his proposal personally in Washington, Higgins had arrived and talked it up—but with an agenda slightly different than Kaiser's. Higgins had been in Washington in early July when the decision to cancel his contract had been made but was not informed until he had returned to New Orleans.

It was not until after Kaiser's speech that Higgins first returned to Washington after the cancellation. He spent as much energy trying to convince the powers that be to change their minds about the decision to cancel as he did in support of the new proposal. And what a soapbox: Higgins was in Washington to testify before congressional hearings devoted to his contract cancellation. After the outcry by Higgins and the public over the cancellation of his Liberty Ship contract, the Senate appointed two subcommittees—one on shipbuilding, the other on iron and steel—to investigate. On July 28, Higgins testified emotionally before the iron and steel subcommittee. The chairman twice had to implore the aggrieved Higgins to sit down. Then Higgins really got going. He referred to the manner of cancellation as "heartless" and banged the table as he asked, "Would you treat a dog like that?"[11]

Oregon senator Charles McNary warned Kaiser's friend Philip Parrish, a *Portland Oregonian* editor, that many people in Washington simply saw Higgins as trying "to save his [recently closed] yard" rather than as genuinely committed to the cargo plane idea. McNary was a vocal supporter of Kaiser's cargo plane idea.[12] Parrish then told Kaiser that McNary "said the situation had been confused somewhat laterally through Higgins's approach. . . . A lot of people are taking the attitude that Higgins is trying to get out from under his problem and that is his reason for pushing this ahead." Kaiser, however, chose not to confront Higgins: "I wouldn't under any circumstances start to fight with him." Instead, he would go to Washington and push his plan himself. Parrish reminded Kaiser how valuable a presence in Washington can be: "You being away [from Washington] and he [Higgins] being there . . . I think you better get back there."[13]

Parrish's advice was a continuation of Kaiser's relationship with the *Portland Oregonian* in particular and the media in general. Palmer Hoyt, publisher of the *Oregonian*, had publicized Kaiser's Portland speech. Hoyt and Edgar Kaiser had become friends when the *Oregonian* followed events at Kaiser's Portland shipyards and before that the construction of the area's Bonneville and Grand Coulee Dams.[14] Hoyt had alerted key members of the press and provided them with advance copies of the speech so the story could reach Monday's eastern newspapers.[15] Parrish helped write the speech.[16] Afterward, Hoyt helped Kaiser find his way through the world of mass media. Kaiser's supporters became a who's who of the media elite. Kaiser acknowledged that his circle of contacts was expanding thanks to Hoyt: "I am spending the weekend with your friend, [*Washington Post* publisher] Eugene Meyer."[17] Hoyt also instructed Kaiser, "Be sure and contact Walter Lippmann, it's very important as Lippmann is all out on Kaiser plan and wants to help."[18] Kaiser complied, then wired Hoyt: "I called Lippmann, as you suggested, with fruitful results."[19]

According to his biographer, Lippmann's "loyal and powerful constituency" included "ten million of the most politically active and articulate people in America." Such a readership rewarded him with tremendous influence among America's policy makers.[20] Lippmann did a series on wartime production in late July and August, noting: "America's secret weapon is the art of mass production, and . . . the masters of this art, men like Mr. Ford and Mr. Kaiser, have proved beyond the possibility of dispute that they can apply it to any object of standardized design, be it a bomber, or a ship or a tank or a gun."[21] Lippmann's piece, entitled "Miracles and Muddles in War Production," also derided Washington's bureaucrats.

Isaiah Berlin, who spent the war at the British embassy in Washing-

ton, wrote of the Kaiser phenomenon in his dispatches to London. Berlin called Lippmann the "clearest spokesman" on behalf of the "great industrialists who represent American genius at its most fertile" and against "the morass of confusion, indecisiveness, and obstruction" of bureaucrats. Berlin believed "Kaiser's shipbuilding achievement is the outstanding miracle of this war in the field of United States production." Writing as a relatively detached observer, Berlin noted that "much indignation— though probably uninformed—on his behalf [for the cargo plane proposal] is expressed in Washington political salons."[22]

The national response to Kaiser's speech was overwhelming. In late July and August, Kaiser and his plan dominated the editorial pages of all kinds of newspapers and magazines. After six Kaiser stories appeared in one newspaper, an employee in Kaiser's New York office wrote, "They are thinking of renaming the 'New York World-Telegram.' 'Kaiser Telegram' would seem to be more appropriate."[23]

Kaiser also had the Time/Life publicity mill on his side. When he wired Hoyt the results of his phone call to Walter Lippmann, Kaiser was "on the train at the moment with . . . [*Fortune* columnist] Eliot Janeway as per instructions of my 'Chief.' "[24] Time/Life also knew what was coming ahead of time. Four days before the speech, Janeway wrote Kaiser: "*Fortune* is so excited about [Kaiser's air transport idea] that it would like you to tell your own story in broad terms under your own name."[25] Kaiser responded: "I feel imperative that significance of air transport be driven home and know *Fortune*, *Life*, and *Time* can assist."[26] They did.

On July 23, Kaiser pitched his cargo plane plan on a *March of Time* broadcast. The evidence Kaiser cited to support his proposal came from— where else? "If *Time* magazine is correct in declaring that 16 percent of the total aircraft of Germany are transports, as opposed to 3 percent on our part, it might well ease this burden if the government could use the country's shipbuilders as a means of providing additional air transport." The role model Kaiser followed in aircraft production was Henry Ford, who "has already pointed out the potential of the automotive industry in producing planes in thousands a month"—an "achievement" Time/Life had widely reported.[27] The day after his broadcast, Kaiser received an invitation to visit Henry Luce at his Greenwich, Connecticut, home.[28] Later on during this heated period, Henry Luce wrote to Kaiser's son Henry Jr., "You and your father are doing an American job in a thoroughly American way, and you have earned the heartfelt thanks and admiration of all of us."[29]

Luce's magazines reflected that sentiment. *Time* promptly reported that

"the biggest, most dramatic shake-up in transportation since the Wright Brothers got their flimsy biplane off the sand at Kitty Hawk is just around the corner."[30] The August 10 issue of *Life* carried a full-page piece in which Kaiser presented his plan. The biggest stumbling block to his proposal appeared to be raw materials. Where would Kaiser get the necessary steel or aluminum without disrupting existing priorities? The subsequent issue of *Fortune* carried an article by Janeway that called Kaiser's plan "first and foremost a bludgeon forcing a new and, for the first time, an adequate raw material program upon Washington."[31]

Amid this publicity, Hollywood could not ignore the Kaiser phenomenon. Even before the cargo plane speech, Harry Cohn, president of Columbia Pictures, had written, "Columbia Pictures is interested in the possibility of bringing to the screen a feature-length production based upon the story of Henry J. Kaiser." Cohn's letter provided evidence of how the various media cross-fertilized one another: "We were very much impressed with the [Gerard Piel] article in *Life* magazine several weeks ago, and feel that there is ample basis for an important picture that would be a credit to Mr. Kaiser."[32] After the cargo plane speech, Twentieth-Century Fox, Frank Capra, and Finney Productions all contacted Kaiser about movies.[33] Republic Pictures released *The Man from Frisco*, a shipbuilding picture loosely based on the Kaiser saga.[34]

Kaiser also reached the audience he sought most: Washington. Congress conducted hearings on Kaiser's cargo plane proposal. A dozen witnesses — most of whom were aircraft experts, including Grover Loening — were asked the identical question: What do you think of Kaiser's cargo plane proposal? Before Kaiser headed east to testify, Fulton Lewis Jr. promised him: "You have a friendly reception awaiting you in Washington."[35]

Lewis was right. Kaiser's name made the rounds in Washington. Congressman Martin Smith of Washington entered Kaiser's speech into the *Congressional Record*, then wrote to Kaiser: "I do not believe that any public utterance in recent months has created as much interest and favorable comment as your address. I think it is the overwhelming consensus of opinion here on Capitol Hill that your proposal should receive thorough and very serious consideration without any delay."[36]

The rumor mill had previously cast Kaiser as a possible replacement for Admiral Emory S. Land as head of the merchant shipping program; now Kaiser was said to be replacing Donald Nelson as head of the WPB. Senator Abe Murdock of Utah, who boasted that he was the one who

had introduced Kaiser to the president, offered an answer to the widely asked question, "Why doesn't the president put Henry Kaiser in charge of the war program?" Murdock wrote Kaiser: "If it were possible to keep your own production activities going, and at the same time have you in WPB, it is my opinion that a great step forward would be taken in our war program."[37] Some went further, pushing Kaiser for president.[38] This was heady stuff.

If only getting this plan off the ground were as simple as the media made it sound. Kaiser's greatest difficulty was in obtaining agreements to help or just good references from existing aircraft producers. Because they already had made agreements with the government, the producers told Kaiser they could not commit any resources—especially raw materials—without permission from the government. Although the WPB gave Kaiser two letters of intent on August 10, such approval was conditioned on Kaiser's not "encroaching upon the requirements of the *presently* approved military program." Donald Nelson also informed Kaiser that he had appointed a committee of aircraft builders "to work on this problem with you."[39]

Kaiser spoke with one member of that committee—Glenn L. Martin— on August 10. Martin had designed the Mars, which Kaiser in his July 19 speech promised to build. Martin was concerned that Kaiser wanted not only his idea but his men: "I understand you want 200 of my engineers." Kaiser did not deny coveting Martin's engineers: "I never mentioned any number to you or anyone else. This is a cooperative job. I only want the men you are willing to let me have."[40]

Their discussion revealed a contrast in style—Martin clearly wanted to move ahead prudently and obtain all necessary clearances. Kaiser had other ideas. Martin said that before the Mars could go into production, "we must fulfill performance tests, and work out specifications to the Navy." Kaiser, anticipating a repeat of President Roosevelt's June intervention on his behalf, responded: "Supposing we found a higher authority to okay production—we could avoid Navy red tape—for example, the Maritime Commission could authorize the building of planes or specifications prepared between their talented man and yours." Martin conditionally agreed: "If you get an order, and the government directs us to help, will do so. . . . We need a directive."[41]

A contrast even starker than that between Kaiser's and Martin's views of how to approach the government was that between their views on production possibilities. Martin pointed out that "your method of manufacture would be different from ours. We shall need 20 months with our

method, so how can we advise you on your 10 month's production program?" Kaiser gave a quintessential response: "Time element, in reality, is a detail. You may be able to build them faster than you think, if we all get in and 'push.'"[42]

Having heard enough, Martin tried to send Kaiser to another manufacturer: "Possibly the Consolidated PB24 would be the better ship, since it is already in production, and [Tom] Girdler [chairman of Consolidated Aircraft] says it will carry more cargo than the Mars."[43] Kaiser knew a brush-off when he heard one. On August 18, he wrote an associate: "I saw Martin [in] New York Saturday. Talked to [Donald] Douglas [head of Douglas Aircraft] Monday from Chicago. Disappointed in telephone conference. Not certain they will help on big ship."[44]

Kaiser then played what he thought was his ace in the hole. He wrote to Grover Loening: "I sincerely believe that the program outlined at the Shoreham [Hotel in Washington] by you, whereby you would proceed to design the plane, assisted by the organization to be supplied by me, would prove highly satisfactory, and may well present the most effective solution in any event. This is most assuredly true if the industry is unwilling to cooperate." Loening, who had been the only truly receptive member of the committee Nelson selected, nevertheless disappointed Kaiser: "I made it clear to you at Shoreham and to Mr. Nelson yesterday that I can assist in your aircraft development only as a consulting engineer in the employ of the WPB to give possible suggestions or corrections on any design or production plans you submit but must also be available to do same for any other company including ones in East like Martin." Loening then tried to encourage Kaiser: "Am confident [your] shipbuilding organization is sufficiently versatile and competent [and] can quickly learn enough aircraft engineering to make a practical contribution by themselves either in production like Mars or a large new design to further meet our difficult and imperative needs for transoceanic cargo airplanes."[45]

Grover Loening was not the final card in Kaiser's deck—Howard Hughes was. If Loening was an ace, Hughes was a wild card. He had inherited a fortune, including his father's Hughes Tool Company, before turning twenty. Being independently wealthy allowed Hughes to turn hobbies in filmmaking and flying into enterprises. He hired mechanics and designers and established the Hughes Aircraft Corporation in the 1930s as a supplier of planes to the federal government. Hughes's proposals received little attention until war broke out in Europe in September 1939.

Hughes, like Chad Calhoun, had a disastrous meeting with Hap Ar-

nold, chief of the army air corps, in 1940. In December 1939, Hughes had written to the air corps that he was working on a new medium-range bomber. Shortly thereafter several air force officials, including Arnold, visited the Hughes hanger in Burbank. They were inspecting plants in southern California and wanted to see the Hughes mystery plane. Hughes's guards were under strict orders that nobody be allowed inside without Hughes's permission. Here was the top-ranking official in charge of the nation's air defense asking to see a plane that might contribute toward that end and being denied entry. Hughes could not be reached, so Arnold angrily drove off.[46]

On August 12, 1942, more than two years after Arnold's abortive visit to Burbank, Chad Calhoun and Edgar Kaiser each received phone calls advising them that Hughes Aircraft was about to lay off two hundred aeronautical engineers from the bomber Hughes could not sell to the government.[47] On August 21, only two days after Grover Loening turned him down, Henry Kaiser discussed his cargo plane plans on the phone with a bedridden Howard Hughes.

Transcripts of their phone conversation allow us the rare opportunity to observe the birth of an enterprise. Hughes told Kaiser, "You have the public behind you." Kaiser made sure Hughes knew it was not just the public but also the White House. Kaiser had lunched with Roosevelt's secretary, Marvin McIntyre, on August 6, and "McIntyre knows what I want to do and is in sympathy."[48] He also told Hughes about his experience with baby flattop aircraft carriers (converted cargo ships). Now the "Army and Navy know they can injure me, but do not think they dare — would make no difference anyway." The implication was that if nobody else came through for them, the president might.[49]

Kaiser was clearly thrilled with the prospect of getting into aircraft production: "I have always said we should get into the air with light materials, but have never had them come out with Big Plane until now — the time is all right. . . . A successful plane will take the world into a new transportation era." Then, like a salesman closing a deal, Kaiser asked, "Can you tell me how you would like to participate?"[50]

There were collateral risks for Hughes, which he explained to Kaiser: "When I make a statement such as you request I am going to antagonize certain people — [army air corps head Hap] Arnold, etc. I have a plane which will be sold to the Air Corps and which will fly in 2 or 3 weeks. I gave this thing a lot of thought before letting [Hughes associate Glen] Odekirk discuss it with you." Hughes told Kaiser he finally decided to go

ahead with the meetings because "I feel that my plane will be good enough so that they will have to buy it whether or not they want to." Now Hughes was selling:

> I have 100 engineers who are as good as any in the country, and with them together with those from Stanford [Kaiser had proposed recruiting a thousand engineers and draftsmen from the University of California and elsewhere]—I know we can engineer this and do it well. . . . I do not know the first thing about production and I feel that you have shown your ability in that direction. I feel I know something about planes. Thought we might get together. You might use my ability to determine the success of this plane from a technical standpoint, and you could handle production, etc. I do not know very much about production and would not take a contract because of that.[51]

Then they ever so briefly discussed "details" of time and money. Kaiser asked, "Would you be willing to start to build the plane as soon as you start the engineers, and take a chance that we will have to do re-tooling after we had flown the first plane?"

"I do not see why it should be necessary to wait."

"You think we could build plant and plane [in such a way that] when the last drawing is off the board the plane is finished?"[52]

Even if he weren't ill, Hughes probably would have gasped. "[That] might be putting it a little strong."

"We want to be flying the plane in a year."

"That is very optimistic, but that is your problem—from an engineer's standpoint could be accomplished."

Finally, money—Kaiser estimated, "Would cost about 1½ million to do it? Have made no arrangements for money. . . . I do not think about profits."

Kaiser had arranged for a radio broadcast that evening and invited Hughes to join him. Kaiser told him: "We could give our statements to the newspapers, but it would be more dramatic this way." Hughes clearly felt rushed: "I am with you 100 percent in theory. I am willing to go ahead and see if we can work out a deal satisfactory to us and then give a statement to the press. I question that we could reach a complete understanding before this evening." Kaiser, who was scheduled to dedicate the second hospital of his health plan, the Richmond Field Hospital, that afternoon, now played doctor: "I think we can work something out and you probably will be well enough to make a statement at 7:30. . . . Will be over about four o'clock—will make arrangements with C.B.S. and N.B.C."[53]

Although Hughes later became the world's most famous recluse, in the early stages of his career he was quite savvy in dealing with the media. In 1938, flying a plane called the *New York World's Fair 1939*, Hughes circled the globe in three days, nineteen hours—a world record—and was rewarded with a ticker-tape parade in New York City.[54] So when Kaiser began angling for the biggest publicity splash they could get, Hughes was entirely in agreement: "*Time, Life*, etc. will pick [the story] up so we must get off to the right start."[55] Hughes was absolutely right: *Time* called them a "Fabulous Team."[56]

By the end of August, Kaiser had become the symbol of the "big plane." He had attracted tremendous support from the nation's media and the public. And just over a month after his Oregon speech, he had landed an experienced aircraft designer—Howard Hughes—as a partner. Yet the WPB Air Cargo Committee had made it clear that Kaiser would not be allowed to mass-produce the Mars, Glenn Martin's seventy-ton cargo plane because Kaiser could not do so without interfering with existing raw materials needs. Therefore, Kaiser and Hughes would have to work on an experimental plane using alternative materials. Eliot Janeway wrote that this was like "telling Mr. Kaiser that, so to speak, he can have a ham sandwich if he can bake the bread, borrow the butter, and steal the ham."[57]

As Kaiser prepared to head east, other members of the media grew impatient with Washington's bureaucrats for stalling his cargo plane proposal. Syndicated columnist Raymond Clapper wrote: "All [Kaiser] has to show is two measly letters from Donald Nelson. . . . Both are signed with the same rubber stamp. . . . Why kid the public into thinking Washington is behind him when nobody there has any intention of raising a small toe to help him? This is a piece of monumental fakery."[58] Kaiser appeared to be no closer to convincing the powers in Washington to give him a green light than he had been in July. Indeed, although in July Kaiser had promised to mass-produce the Mars, in late August as he prepared to return to Washington, he had backed off from that idea: "You can readily understand at this time I am unable to divulge to you the details of this proposal."[59] It took a government investigation of Kaiser—and reaction to it—to get approval for his project.

In late August, at the very apex of the Kaiser summer of 1942, the Office of Price Administration (OPA) accused Kaiser of paying above-market prices to obtain steel for his new southern California steel plant, where ground had been broken just the month before. The OPA's regional attorney in Cleveland said that "Kaiser Company, Inc. has branded itself as a 'scoff-law' participating in illegal transactions . . . to snatch steel from

other steel-famished war industries." He also accused Kaiser of being a willing accomplice to others: "By paying profiteer prices, it enabled the Builders Structural Steel to violate the law."[60]

It had seemed inevitable that someone like Kaiser with deeply anti-bureaucratic values would run into trouble with wartime agencies devoted to rationing and price control. In this case, Kaiser appeared to cross swords with an old ally, Leon Henderson.

The OPA's action was in response to Andrew Jackson Higgins's testimony before a Senate committee in late July. Higgins wanted to know why the Maritime Commission canceled his contract because of insufficient availability of steel without informing him of the problem or allowing him to try to solve it. He offered a few ideas: "Maybe they would stop using steel for guard rails along the highways. . . . Maybe they can stop the 'black market.' Maybe they would permit me to get my steel from the 'black market.' "[61] Higgins was implicating Kaiser.

The wording of the OPA's press release reflects the extent of Kaiser's 1942 publicity: "An injunction preventing Henry J. Kaiser, West Coast miracle shipbuilder, from buying hot steel was issued today by Federal Judge Robert L. Wilkin in the United States District Court in Cleveland." Even when it was on the verge of prosecuting Kaiser, the OPA used superlatives to describe him. The press release also revealed that the Kaiser case was catalyzed "as a result of an investigation launched by the Office of Price Administration into the activities of the Higgins Shipbuilding Yards in New Orleans."[62]

A hearing date of September 5 was set. If the OPA made the charges stick, then the Justice Department would prosecute Kaiser—the same Justice Department that had been so delighted when Kaiser helped out in its battles with forces of monopoly and oligopoly. For help at this point Kaiser turned to Thurman Arnold, head of the antitrust division of the Justice Department. Arnold, who was from Wyoming, shared other westerners' suspicions of the concentration of economic power in the East. He wished to see the battle against "entrenched special privilege" carried out by challenges from the private sector instead of administration economic planners. Even after the war began and industrial giants had descended on Washington to head agencies and secure contracts, Arnold was optimistic: "I believe that men like Henry Kaiser are going to get strong enough through this that they cannot be stopped."[63] Arnold, like other administration antitrusters, was an enthusiastic supporter of Kaiser's efforts in steel and magnesium. Arnold also sought competition for Alcoa in the aluminum industry.[64]

On August 28, Arnold reassured Kaiser: "I am not empowered to make a deal, but can say that OPA is kindly disposed to suggestions." Arnold told Kaiser he would not need to move up his planned trip from the West Coast to settle the matter to his satisfaction. Arnold said he could obtain "a decree which will relieve you of any stigma of lack of patriotism—we can get it cleared up in about 2½ hours." Arnold thought the "matter can be worked out by sending your Attorney." According to Arnold, the OPA was as eager as Kaiser to avoid a potential fight and the related publicity.[65] But it was too late; Kaiser's publicity mill was operating at full speed: compounding the criticism, provoking conspiracy theories, seemingly confirming what everyone already knew about the federal government.

John B. Hughes, a West Coast radio commentator who had warned in the spring that "a fifth column, foreign agents, and American obstructionists" were "concentrating their efforts toward slowing down the shipbuilding program," sensed another conspiracy. For an August 27 broadcast, Hughes asked Kaiser to "wire me a statement about your purchase of steel on so-called black market." Hughes asked, "Do you feel Cleveland injunction is deliberate attempt to block your plans? If possible give me a hot statement on faulty distribution system making so-called black market purchase necessary in order to get production."[66]

After speaking with Kaiser, Hughes said in his broadcast, "The plain truth of the matter is that there has been some skullduggery here of some sort and it looks as if there has been a deliberate attempt to interfere with the development of industrial resources in the West." Hughes went on to suggest that Bethlehem Steel was obstructing Kaiser's efforts to get his Fontana steel plant up and running and that the case might "expose not a company doing wrong, but a practice countenanced by the government for the benefit of special private interests."[67]

The office of Leon Henderson, head of the OPA, denied any prior knowledge of the action against Kaiser, and Kaiser showed no evidence of suspecting any hidden agenda by Henderson.[68] Kaiser attempted to put the matter on the personal basis that had worked so well for him in Washington. He issued a press release on August 27 that began: "I know Henderson personally. I know that he knows my record and I believe he has absolute confidence in my honesty and integrity."[69] In a speech at a launch the next day, Kaiser said, "I firmly believe that Leon Henderson is trying to do a good job" and what was needed was a change in policy.[70] Kaiser had, in fact, submitted the speech to Henderson's office for review before the launch.[71]

Kaiser had made other arrangements, as well. He hired Beverly Hills

publicist Russell Birdwell to draft another press release. The statement was direct: "Upon investigation I find that neither I, nor any one connected with me, have at any time bought steel on the so-called black market. . . . I hereby defy anyone to try and prove the contrary."[72]

Kaiser's damage control worked. On September 2, Leon Henderson announced the decree Arnold promised, and the matter was settled without a public hearing.[73] Avoiding a fight did not, however, prevent additional favorable publicity for Kaiser. If anything, being tarred with the brush of black market dealings helped rather than hurt Kaiser's image. Kaiser the rule breaker would become even more popular than Kaiser the record breaker. He shifted from being an archetypal miracle worker to an archetypal entrepreneur for whom the rules did not apply. In so doing, he tapped into some of America's most deeply held self-conceptions.[74]

Kaiser's breaking of the rules dovetailed well with a theme *Time* used in its very first article on Kaiser—breaking nature's rules: "He refuses to believe in clocks or calendars." The lesson was that "time is no obstacle to men of energy and purpose."[75] Nor are the rules set by bureaucrats. Americans complained a good deal about all the rules and controls, but few actually broke the law. Most settled for vicarious rule breaking through public figures.

In 1938, Douglas Corrigan had become a national hero by thumbing his nose at the Department of Commerce. After failing to receive permission to fly the Atlantic, Corrigan set out to fly from New York to California and "accidentally" ended up in Ireland. A hero was born: southern California children were given a half-day off from school to celebrate, and more than a million people turned out at his New York ticker-tape parade, more than had cheered Charles Lindbergh after his 1927 solo flight. As Jonathan Yardley points out, Americans have always loved those who have flown in the face of authority, and Corrigan had literally done just that.[76]

Such sentiments were intensified by the war. Because "everyone who read the newspapers knew what [Kaiser's] results were," most bureaucrats knew well enough to leave Kaiser alone. Eliot Janeway noted that "they philosophized that the men who got results are invariably men who break rules," and once the war ended it would be up to Congress to determine if such behavior helped or hindered the war effort.[77]

Typical of the public reaction to the OPA-Kaiser spat was a Scripps-Howard Newspapers editorial called "Lincoln, Grant, Whisky—and Kaiser." It emphasized Kaiser's results: "Whatever steel Kaiser has been using has been going into victory ships and other war implements." The editorial then compared complaints about Kaiser's steel purchasing to rumors

about General Ulysses S. Grant's drinking and closed with Abraham Lincoln's famous response: "Send a barrel of it to my other generals."[78]

In the same spirit, Raymond Clapper weighed in with a piece in which he admitted that "I'm apt to be a sucker for a fellow who gets things done. . . . The indictment is not against Old Man Kaiser but against this arsenal of bureaucracy." Responding to the label the OPA tagged on Kaiser, Clapper wrote: "If you have to be a scofflaw to get steel . . . then I hope the old fellow breaks every law on the books. Winning the war is more important than any regulation of any Washington bureaucracy. . . . Give us a dozen such scofflaws around this town and it might shorten this war and save thousands of lives." *Time* ran a segment of Clapper's column, saying that he "well expressed the public sentiment."[79]

According to the *New Republic*, "Kaiser is a producer in the heroic American mold. We need him, and others like him. . . . A lot of bureaucrats would rather lose the war by orthodox means than win it by unorthodox ones."[80] So it went. Instead of being derailed by this story, the engine of Kaiser's public image picked up steam: learning that their man may have broken the rules seemed to escalate the commitment of Kaiser's many supporters. This seemingly excessive response was no doubt due to the overheated environment created by reactions to Kaiser's cargo plane proposal.

That same day, Drew Pearson's column hinted darkly at a conspiracy against Kaiser by top government officials. The liberal, pro–New Deal Pearson was another advocate for Kaiser. His syndicated column, "Washington Merry-Go-Round," had begun in 1932 on the eve of Washington's ascendance as a news center, and Pearson added a radio program in 1940.[81] Nevertheless, Kaiser attained such public stature during the war that their association was viewed as a boon to Pearson's reputation. Isaiah Berlin reported in August 1945: "An interesting sidelight on the influence and prestige of the columnist Drew Pearson is to be seen in the fact that the following national figures have been prepared to take over his column for one day each during Pearson's vacation—Fred Vinson, Henry Kaiser, Leon Henderson, Herbert Brownell, and Philip Murray."[82]

Pearson had written glowingly of Kaiser's shipbuilding performance in April 1942, then in the summer began collecting material for another Kaiser story. As part of the process, Pearson spoke to Kaiser's erstwhile lawyer/lobbyist Tom Corcoran on August 3, and Pearson's notes from the conversation indicate that Corcoran believed that the man and the moment had met: "Kaiser is a great success in [a] period like this . . . when money doesn't count, when it has to be spent like water to win." In peace-

time? "Kaiser would go broke in another era."[83] Corcoran told Pearson that Kaiser "sees things broadly. Has great dreams, sees them through." Pearson agreed and two weeks later wrote a story entitled "Miracle Man Kaiser May Make WPB Swallow Its Big 'If' on Those Cargo Planes."[84] Pearson's story did not go as far as Corcoran had gone on the phone; he had argued to Pearson that Kaiser should head the WPB because he was "not afraid to take chances."[85]

In his September 2 column, Pearson described a luncheon discussion in late August, which included Admiral Land, chairman of the Maritime Commission, Donald Nelson, head of the WPB, and Robert Sherwood, speechwriter for the president. Land was expressing a common sentiment in the wake of Kaiser's cargo plane promotion: "Damn these newspapermen, playing up Henry Kaiser. However, I don't blame them as much as I do Kaiser; he is the one who stirred up the whole rumpus." Then came his real beef: "[Kaiser] ought to know we have plenty of transports, and don't need cargo planes." Donald Nelson, wrote Pearson, then interrupted Land: "Jerry, you may be interested in knowing that we are going after Kaiser. I just talked to Leon Henderson about it and we've caught him buying steel in the black market. Leon's decided to crack down on him." The next day, Henderson's Cleveland office did just that.[86]

Pearson's column offered all the elements that might explain to paranoid Kaiser supporters why he had not yet received government permission to proceed on his cargo plane project. Admiral Land headed the agency that built the ships the cargo planes were supposed to replace. Nelson and Henderson were heads of the two most visible wartime agencies, and Sherwood was proxy for the president. There was ample power in that group to take Kaiser down a notch or shut him out entirely—if that was their goal.

Yet there was even less reason to believe that Land was out to get Kaiser than that Henderson was scheming against him. Land had testified at the Higgins hearing that "probably I am responsible more than any other man in the United States for getting Henry J. Kaiser and associates in the shipbuilding business."[87] In late July, Kaiser had been invited to chair the new United Seaman's Service (USS), a USO equivalent for the merchant marine. Kaiser protested that he had little time for such things and skillfully pointed out that regardless of his shipbuilding achievements, "[Admiral] Land criticizes me terrifically, personally, without any restraint, for doing too much and spreading myself too thin. If I undertake something like that, he will have something to say." Kaiser even mentioned an allusion Land had made, probably about Kaiser's rival Andrew Jackson Higgins: "He told me the other day I was like some-

one else only 'he isn't in every spot in the country you are.'" Kaiser wryly granted, "He is about half right too." Kaiser finally agreed to serve under one condition: "Get Admiral Land to call me and tell me he wants me to do it. Then I can blame him."[88]

Land approached Kaiser about the USS less than a week before the OPA blowup.[89] This was about the same time that Kaiser informed Land that he wanted the cargo plane program to operate under the auspices of the Maritime Commission.[90] If Land were out to get Kaiser, it would make no sense to do so at the same time that he ordered Kaiser to head the USS or when Kaiser might be able to involve him in an exciting new program.

As for Roosevelt, in June he had overruled top navy brass to award Kaiser a contract to build fifty aircraft carriers and in August had his secretary, Marvin McIntyre, meet with Kaiser about the cargo plane plan. Roosevelt, of course, had earlier been an enthusiastic supporter of Kaiser's efforts to offer new competition in the cement, magnesium, and steel industries.

When Pearson's column about the luncheon appeared in the *Washington Post*, Chad Calhoun asked publisher Eugene Meyer about it. Meyer did not admit that Pearson had his facts wrong but did suggest that Calhoun "not pay too much attention to the Pearson article, but continue your relationship with Nelson for the time being on the basis of what you have said to Nelson and Nelson has said to you."[91] Indeed, the same September 2 issue of the *Post* had carried a story saying, "Nelson denies he ordered change in Kaiser arrangement," and "[Nelson's] position on Kaiser's [cargo plane] proposal remained unchanged."[92] Pearson, as Meyer's advice to Calhoun suggests, may have had his own agenda. Perhaps he agreed with Tom Corcoran's suggestion that Kaiser, not Nelson, should be head of the WPB.

Donald Nelson responded immediately, sending a letter to Drew Pearson the day the story appeared (copies of which went to Henderson, Kaiser, Meyer, and Land). It began: "I have not before commented upon many inaccurate, misleading, and often insidious statements which you frequently have made about me in your column, the Washington Merry-Go-Round." Nelson wrote that he "knew nothing about the case against Mr. Kaiser brought by OPA. . . . As a matter of fact, my attention was first called to the case by a newspaper man, and I later called Mr. Henderson to find out whether or not there was any truth to it." Nelson concluded: "Furthermore, I have believed in and supported Henry Kaiser, still believe in him and still support him in his effort to get more war production."[93]

Henry Kaiser's reputation was such in the summer of 1942 that one of the best ways to maintain job security was to profess belief in him; it was tantamount to a loyalty oath.

In 1942, Kaiser had gained so much clout through public opinion and the press that he could pursue enterprises that had not yet been proposed inside the government. The cargo plane idea had been discussed but had not yet developed a cast of administration supporters like that he had relied on when he launched previous enterprises. Nevertheless, within six weeks, the public's overwhelming response led Roosevelt to move—as Kaiser suggested he would. The president ordered embattled WPB head Donald Nelson to give Kaiser and Howard Hughes the go-ahead. They signed a contract on September 10. For Kaiser, however, it was a hollow victory: he and Hughes were to produce three two-hundred-ton prototypes, at no profit, and could not use strategic military materials—so Hughes began working with wood.[94]

With public opinion on his side, Kaiser was better able to weather a direct attack, such as that of the OPA, than a more convoluted process, such as that initiated by the WPB. The WPB achieved its goal: to get Kaiser and the public off its back. A letter from the WPB's director of aircraft production appears to bear this out. In summarizing the situation for Jesse Jones, he wrote, "We have tried for many weeks to bring this matter to a *definite conclusion.*"[95] A cargo plane contract was thought by many to be a new beginning, but to some within the WPB this would be the end of it, and for the most part they were right—at least for Kaiser. Andrew Jackson Higgins, by contrast, appeared to be just getting started.

In September 1942, President Roosevelt conducted a "secret" tour of defense facilities, and one of his stops, on September 23, was Henry Kaiser's Portland shipyard. Roosevelt visited Andrew Jackson Higgins's facilities in New Orleans on September 29. The two shipbuilders—linked in the public mind and in the mass media—apparently were linked in the president's mind as well. On October 19, both Kaiser and Higgins visited Roosevelt at the White House.[96]

Higgins parlayed public support and the visit by the president into his own new enterprise, which appeared to trump Kaiser. Whereas the WPB asked for only three prototype cargo planes from Kaiser, Higgins secured a contract calling for production of twelve hundred cargo planes—the largest aircraft contract in history.[97] The main reason Higgins was able to secure a huge contract while Kaiser was not is that Higgins contracted to produce an existing design—the C-76 Curtis Commando transport—using plywood, which was not an essential war material.

Time/Life could not resist comparing the two shipbuilders. When Higgins had "practically" landed his biggest aircraft contract, "this meant that Higgins had stolen a march on his friend and archrival, Henry Kaiser, the Wizard of the West Coast." How did he do it? "By using a double dose of Kaiser's own technique—rough and tumble action plus fortissimo publicity." Publicity by whom? Time/Life was being self-referential about its role. Even Time/Life's *Time Capsule/1942*, a condensation of the magazines' stories assembled more than twenty-five years later, displays pictures of Kaiser and Higgins side by side.[98]

Henry Kaiser and Andrew Jackson Higgins were comparable not only for their publicity-attracting efforts in 1942 but for the ultimate outcomes of their respective cargo plane ventures. Higgins's was altered in 1943, then canceled in 1944.[99] Even with his modest contract, Kaiser fared no better because of problems with his partner.

In mid-September Kaiser had sought Jesse Jones's evaluation of Howard Hughes. Jones told him: "You are safe in proceeding with Howard Hughes. I have known him since he was a boy—and I knew his able father before him—and I know of no more capable and reliable man than Howard Hughes. . . . Now, whatever you do, Henry, do not interfere with Howard. He is thorough and he is a genius and do not interfere with him."[100] Kaiser's experience with Hughes would be different than what Jones had led him to expect.

In September and October, Eugene Trefethen and Noah Dietrich, the right-hand men of Kaiser and Hughes respectively, worked together on the formation of a new corporation.[101] On October 7, the day Trefethen submitted their plans to the Defense Plant Corporation, a Hughes employee wrote Kaiser a letter that suggested that the principal difficulties of the new enterprise might come from his prospective partner rather than from established aircraft producers or the government. Leonard J. Strong, night superintendent of Hughes Aircraft, raised serious doubts as to whether Hughes would deliver on his promises:

The Hughes Aircraft Company will not and cannot operate in any way approaching an efficient manner under the present management. Mr. Hughes has saddled himself with a gang of the men who built his famous racer and these men to all indications are still living in the dubious limelight of that accomplishment. He selected Mr. [Glen] Odekirk for Plant Manager due to the fact that he was in charge of the preparation of the Lockheed transport which was used on the Round-the-World flight and as this was merely a rework job it was accomplished

without too much trouble. . . . Mr. Jerman, his assistant['s] only claim to fame with this organization lies in the fact that he designed a silencer for a shotgun which was purchased by Mr. Hughes and presented to Miss Ginger Rogers.

Summarizing, Strong wrote: "We have some of the best mechanics and engineers in the business and they have had their hands tied for the lack of efficient management for so long that a great many of them have quit and gone elsewhere. . . . This may appear to be a very bleak picture (which I intend that it shall be) but it is in no way one whit blacker than the actual facts — it could not be." As for Kaiser and his new partner, "Mr. Hughes will not say yes or no and . . . one of the greatest troubles here is that you can never get a direct answer on any questions and that is one of the prime requisites of an executive. . . . You, in your present position, cannot afford to be associated with an organization in the state that this one is foundering in. . . . The nation looks to you as a builder and we here are proud to be with you but not under the shadow of failure that will dog us through this project."[102]

There is no evidence to suggest that this letter slowed Kaiser down at all. Nevertheless, Strong's predictions came true. Although at face value the combination of Hughes, the design genius, and Kaiser, the production miracle worker, seemed ideal, their styles proved fundamentally incompatible. This was particularly the case with their contrasting attitudes toward deadlines: Kaiser was fanatical about adhering to them, whereas Hughes was cavalier about ignoring them.

The first leg of the project was Hughes's responsibility, but Kaiser wanted to keep close tabs on it. Soon it became clear that was not happening. Kaiser — a man said to be impossible for his executives to escape from, even while on vacation — simply could not track down Hughes to find out how things were going. In April 1943, eight months before the deadline for completion of the first plane, Kaiser wrote Hughes:

I regret that you did not keep the appointment which you made with me and which I made several weeks ago in order to permit you to make your plans so you could see me here.

I am disappointed more than you can possibly know. Mr. Don Nelson advised me that under no condition was I to be relieved of the responsibility of the delivery of these planes within the time scheduled, and since my reputation is at stake as well as yours I request that you immediately advise me by letter the actual schedule, number of man hours

per day, and a chart showing how these planes are being completed. . . . I have no information from you whatsoever except that you too are concerned about the management. If I am again asked by either Mr. Jones or Mr. Nelson I shall be compelled to tell them the truth.[103]

Kaiser fared little better until October, when he learned the planes were going to be heavier than expected.[104] In February 1944, the contract was canceled.[105] Kaiser's partnership with Hughes ended without a single plane having been produced. Hughes proceeded alone, completing one of the three planes, called the "Spruce Goose." It flew only once, November 2, 1947, with Hughes at the controls.[106]

Ironically, Kaiser's initial proposal from his July 19, 1942, speech—to mass-produce the Mars—might have fared better. In a letter to Senator Harry Truman about the contract cancellation, Donald Nelson pointed out, "The Martin Mars is now being built. It is a much better plane."[107] *New York Post* columnist Samuel Grafton had sensed in August 1942 what was happening. He wrote that Kaiser was a victim of the WPB's "broadening out the issue . . . until the issue is lost." The original issue was mass production of the seventy-ton Mars, but the WPB avoided consideration of that proposal by "concentrat[ing] thrilled attention on a 200-ton plane, which can't possibly have its first test for two years." This was a common Washington ploy: "achieving postponement of the possible [by showing] keen interest in the impossible."[108]

Chad Calhoun later lamented, "Mr. Kaiser was given perhaps the greatest run-around of all time last August by the aircraft industry and its minions in Washington D.C. It was the aircraft industry primarily who scotched Kaiser's cargo plan and kicked it off with an order for three prototype planes for Kaiser and Hughes."[109] This was a far cry from a contract to build thousands, or even hundreds, of planes. Nonetheless, at the time, Kaiser entertained hopes that the three prototypes would lead to something bigger.[110]

Although the power of public opinion was sufficient to give Kaiser a hearing when the government had not made up its mind on an issue, it proved not as helpful as already having key government officials lined up to support a project. Kaiser succeeded most often when he was acting as a private sector extension of public policy, rather than as someone trying to change public policy. His Washington office was set up to determine where policy was headed rather than to influence it.

After bowing out of the cargo plane project, Henry Kaiser remained

a household name. By then, the great shipping crisis of 1942 had passed, and the Allies' outlook in the war was considerably brighter. Even more important, by 1944 Henry Kaiser had graduated into the ranks of industrial statesmen—those sought for advice beyond the realm of their own enterprises or industries.

I am a builder,

not a politician.

Henry J. Kaiser,

1946

8 ———— SEND FOR KAISER

In May 1943, Associate Solicitor General Oscar Cox wrote to Roosevelt aide Harry Hopkins that "[Henry] Luce, [Wendell] Willkie, and some of the other Republicans are trying hard to seduce Henry Kaiser into their camp."[1] As recently as a year before, Cox and the Democrats would have cared little which way Kaiser went. In the interim, however, two significant things had happened. First, Kaiser had become a national hero because of his shipbuilding achievements and his cargo plane proposal. Second, Kaiser had gone beyond his accustomed role as government entrepreneur—seizing opportunities when they appeared in Washington—to tackling issues of national policy. Certainly the ques-

tion of whether the War Production Board would approve production of giant cargo planes in the summer of 1942 constituted a policy issue, but in December Kaiser had gone well beyond that, to postwar domestic policy.

Speaking at a black-tie dinner of the National Association of Manufacturers (NAM) on December 4, 1942, Kaiser issued a challenge to American business: to meet America's peacetime civilian needs.[2] Less than a year after Pearl Harbor, in a speech entitled "Management Looks at the Postwar World," Kaiser announced that "the problems of peace are already at hand."[3] Some of Cox's fears about "losing" Kaiser to the Republicans may have arisen from concerns about the audience Kaiser addressed: the NAM included proprietors of many small businesses, a group traditionally more conservative than the organization men of Main Street. Isaiah Berlin, for one, mistook venue for message, writing on December 8 that "[Kaiser] is certainly the most spectacular spokesman of American business against the New Deal that has so far emerged."[4]

In his speech, Kaiser said, "Our preparation for life after the war should begin tonight: The mobilization of the tremendous forces of American production, launching out boldly *for housing, for transportation, for highways, for essential medical care.*"[5] This was not just a builder speaking, or even a garden-variety industrial "statesman." America was accustomed to having men like Charles E. Wilson of General Motors talk about how to solve problems in his own industry or men like Bernard Baruch or Owen Young offer advice on larger economic issues. Kaiser, however, was unique in backing up his advice with the possibility of establishing new enterprise. As it turned out, Kaiser would follow through with housing developments in California, with Kaiser Aluminum in the Pacific Northwest (and later nationwide), and with the Kaiser Permanente health care plan and hospitals on the West Coast (and later, nationwide).

Kaiser knew he was launching a bombshell. He sent an advance copy of the speech to Eugene Meyer, publisher of the *Washington Post*, with the warning: "I am afraid you never will love me again when you read the enclosed copy of the address which I shall make before the annual meeting of the National Association of Manufacturers. Please note that in the address I did not mention which friend advised me against 'talking post-war.'"[6] A few weeks after delivering the speech, Kaiser wrote Meyer again: "I know how you feel about post-war planning, and I remember the lecture you gave Edgar and me; however, I don't know of any doghouse better than yours to be in."[7]

Kaiser did, however, receive a positive response from certain members of the press such as the *New York Herald Tribune*, *Time*, and Walter Lipp-

mann. His most visible critic was not a journalist but Joseph Frazer, head of the Graham-Paige Auto Company. Kaiser's principal challenge, after all, had been to the auto industry: did it have "the courage now to design and announce 1945 models for delivery six months after the close of the war?"[8] The Roosevelt administration had castigated the auto industry in 1941 for hesitating to switch from civilian to wartime needs. Implicit in Kaiser's 1942 speech was a threat to enter the auto business if the industry did not move quickly enough to meet postwar demand. Needless to say, automakers were not thrilled. Joseph Frazer called Kaiser's ideas "half-baked . . . stupid bushwah."[9]

Paul Cadman advised Kaiser: "Very confidentially I learned this morning that Mr. Frazer was so angry at the seat which had been assigned to him and his party at the banquet that he took his guests across the street to a night club. They returned to the banquet hall at the very moment when you were turning the heat on the automobile industry. I judge from this that Mr. Frazer is a very unhappy man, and it is very well that you did not dignify him with an elaborate reply."[10] Kaiser would need such restraint for his next role as government entrepreneur: industrial statesman.

Americans traditionally speculate as to whether a charismatic leader from a sphere besides politics—such as the military or business—could do a better job solving social problems than the incumbent public servants. As early as the spring of 1942, such speculation arose about Kaiser. Kaiser's December speech to the NAM showed that he now believed the speculation, too. This, combined with his already legendary track record and his appeal to members of both political parties, made Kaiser, as Oscar Cox recognized, a potentially formidable force.

What hold did Luce and Willkie have over this man? Cox may not have realized that Kaiser had more of a relationship with Time/Life writers such as Gerard Piel and Eliot Janeway than he did with Henry Luce.[11] Kaiser's relationship with Luce, as Luce later pointed out, tended to be based on the tone of the most recent Time/Life story on Kaiser, rather than on any political agreements or differences between the two.[12] Indeed, one of Kaiser's biggest blowups against Luce and Time/Life took place shortly after Cox wrote Hopkins. Luce met with Kaiser over objections Kaiser had to an upcoming story in *Fortune*.[13] In the fall of 1943, a three-part series on the Six Companies appeared in *Fortune*, along with a feature article on Kaiser. These articles would be the most widely used reference material on Kaiser for the remainder of his life. The four articles proved sufficiently satisfactory to Kaiser and his staff that they would cooperate with *Fortune* many more times.

The road to detente was rocky, however. In a June 1943 meeting with two representatives of *Fortune* to discuss the upcoming Kaiser article, tempers flared. Kaiser said, "I believe this is a 'Kaiser hate' article. . . . I don't expect you to write anything but what is bad." Kaiser threatened to furnish affidavits to contest statements in the article. Then Kaiser really began to apply his temper: "I hope I'll never find another individual who will talk to me as you have talked to me. . . . When you question my word you do me intentional injury. You don't know how far-reaching it is. That is why you are bringing out the very worst in me." Kaiser said: "What does bother me is the misleading information as to what [Kaiser's] profits are. I know what I am doing. As to opposing [the *Fortune* story], I probably shall write an article. It really will hurt *Fortune*. I am going to tell Luce he is doing a great injury." As with so many Kaiser typhoons, this one blew over quickly. Kaiser apologized before leaving the room. Kaiser said that "this is the only [Time/Life article] I have objected to"; it would not be the last.[14]

Henry Luce's friend Wendell Willkie may have seduced Kaiser, but he did it the old-fashioned way: his 1940 campaign had aroused some of the strongest passions of any Republican nominee in the twentieth century. Willkie offered a unique political package: a onetime Democrat, as a lawyer and utilities executive he had led the battle against government ownership of power companies represented by the Tennessee Valley Authority. Willkie's beliefs in civil rights and in internationalism, which he shared with Roosevelt, not only made it difficult to differentiate between his policies and those of the president but also gave rise to doubts as to whether he had completely abandoned his Democratic roots (he switched parties in 1939).

Although Kaiser had never supported individual political candidates through fund-raising or other forms of support, national magazines did report that he voted for Willkie in 1940.[15] As Kaiser had increasing contact with magazine and newspaper publishers, he rubbed shoulders with a largely Republican crowd. Indeed, in the 1944 campaign, more than two-thirds of publishers surveyed opposed Roosevelt, and less than 20 percent supported him.[16] Among publishers, none was more supportive of Willkie than Henry Luce and his Time/Life magazines. In 1939 and 1940, a series of Time/Life features had helped propel this virtual unknown into national consciousness, then to the Republican nomination.

It was probably Kaiser's appearance as a player in national policy discussion, more than any move by Willkie or Luce to "seduce" Kaiser, that caught Cox's attention. Cox suggested that Hopkins and Roosevelt see Kaiser "once in a remote while" in order to "counteract the influences that

are being brought on him." Cox offered a bone that they could toss to Kaiser: "One project that might currently be discussed with him is an idea he has for taking care of the children of the women and men workers in his plants."[17] Finally, Cox acknowledged Kaiser's value as a role model to others: "It's not earth-shaking, but if Kaiser does it the symbolic example might get others to do it."[18] Cox believed Kaiser was the sort of business-man with whom the administration should continue to work and that it should not risk losing his active support.

Oscar Cox, like some of the eastern press, treated westerner Kaiser as an innocent: "At heart his urges are the other way. But he is not completely un-naive in this field." Kaiser was not totally naive; he commissioned a 1943 poll to determine public attitudes toward himself. It is not clear whether this was for political purposes or was an early move in marketing Kaiser's enterprises to the postwar world. In any event, the poll, which was conducted in fifteen cities, found that more than 75 percent of Ameri-cans responded only positively to Kaiser's name and fewer than 2 percent only negatively. Subsequent polls confirmed Kaiser's enormous popularity. A 1944 poll of newspaper editors would name Kaiser "industrial man of the year" by a wide margin.[19] Although Kaiser Steel would produce only 1 percent of the nation's steel by the end of the war, Kaiser achieved greater name recognition than the chairmen of U.S. Steel and Bethlehem Steel.[20] In responses to the survey question: "Which one person in the steel indus-try do you think of first?" only Andrew Carnegie and Charles Schwab— both dead—outpolled Kaiser.[21] Finally, a 1945 Roper poll would credit Kaiser more than any other civilian (except FDR) with winning the war.[22]

The clout provided by supportive public opinion allowed Kaiser to en-gage in broad-gauged discussions in which his agenda not only brought him access to the president but made him the subject of White House re-quests. At a time when a song entitled "Send for Kaiser" was making the rounds, the White House shared the public's faith that the "can-do" in-dustrialist would get the job done.[23] The president did not have time to meet regularly with one industrialist, no matter how visionary or popular the businessman happened to be.[24] Instead, two lawyers acted as inter-mediaries between Kaiser and Roosevelt: Oscar Cox and Sam Rosenman.

Cox is largely forgotten now—even in Washington—but he was one of the most ingenious, creative, and activist lawyers in Washington and a superb legislative craftsman. As assistant to the general counsel of the Treasury Department, Cox made a name for himself as one of the ad-ministration's most able individuals in finding means to help France and England before Congress endorsed such a policy.[25] When the president

decided to legitimize such assistance with legislation, Cox drafted the Lend-Lease Act of 1941.[26] As general counsel of the Lend-Lease Administration, Cox came into the orbit of Henry Kaiser, who was supplying ships to both European and Asian allies.[27]

Oscar Cox's wartime career in Washington was a testament to the administration's organizational style. Cox simultaneously held a variety of positions and served different bosses. He served simultaneously as general counsel of the Office of Emergency Management, general counsel of the Lend-Lease Administration, and associate solicitor general of the United States. Cox also joined the group Rosenman called upon for assistance in writing the president's speeches.[28]

Rosenman, a longtime friend of Franklin Roosevelt, had been counsel to FDR during his term as New York governor. Rosenman's subsequent election to the New York Supreme Court did not prevent him from writing speeches for Roosevelt in his spare time.[29] Rosenman not only helped frame administration ideas for public consumption but also brought ideas to the White House. As early as 1933, Supreme Court justice Brandeis sought out Rosenman to keep FDR "apprised of his position on the issues." Rosenman did the same for Justice Felix Frankfurter once Tom Corcoran left the government. Frankfurter sent Rosenman memos ranging from brief ideas to "complete drafts for future speeches." Even then, Frankfurter was careful to cover his tracks: after Roosevelt delivered a Frankfurter-drafted speech, "an effusive message" of praise from Frankfurter would arrive the next day on the president's desk.[30] Rosenman was therefore well versed in the boundary-free nature of the New Deal and was an excellent contact for other outsiders, such as Henry Kaiser.

When Roosevelt created the position of White House counsel in September 1943 (a job Roosevelt had considered establishing for Corcoran in the 1930s), Rosenman quit the bench to accept the position.[31] As White House counsel, he became a good friend of both Kaiser and Calhoun, offering them vital advice on how to approach the president. If Kaiser had a proposal for the president—and he had many—Calhoun would first meet with Rosenman, who might offer suggestions on both timing and content. When Rosenman agreed that the time was right, he would suggest which points to emphasize and which to leave out, then would edit Calhoun's formal proposals.[32] This helped align Kaiser's proposals with the president's thinking, which was constantly evolving. Calhoun reciprocated by offering ideas for drafts of the president's speeches, which Rosenman would write.[33] Kaiser's own speeches, which Calhoun helped write, were thus well attuned to those of the administration. One of the most memo-

rable echoed Roosevelt's "Four Freedoms" speech and identified a "Fifth Freedom"—the freedom to produce.[34]

As gatekeeper to the president, Rosenman helped Kaiser's cause in many ways, from helping Calhoun draft a letter from Kaiser to the president regarding a plan to relieve industrial manpower shortages to floating Kaiser's name to the president as a candidate for a commission on absenteeism in war plants.[35] The appearance of Kaiser's name for such a position did not surprise anyone; by early 1943, Kaiser was the role model against which other wartime producers were measured.

Naturally, much of the attention focused on his performance as a shipbuilder. In late March, the American Federation of Labor suggested that Kaiser and Higgins could handle the Maritime Commission's entire building program.[36] In April, Kaiser was offered another platform from which to pontificate on labor relations and shipbuilding. The Special Committee to Investigate the National Defense Program invited Higgins, Kaiser, and two other shipbuilders to Washington. The committee's primary mission was to expose problems or abuses of defense contractors, but this time they wanted the four shipbuilders to reveal their formulas for success.[37] They asked Kaiser to explain "how you have achieved the efficiency you have achieved."[38]

A good example of the ascent of Kaiser's reputation within the government came in the industry that had bedeviled him the most, aircraft. In September 1940, the head of the army air corps had all but thrown Chad Calhoun out of his office for trying to secure aircraft work without prior experience. In early 1943, Kaiser still had never built planes, but he was approached separately by two individuals who asked him to solve an aircraft problem the government was having. An administration whose management of the defense effort had been widely criticized in many circles stood to benefit from association with the nation's greatest home front war hero. Each industry in which this enlightened industrialist participated meant a chance for the administration to influence industry policy such as labor relations. It seemed natural that the administration was calling on him to help solve their problems. The Brewster Aeronautical Corporation on Long Island, on which the government was counting for the production of aircraft, had been plagued by labor problems. Roosevelt ordered the navy to take control of Brewster in April 1942.[39] So in March 1943, as a favor to Under Secretary of the Navy James V. Forrestal, Kaiser took over as chairman of the company.[40]

Cox wrote to Kaiser: "I am sure you will do a bang-up job running Brewster. We need your kind of imagination, drive, and concept of the

public interest in the aircraft field for the war and after."[41] Neither Cox nor the navy people now seemed concerned about Kaiser's lack of experience in producing aircraft. By October, when little progress had been made at Brewster, congressional hearings were called. Kaiser subsequently turned things around, increasing production from 14 planes in October to 123 in April 1944; the navy assumed management of the plant in May.[42]

By then, Kaiser's name was a household word at 1600 Pennsylvania Avenue. If ideas or support were needed from the business community, Kaiser got the call.[43] When Navy Secretary Frank Knox died in late April, Under Secretary Forrestal became acting secretary.[44] A week later, Cox mentioned Kaiser to Rosenman as a possible successor. Rosenman said the same idea had occurred to him. Rumors began to fly that Forrestal, whose term as acting secretary would last until the end of May, would be replaced by a "practical" shipbuilder such as Kaiser or Higgins. Within a week, Cox had drafted a memo to Rosenman, urging the selection of Kaiser for navy secretary. Cox cited Kaiser's "energy and vitality" and noted that "he has also captured the imagination of the American public—particularly the younger people—by doing the kind of things that most people said were impossible."[45]

In an election year, White House decisions are often shaped by dictates of the campaign, and Cox's memo indicates that 1944 was no exception: "In the coming election California—as in prior elections—is likely to be a key state. [Kaiser] has more than 100,000 workers in his plants in California. Most of them think very highly of him. He also rates well in Oregon and Washington [where Kaiser also had shipyards]."[46] Roosevelt named Forrestal as Knox's permanent successor a week later, but that did not mean he disagreed with Cox's assessment of Kaiser.[47] It took the president little time to consider Kaiser for a position that would capitalize on his potential electoral pull.

On May 22, Roosevelt's cousin and confidante Margaret Suckley asked if he had chosen a running mate for the upcoming campaign. Suckley's diary includes Roosevelt's response and the ensuing discussion:

"I haven't even decided if I will run myself."

"What is going to decide you? For you are practically nominated already."

"What will decide me, will be the way I feel in a couple of months. If I know I am not going to be able to carry on for another four years, it wouldn't be fair to the American people to run for another term."

"But who else is there?"

"I *have* a candidate—but don't breathe it to a soul—there is a man, not a politician, who, I think, I could persuade the country to elect. There would be such a gasp when his name was suggested, that I believe he would have a good chance if he were 'sold' to the country in the right way!"

I did gasp a little when he mentioned the name of Henry J. Kaiser. As the P. says, it was a sudden thought on his part, but the more he thinks about it, the more he sees in it. Henry J. Kaiser has proved himself a genius in production. The P. thinks he can learn where he is ignorant & without experience, such as politics, dealing with Congress, International affairs, etc.

I asked *how* he would get on with the Churchills, Stalins, etc.

The P. said: "He's more like them than I am."

The P. didn't answer that. A little later he said he thought Mr. Kaiser would ask his teaching & guidance in dealing with other nations. Perhaps he is right—he usually is, and perhaps Mr. Kaiser is just the sort of dynamic person the country needs at the present time, *if* the P. does not feel up to going on with the job.[48]

We now know that nothing came of this discussion, but that does not diminish its significance. The president had a reputation for adopting the point of view—or appearing to—of the person(s) with whom he had most recently spoken, and it had been only four days since he had last seen Kaiser.[49] Yet this may be the only surviving record of Roosevelt discussing a possible successor in 1944.[50] Although we can only speculate about how Kaiser would have responded to such a proposal, it is fair to say that any campaign by the president to "sell" Kaiser to the public would have been little different from the efforts performed on Kaiser's behalf the previous two years by the national media.

Not long after the discussion with Margaret Suckley, Roosevelt made known his plans to run for a fourth term, at which point Sam Rosenman pushed Henry Kaiser for the vice presidency. As early as April 1944, the administration was considering possible running mates for Roosevelt and had even sent up Kaiser's name as a trial balloon.[51] In June, Roosevelt was serious enough about a Kaiser candidacy that he directed Rosenman to obtain an FBI report on the industrialist. The president wanted to "find out all we can about Henry Kaiser. . . . What he's said in his speeches, his family life, whether he's belonged to any cults."[52] Kaiser's speeches, written by Calhoun and economist Paul Cadman, proved sufficiently liberal for the president's taste—with one exception. Before a group of St.

Louis bankers, Kaiser had urged a 10 percent sales tax. Unions would not like such a regressive tax, noted Roosevelt, who asked Rosenman, "What the hell did he go and say that for?"[53] Rosenman reminded the president that he had committed a similar gaffe years before: "For the same reason you advocated a 25 percent reduction in government spending in your 1932 Pittsburgh speech."[54] The FBI found nothing that might discredit Kaiser any more than that speech.

The FBI report actually revealed so little that Sam Rosenman attached to Roosevelt's copy of the report the 1943 *Fortune* articles that had provoked Kaiser's explosion. Rosenman wrote to Roosevelt that the articles "give a pretty clear picture of what [Kaiser] does."[55] Here was more evidence of the role Henry Luce's publications played in the Kaiser saga. The Luce press version of events came to be accepted as gospel at the highest levels of government. When seeking information about Japan during the war, the Office of Strategic Services (forerunner of today's Central Intelligence Agency) obtained permission from *Fortune*'s managing editor to debrief Time, Inc., staffers who had contributed to a special *Fortune* issue devoted to Japan. Although there was considerable friction between Luce and Roosevelt, Rosenman had become accustomed to passing *Fortune* material on to the president. *Fortune* had, after all, gained considerable credibility at the White House during the 1936 campaign. A poll by *Literary Digest*, one of *Time*'s principal newsmagazine competitors, indicated that Republican challenger Alf Landon would beat Roosevelt. Meanwhile, *Fortune*'s Roper poll had accurately predicted the Roosevelt landslide. Roosevelt, who was fascinated by the possibilities presented by new polling techniques, had Rosenman provide him with advance copies of subsequent Roper surveys.[56]

When Harold Ickes, an old Kaiser supporter, learned that the westerner had made Roosevelt's short list, he called it "a strange political fish to appear on the platter." According to Ickes, a onetime ally did in Kaiser's chances. At an Oval Office meeting days before the Democratic National Convention, Tom Corcoran mentioned rumors that Kaiser was a Jew. It is not clear where such rumors originated, but they may have come from Nazi propaganda. In May 1943, the German newspaper *Voelkischer Boebachter*, following up on criticisms of Kaiser by Radio Rome in 1942, had referred to "the Jewish shipbuilder Kaiser."[57] Rosenman, still in Kaiser's corner, was thrust into an awkward situation. Despite being one of the Jews in Roosevelt's inner circle, Rosenman had to defend Kaiser's selection by pointing out that the industrialist was not Jewish. Nonetheless,

Kaiser's case for the vice presidency went no further.[58] Rosenman later sighed, "If only we had pushed just a bit harder."[59]

Kaiser's association with politics in 1944 was not limited, however, to the Kaiser for President clubs early in the year and the vice presidential machinations before the July Democratic convention. His most visible and significant activity did not involve running for office. Kaiser chaired a nationwide get-out-the-vote effort called the Nonpartisan Association for Franchise Education. The association's—and Kaiser's—involvement are forgotten aspects of the 1944 campaign, but they bear close examination both because of the White House's behavior toward them and because of the significance of voter turnout in the election's outcome. Attempts to get out the vote (by a Democratic congress, by the CIO, and by the association) rank with the president's health and the disappearance of Wendell Willkie from presidential politics as the big stories of the 1944 campaign. These issues were not independent of one another: the end of the Willkie candidacy was the association's genesis.

Wendell Willkie's candidacy for president represented the high tide of liberal Republicanism in the twentieth century. Since his 1940 defeat, Willkie had published the influential 1943 book *One World*, which was an attempt to bury isolationism. Whereas internationalism in 1940 meant a willingness to intervene in the European conflict, in 1944 it meant an effort to create a body to promote international peace. Despite the boost to his presidential hopes provided by the book, in 1944 the Willkie race ended much more quickly than in 1940. Willkie declared his candidacy in mid-February and pulled out of the race the first week of April. Willkie's Waterloo was Wisconsin, where he finished a disappointing fourth behind New York governor Thomas Dewey, Minnesota governor Harold Stassen, and General Douglas MacArthur; only Willkie failed to gain a single Wisconsin delegate to the convention.[60]

Just as Time/Life had been instrumental in lining up the opposition for Roosevelt in 1940, now its postmortems on Willkie helped shape the 1944 general election in a way that would benefit the president. On May 29, *Time* angrily reported that low voter turnouts in the primaries were sabotaging the political system. Voter turnout had plunged since 1940 to record lows in the 1944 presidential primaries. An article entitled "Government by Default" noted that in New Jersey, with the exception of one county, only 15 percent of those eligible actually voted. Then *Time* vented about the real disaster: "Even in the Wisconsin primary, when Wendell Willkie staked his Presidential chances on the outcome, only 33 percent of

the qualified bothered to vote. Forty years ago reformers crusaded for primaries in the confidence that they would 'take Government out of the hands of the politicians and return it to the people.' Now a politician could rightly say that the people didn't seem to care."[61] And the people lost Willkie, *Time*'s onetime choice as best man for the job.

Getting out the vote was a much larger issue in 1944 than in the usual election year. The 1944 election, after all, would be America's first national election during wartime since the Civil War. Even democracies do not always run the risk of conducting a national election during wartime; England, for instance, suspended elections during the war. So America's 1944 election carried worldwide significance, and high voter turnout might send a symbolic message to both America's allies and opponents about democracy in action.

In politics, the transcendent concerns are accompanied by questions of self-interest. In addition to any international impact, high voter turnout in America would help one political party (the Democrats) more than the other. Get-out-the-vote efforts usually bubble up a cauldron of spirits, from the patriotic to the political. One is the issue of race. That is why, after Democrats in Congress proposed a bill in September 1943 to allow civilian war workers and servicemen and servicewomen overseas to vote in the 1944 election, the National Negro Congress urged defeat of such a bill unless Negro ballots were assured in poll-tax states. Southern Democrats were not enthusiastic about get-out-the-vote efforts, which might increase black voting.[62] Debate over this bill was the most widely covered issue on the home front in the two months before the Wisconsin primary.

The Gallup poll concluded that the soldier vote could decide the 1944 election, and many sources estimated that the Democrats would get 70 percent of servicemen's votes.[63] Roosevelt, of course, supported this bill.

In January, before announcing his candidacy, Willkie endorsed the "soldier voter" also.[64] At any rate, Willkie aligned with the president—and against conservative members of his own party—on this issue, as he had on many others. This foreshadowed efforts by the two to establish a liberal party. A states'-rights offensive of southern Democrats and conservative Republicans managed to revise the measure substantially, so Roosevelt allowed the watered-down bill to become law without his signature just before Willkie's departure from the race.[65]

After the Wisconsin primary, a group of erstwhile Willkie supporters formed the Committee on Voting, which sought to increase voter turnout. The committee included Frank Graham, president of the University of

North Carolina; syndicated columnist Raymond Gram Swing; Representative Joseph Clark Baldwin; and Jean Macauley.[66] The founders argued that while American troops were fighting for democracy and majority rule overseas, it would be embarrassing and disheartening for America to produce less than a majority vote in the 1944 general election.

As is often true of presidential politics, the manner in which the committee chose a leader proved more revealing about the political climate of the time—and the priorities of the White House—than anything Henry Kaiser later did as chairman. On June 8, the group—which had renamed itself the Nonpartisan Association for Franchise Education, Inc., to help achieve status as a nonprofit organization—invited Kaiser to serve as national chairman.[67] This was not a cold call; Macauley had become acquainted with Kaiser when they worked together to create the United Seaman's Service in the fall of 1942.[68] The position of chairman would be largely symbolic; Kaiser's name was expected to attract money to the organization even without his day-to-day involvement. Nevertheless, Kaiser turned them down.[69]

Four days later, on June 14, Macauley tried again. She pointed out that demands on Kaiser's time would be minimal because daily responsibilities would be in the hands of executive director Randolph Feltus, a public relations man from New Orleans. She wrote that they sought "someone who is not identified with partisan politics, who commands public response, and whose name and accomplishments are such as to catch the imagination of the American people." She concluded that Kaiser should recognize that he was "the only man in the country who meets these requirements."[70] Feltus followed up with a letter of his own, describing the gravity of the voting problem. He cited the May 29 *Time* article about declining voter turnout. Despite this second set of pleas, Kaiser turned them down again.[71]

The same day that Feltus wrote to Kaiser, he also enlisted the support of Palmer Hoyt, the *Portland Oregonian* publisher, who had helped vault Kaiser into the public eye in July 1942.[72] Hoyt, who in January had resigned as Office of War Information domestic operations director, wrote Kaiser that he had "just talked to Leon Henderson, [Supreme Court justice William] Douglas, and Mrs. Macauley. . . . This is purely honorary and obviously worthwhile. . . . Use further consideration before refusal."[73] While trying to convince Kaiser to serve, Hoyt was not setting an example: he refused Feltus's request that he serve on the association's board.[74] Kaiser declined Hoyt's invitation, but it is likely that Hoyt convinced him to reconsider before sending his regrets to Macauley.[75] After conferring with

Cadman and Chad Calhoun—who advised against it—Kaiser made his decision.[76] On July 11, Randolph Feltus sent a deflated message to Macauley: "Kaiser has just declined finally. Funds still slow."[77]

As he did with most of the avalanche of requests he received by now, Kaiser cited other commitments and demands on his time as reasons to decline. If he was also trying to avoid involvement in partisan politics, Kaiser had—for the time being, anyway—dodged a bullet. The same day that Hoyt had written to Kaiser, June 27, Randolph Feltus had sent a copy of the association's prospectus to journalist Herbert Bayard Swope. Feltus described the association's nonpartisan "object and approach." He then reminded Swope that "the Democratic National Committee is quite interested in the matter because they feel that a large vote will inure to the benefit of the Democratic candidates in the November election." After enticing Swope with such bait, Feltus insisted that his main motivation in meeting with Swope the next day was "principally to get your advice on securing persons on both sides of the political fence for membership on our National Committee."[78]

Feltus had made a more direct appeal for partisan reaction a few days earlier, in approaching Chicago businessman John J. Mack: "Inasmuch as the prospectus is pitched in rather high-flown nonpartisan terms, you might tell your friends who are pro-Roosevelt that any votes over forty million will go to the President by about 75–85 percent. The statistics of recent elections support this. Also, the greatest curtailment in voting is among younger people (armed forces) and migratory voters. Both groups are largely pro-Roosevelt. If we can get soldiers and workers, and the families of both groups to register and vote, the Democrats will benefit."[79]

Feltus's appeal to Mack was not the usual form letter: "Of course, this story would not be told to anti-Roosevelt people. They can be appealed to on the basis of the dangers to democracy inherent in a declining vote rate. This, of course, is a very real reason for bestirring ourselves. Majority vote calls for exercise of the voting franchise by a majority of the people. The person who fails to vote is letting down the boys who are fighting and dying to preserve democracy."[80]

Feltus and the association were asking opponents of Roosevelt to act on high-minded ideals, while providing an opportunity for supporters of Roosevelt to act based on political instinct. Naturally, the pro-Roosevelt forces were glad to help. Finding conservatives to support get-out-the-vote initiatives has traditionally been difficult, and for Randolph Feltus it proved a supreme challenge in the summer of 1944, as demonstrated in Feltus's approach to Leon Henderson. Feltus sent Henderson a prospectus,

then followed up with a plea: "A word from you to a few prominent persons, preferably conservative, would help immeasurably in securing names for the national committee and in getting the necessary funds."[81]

What motivated Roosevelt's opponents to participate? After Wendell Willkie's Wisconsin debacle, a question lingered: if 50 percent of the people in Wisconsin had voted, would Willkie have gone on to win the nomination? Just as American politicians and armed forces often seem to be fighting the last war, three months after the fact the association may have been fighting the Wisconsin primary over again. It is probably no coincidence that the law firm used by the association was Willkie, Owen, Farr and Gallagher.[82]

Regardless of their motives, Republicans who supported the association were helping the Democrats' cause. The Democrats could not have dreamed up a better scenario: to have their opponents do some of their work for them. If the association had not come along, the Democrats would have had to help create it. In fact, a memorandum in the papers of the association suggests that the Democrats may have done just that. Dated April 10, 1944 (only five days after Willkie's departure from the race for the Republican nomination), the memo entitled "Gallup Vote Total 1944 Predictions and Deductions" is in a folder titled "material for writers" and appears to have been used by Randolph Feltus throughout the summer.[83]

The memorandum includes the principal piece of information that seems to have been common knowledge in the Roosevelt campaign, but which the association avoided mentioning when recruiting Willkie sympathizers and more conservative Republicans: "[Pollster George] Gallup has told Dewey that he ought to win the election on a maximum [voter turnout of] forty million. . . . All good political analysts will agree that Roosevelt is progressively helped by every million votes above forty million."[84] The goal of substantially exceeding the forty million threshold was a key component of the association's approach to Roosevelt sympathizers.

The memorandum was clearly conceived by someone who wanted to use Wendell Willkie's departure from the campaign work to the political advantage of the president: "SUGGESTION: Some progressive group should be headed by a Willkie, a Norris, or Eugene Meyer, called 'Votes for Victory.' It is possible [William T.] Evjue, the Madison, Wisconsin publisher who has lost Willkie and controls the Progressive sentiment of Wisconsin, might be a western Committeeman. . . . The radio division of publicity should be headed up by George Fielding Eliot, who at the present time is President of the Radio Broadcasters, who is a personal friend of Willkie,

and who works for Mrs. Ogden Reid, and has a large newspaper syndicate as well as a radio audience."[85]

Indeed, the association approached a paragon of Wisconsin Progressive sentiment, in fact its rightful heir, Senator Robert LaFollette Jr. LaFollette's father had been the state's principal figure in the Progressive movement and had run for the presidency in 1924. Feltus wrote to LaFollette, "Believe it or not, we are keeping it strictly nonpartisan and people of widely divergent political views are finding in it a common ground." Feltus then reminded LaFollette that Wisconsin voters seemed to be neither thinking globally nor acting locally: "In your own state, according to *Time* magazine, less than a third of the registered voters went to the polls in the recent 'Willkie primary.'"[86]

The April memorandum's author also realized that involving Willkie supporters would keep the Democrats' fingerprints off the project: "The majority of front names should include few New Dealers and a minority of Democrats. . . . The work cannot be done by the Democratic National Committee; by the [Sidney] Hillman [CIO Political Action] Committee; or by any other selfish group. . . . The idea should be started by an independent or progressive middle sized guy and should never contact [Robert] Hannegan [chairman of the Democratic National Committee] or Hillman."[87]

What was the sense of urgency? "Unless there is a real crusade working through the women and the preachers and the liberal publications [most publishers opposed Roosevelt], the efforts of the Democratic Party and the Hillman Committee will be found 'too little, too late.'"[88]

The memorandum also offered ideas on how to interest as broad a spectrum of voters as possible in a project sure to help the president's reelection chances: "A 'Votes for Victory' or any other 'Get out the vote' organization must start immediately, be entirely nonpartisan, and be designed to have every mother, father, brother and sister, of every soldier vote for the absent one. The big appeal is that the soldier has been robbed of his vote and has to depend on the people at home to vote for him. One slogan could be 'Register and Vote as your Soldier Believes.'" Another proposed slogan was "Work, Fight, Vote."[89]

As for the role of the president,

> Roosevelt might, two weeks before anything else happens, as President of the United States, speak briefly in a general Fire Side Chat on the condition of the nation and put in there two strong paragraphs on the duty of all to vote regardless of whom they vote for and carry it

down to the voting for Sheriffs and Judges and Governors. The idea, of course, of any Roosevelt statement would be that we must keep clean Government no matter how they vote, and that clean government beginning in the precinct, in the County, in the State, with the myriad of government officials—that is, not confined to Washington and the Federal Government. This to give a States Rights flavor and to take the broad appeal from the candidate Roosevelt. Then Roosevelt should never again speak of the matter or entertain any delegations or individuals who are connected with getting the vote.[90]

This was not the first attempt to exploit the wartime hothouse of patriotism (or desire for peace) for political gain, but it is among the most clearly thought-out and articulated blueprints for the benefit of (although not necessarily at the behest of) a sitting president.

Throughout the summer, executive director Randolph Feltus and the association apparently followed this blueprint. A majority of the people making major commitments to the association were onetime Willkie supporters, and very few Democrats or New Dealers played visible roles. Meanwhile, the principal beneficiary of the association's efforts, President Roosevelt, kept a safe distance from the association.

None of this would matter, however, without the right chairman, and Feltus expressed his frustration at the association's inability to line up the man they wanted: "Henry Kaiser let us down after being carefully primed and pressured by such experts as Leon Henderson, Palmer Hoyt, Justice Douglas, Mrs. Macauley and others. This took time and we were encouraged almost daily."[91]

The plot thickened considerably, however, in July. For one of the few times in his career, after Kaiser abandoned an enterprise things became considerably more interesting. On July 13, Feltus met with Wendell Willkie and offered him the chairmanship of the association: not a bad second choice for a group of disappointed Willkie supporters. Presumably Willkie had not been first choice for chairman because of the association's decision "to have no candidates for office on the Board of Directors of the organization after it was formally organized."[92] In addition, despite his embarrassing defeat in Wisconsin, Willkie and his supporters may have still entertained hopes that the Republican convention in late June would deadlock, then come to him. That did not happen, and the nominee was New York governor Thomas Dewey, for whom Willkie had utter contempt. Willkie turned Feltus down but promised to give Feltus "entrée to several Republicans."[93]

Feltus had no way of knowing that over the previous three weeks, Willkie himself had sought entrée to the leading Democrat: President Roosevelt. Convinced that the alignment of Republican conservatives with Governor Dewey had cost him the 1944 nomination, Willkie approached Gifford Pinchot, onetime governor of Pennsylvania, with a daring idea. Willkie would lead the liberal wing of the Republican Party into alliance with the liberal Democrats, creating a new political party. Presumably the conservatives from each party would subsequently join together.[94]

Roosevelt saw sufficient promise in the idea that he sent White House counsel Sam Rosenman to meet Willkie at the St. Regis Hotel in New York City on July 5. Willkie was so concerned about being seen with a Roosevelt envoy—and recognized—that when room service brought lunch, he ducked into a bedroom, out of view. Willkie told Rosenman that the "proper time" to pursue the idea would be after the election. Roosevelt, however, could not wait, and he sent a letter inviting Willkie to visit either the White House or Hyde Park.[95] This was on July 13, the same day Willkie met with Feltus.

The contents of the letter were leaked to the press, and when reporters asked the president about it in late August, he denied having written such a letter. Angered by the president's denial, Willkie's friends threatened to publish the letter. Roosevelt wrote Willkie again, attempting to explain the awkward situation and inviting Willkie to visit. Willkie did not follow up; he did not want to muddy the idea with current-year campaign concerns. Instead, he wanted to wait until after the election. The two never did meet to discuss party realignment; Willkie died of a heart attack in October. This episode shows that the White House was ever conscious of the consequences of Willkie's departure from the campaign and was ever poised to make the most of the opportunities to win over disaffected Willkie supporters in the general election.

When Randolph Feltus left Wendell Willkie's office on July 13, prospects for the association looked dim. The next day he wrote to Randolph Paul, who had just retired as general counsel of the Treasury Department.[96] Calling it a report of "progress and lack of progress," Feltus wrote: "I have seen just about everybody in New York and have degenerated into a medium-, and sometimes high-pressure money raiser. Results are not too good so far, but there are many promises. The next ten days will tell the story."[97] The next ten days brought little cause for hope of finding the right chairman, nor did the next twenty after that.

Jean Macauley, who in June had been so firm about barring elected officials from the association's board, now appeared ready to open the door to

that possibility. She suggested that Randolph Feltus follow up on Palmer Hoyt's suggestion of California governor Earl Warren for chairman.[98] Warren was an elected official and a Republican. Macauley's convictions were not tested further, however: nothing came of the Warren idea.

Meanwhile, a form letter was worked up for the association, mentioning those already willing to serve on the national committee. Listed were founders Raymond Gram Swing and Frank Graham, along with George Fielding Eliot, the president of the Radio Broadcasters Association—and Willkie friend—mentioned in the April 10 memorandum, and various luminaries, including Andrew Jackson Higgins.[99] Higgins did not last; he ended up head of Businessmen for Roosevelt, which was more in keeping with his family's tradition of loyalty to the Democratic Party than a "nonpartisan" group would be.[100]

When the association still could not find a chairman by August 8, desperation began to set in. Owen Young, onetime head of General Electric, turned them down "after careful preparation and well planned attack." Feltus informed Macauley: "Another long maneuver has been begun. I fear it will end the same way. . . . I have the usual quota of good promises and high hopes from everyone interested, but no real money and no chairman. Everybody seems to have contacted everybody else, with no result."[101]

Feltus was also clearly dissatisfied with his own role: "I never professed to be a money-raiser, nor did I claim to have the magnetism which would attract a large group of conservative dignitaries to a national committee. . . . I am a public relations man, and that was what this job was supposed to require. . . . If one of the long maneuvers succeeds, or some of the high hopes are realized, so much the better. I, however, will believe it when I see it; not before." Yet embedded in this letter was the ultimate solution to his problem: "As I have maintained repeatedly, the only way to get the kind of conservative chairman we need and the funds necessary to do the job, is to have orders come from the Great White Father."[102] That is just where the crucial orders would come from less than two weeks later.

On August 20, one of the president's secretaries called Kaiser, asking him to fly from Oakland to Hyde Park right away.[103] Kaiser rarely flew; instead, he usually took the train cross-country. For him to change his habits in August 1944 was special: the commander in chief was calling, and there was no time to waste.

Kaiser asked Calhoun to find out what the meeting was about, and Calhoun in turn called Cox. Cox believed Roosevelt was about to offer Kaiser the job as director of Office of War Mobilization and Reconversion (OWMR); he expected incumbent James Byrnes to resign.[104] (Cox turned

out to be wrong on both counts: Byrnes stayed on until April 1945).[105] Cox called Rosenman, who then spoke to Kaiser. Rosenman had just visited Kaiser on the West Coast at the beginning of the month as part of the president's visit to Pearl Harbor.[106] He told Kaiser he did not know why the president wanted to see him.[107] Meanwhile, another of Roosevelt's secretaries called Rosenman, saying that the president wanted to know what he was supposed to talk to Kaiser about. Kaiser and his wife landed in New York at 4:00 P.M., then drove up to Hyde Park. Meanwhile, Roosevelt sent an army plane to fly Rosenman from Washington to West Point so he could arrive in time to tell the president what to say to Kaiser over dinner.[108]

Roosevelt was a sick man in August 1944, but it is hard to imagine him fretting about dinner conversation unless a potentially delicate situation loomed. If the president had invited Kaiser to Hyde Park but did not want personally to invite him to accept chairmanship of the Nonpartisan Association, he *would* need Rosenman's counsel on how to proceed.

The evening of the twenty-first was pleasant—Mrs. Kaiser was charmed by the president—if apparently not as substantive as the urgent arrangements and "off the record" nature had suggested.[109] Even though he had been called on short notice and flown across the country for a particular reason, Kaiser, as was his custom, broached his own set of issues over dinner, ranging from employment to transportation to housing to medical care. An observer who did not know better might have been surprised to learn that Kaiser was not the one who had called for this meeting. Yet the only request made of Kaiser came from the First Lady. Eleanor Roosevelt asked Kaiser if he would head up the Nonpartisan Association for Franchise Education. The president may have asked Rosenman what to talk about because he knew he had to delegate the principal business at hand to avoid injecting "partisan" politics into the "nonpartisan" association.

Kaiser did not give an immediate answer. In fact, he rode to his New York office the next day and composed a letter to Mrs. Roosevelt. Kaiser began by acknowledging her request: "I, too, am concerned about getting out the vote, and I am going to talk to some of the other people who are interested in it. I will let Sam know shortly whether I think a job can be done and whether I can do it." Kaiser was more interested, however, in the proposals he had made that evening: "On the more important things which we talked about last night, we have drafted a tentative program of which I am sending you a copy. Sam is going to discuss them with the President, and I know you will be interested in helping us get these issues

before Congress and the people. The intense concern which you exhibited last night encouraged me to send this to you and to enlist your help."[110] Kaiser had the good sense to substitute "other important things" for "more important things" in the final draft.

Rosenman then rode back to Washington with Kaiser, spending the whole time talking about the Nonpartisan Association, not Kaiser's proposals.[111] What could Kaiser do? He obviously did not want to head this association, but the request came from the head of his only customer of consequence—the federal government. Kaiser finally bowed to the president's wishes. Three days after meeting with the president, Kaiser sent off the first of a series of letters enlisting the support of luminaries such as David Selznick, Charles Evans Hughes, John J. Pershing, and Henry Luce: "I have agreed to accept the chairmanship of the Nonpartisan Association for Franchise Education."[112]

Although the April 10 blueprint called for no presidential involvement, when the association had involved the president as a last resort the request was skillfully made—and not by the president. The urgent request that Kaiser fly cross-country provided sufficient gravity that Kaiser responded (after having turned down the association three times before) as the president might expect a citizen to do when given an order by the commander in chief.

Who notified the president that the association needed his help? The historical record allows no definitive answer. One possibility is Leon Henderson. After leaving the Office of Price Administration in 1943, Henderson was without portfolio. In June and July 1944 he recruited Kaiser for the association, then in the fall headed the pro-Roosevelt National Committee of Independent Voters. Henderson visited with Roosevelt in July and left long notes about the president's deteriorating physical condition. There is no reason to believe Henderson did not tell the president about the association then, that is, if the president did not already know.

Another possibility is Tom Corcoran, one of the most savvy political advisers the president ever had. Corcoran's first activity after leaving government service in 1940, after all, had been on behalf of the National Committee of Independent Voters for Roosevelt and Wallace.[113] Corcoran had subsequently kept his hand in and had played a role in the vice presidential selection process earlier in the summer. Furthermore, like Henderson, he had been sent one of the association's prospectuses.[114]

The most likely messenger, however, was Jean Macauley's husband, Captain Edward Macauley of the U.S. Maritime Commission.[115] Captain Macauley was an old friend of the president. He had served as FDR's chief

of staff on a 1918 European inspection trip, and Roosevelt subsequently kept in touch with "Eddie."[116] Macauley was also a Democrat.[117]

Kaiser was quick to put his own stamp on the association, naming Chad Calhoun as treasurer.[118] The association also switched from Willkie's law firm to one Kaiser had worked with: Root, Clark, Buckner and Ballantine.[119] Marshall Skadden of Root, Clark lobbied successfully to become secretary of the association.[120] At the association's first meeting, on September 20, the ever-enthusiastic Kaiser proposed assessing fines against all people who do not vote, based on the Australian model.[121] That same day Kaiser completed the circle begun a month earlier at Hyde Park. He sent Roosevelt a request for "a short statement giving your views on the importance of exercising the franchise this year." This was pro forma: Kaiser sent similar notes to Governor Dewey and to vice presidential nominees Harry Truman and John Bricker. Kaiser noted, "The views of both the Presidential and Vice Presidential candidates will be used on a patriotic nonpartisan basis." The goal was for America to set an example for the world by "exercising the fundamental right for which they fight."[122] He did not mention the Australian plan.

Many interpreted Kaiser's involvement, or the group's mission, as anything but nonpartisan. White House enthusiasm for the project alone might be sufficient to raise such doubts, as would Oscar Cox's providing Kaiser with information to help promote the association's mission.[123] Even better evidence was the reaction of some of Kaiser's other friends. In mid-September, Mrs. Ogden Reid (wife of the publisher of the *New York Herald Tribune*) wrote to Kaiser: "Some one told me that you are organizing a drive for the president." This was not a disinterested observation: Mrs. Reid and the *Tribune* had a history of supporting Republican causes. She had called Wendell Willkie's 1940 candidacy "heaven's gift." Now she wrote, "The news made me a bit sick for, in spite of our not having been able to get the man about whom you and I were enthusiastic [Willkie], I firmly believe that the present administration should be eliminated from office."[124] Kaiser must have done a good job of answering her concerns because she accepted a position on the association's national committee a few days later, joining her employee George Fielding Eliot.[125]

By now, the association had a strong cast of onetime Willkie supporters. One member of the national committee, advertising executive Albert D. Lasker, was one of Willkie's closest friends—and onetime assistant chair of the Republican National Committee—and had been a fund-raiser in the 1940 campaign.[126] Gardner Cowles Jr. was another. Cowles was publisher of the *Minneapolis Star*, the *Minneapolis Tribune*, and the *Des Moines*

Register. Cowles also published *Look*, the principal competitor of Luce's *Life*, and was introduced to Willkie in 1940 by Russell Davenport, a *Fortune* editor.[127] Willkie's lieutenant and speechwriter Bartley Crum also helped out.[128]

Many political analysts attribute Willkie's rocketlike ascent in 1940 to his support from the press, and Willkie biographer Ellsworth Barnard singles out a handful of publishers in particular. Among the publishers of those magazines and newspapers, Henry Luce, Gardner Cowles Jr., and Mrs. Ogden Reid all substantially supported the association.[129]

Mrs. Reid's concerns about Kaiser's role in the campaign came to pass nine days later. Roosevelt formally kicked off his reelection campaign at a Teamsters dinner, delivering what many experts consider the greatest political speech of his career.[130] Roosevelt attacked the Republicans throughout: "The whole purpose of Republican oratory these days seems to be to switch labels. The object is to persuade the American people that the Democratic Party was responsible for the 1929 crash and the depression, and that the Republican Party was responsible for all social progress under the New Deal." Then, aligning himself with the Willkie faction, Roosevelt continued: "Of course, it is perfectly true that there are enlightened, liberal elements in the Republican Party, and they have fought hard and honorably to bring the Party up to date and to get it in step with the forward march of American progress. . . . But these liberal elements were not able to drive the Old Guard Republicans from their entrenched positions. Can the Old Guard pass itself off as the New Deal? I think not." Finally, Roosevelt responded to accusations that he had sent a destroyer to look for his dog at taxpayer expense: "The Republican leaders have not been content with attacks on me, or my wife, or on my sons. No, not content with that, they now include my little dog, Fala."[131]

Roosevelt's effort to "deliberately stir up the mud" was in recognition that voter apathy would work in favor of his opponent. Roosevelt may have been inclined to give such a speech toward the end of the campaign, but he needed to strike early because voter registration would end in mid-October in many states.[132] This was as political and partisan as it gets, and who was photographed sitting at the dais with the president? Henry Kaiser, chairman of the Nonpartisan Association for Franchise Education. That alone would have been a sufficient problem for Kaiser if the president had stuck to his text—but he did not.

One of the president's habits, which kept his advisers and speechwriters on edge, was to ad-lib during major addresses. Their concerns that he might get "off message" were similar to those of staffers to the twenti-

eth century's other "Great Communicator" in the White House, Ronald Reagan. Harry Hopkins, Robert Sherwood, and Sam Rosenman organized "The Society for the Prevention of Ad-Libbing."[133] The creators of the Nonpartisan Association came to regret the society's failure on this point: after acknowledging labor's achievement in helping produce nineteen thousand tons of cargo ships per year, Roosevelt turned to Kaiser and ad-libbed, "and Henry Kaiser is here tonight, I am glad to say."[134] This statement was particularly difficult to ignore. Broadcast of the speech attracted more than 82 percent of the total radio audience.[135] Such attention for their chairman at a partisan political event is not what the creators of the Nonpartisan Association had in mind.

Kaiser demonstrated some genuine naiveté if he expected to maintain a nonpartisan reputation while attending this—or any—labor union event. The president had announced in late August his intention to make a speech that "might have a tinge of politics" at the Teamsters dinner.[136] Kaiser had been invited to the dinner by Teamsters president Daniel Tobin, not Roosevelt, and was probably surprised to be singled out by the president. But Kaiser, the old professional photographer, should have expected that if he were a mere two seats from the president, that would make a good "shot" for the wire services.

Some of Kaiser's supporters responded with disappointment. Mrs. Irving Gates sent Kaiser a blunt critique: "The question is arising here among many of us [in Kirkwood, Washington] concerning your Nonpartisan Fund. I volunteered to ask you. Can you be nonpartisan when only last week, photos are printed from coast to coast, of you cheering in the company of the New Deal, C.I.O., P.A.C., et al., or are you planning a similar picture with the other party? All we have previously learned of you has led us to believe you are honest and a 100 percent straight shooter."[137]

Maury Maverick, head of the Smaller War Plants Corporation and unapologetic New Dealer, was delighted. He could not resist teasing Kaiser about the Teamsters dinner. Maverick had received one of Kaiser's fundraising letters and now responded: "Herewith $1.00—I wish I had $25,000 —and this is for you personally and to pay you for the smile you had the other night at the Teamsters Union meeting. In reply to your letter about the nonpartisan business, I want you to know I am with you 100%— 1,000,000%—and in the strictly nonpartisan way that you are. Yes, sir! I am nonpartisan, *just like you*. Also, I am going to do everything I can everywhere to get our people to vote—in the same nonpartisan way as you are going to do." Maverick then dug the needle in deeper: "Please do not waste this $1.00. This is no time for waste, but if you will just continue

that nonpartisan smile, we can get a lot of people to register and vote, and I hope to Christ they vote right." Maverick signed as "Your nonpartisan friend."[138]

Palmer Hoyt was not amused. He wrote Kaiser a blistering letter: "It seems to me that our Nonpartisan Association is taking a very bad slant for Mr. Roosevelt [including] [y]our presence at the Tobin dinner which was mentioned in Mr. Roosevelt's speech and in wire photos sent all over the country." Hoyt then pointed out what everyone else knew: "Pro-Roosevelt commentators such as Marquis Childs have repeatedly made the point that an increased vote adds insurance to Roosevelt's election." Hoyt then noted, "It is very important that the organization assume its proper nonpartisan position in the eyes of America proper. I think it is important to everyone, but particularly to Henry J. Kaiser." Hoyt suggested that the association give equal attention to "the conservative side." Hoyt also addressed himself to Kaiser, proposing to arrange for Kaiser to appear at a Dewey meeting "preferably with Dewey as speaker, and there be photographed." Finally, he suggested that Kaiser hold a press conference to "differentiate between the purposes of the Association and the C.I.O. PAC—with which it is sadly confused."[139] As an indication of the level of concern in Republican circles, Hoyt sent a copy of the letter to Herbert Brownell, chairman of the Republican National Committee.

Kaiser's response was defensive, reminding Hoyt that he was "responsible for getting me into this thing."[140] Though he agreed to appear with Dewey, that photo opportunity never took place.

It is not clear which hurt Kaiser more, the amusement and anger of his friends or the slings and arrows of his enemies. In any event, he responded, calling for a meeting of the association's national committee for the first week of October. At the meeting, Kaiser said that "Winthrop Aldrich and other Republican members of the committee had questioned the association's nonpartisan position." Kaiser then acknowledged the four principal criticisms leveled at the association: first, that its literature had been distributed by political groups; second, that Kaiser had "given the impression that he was pro-Roosevelt when he appeared at the Teamster's dinner"; third, that the "association's first appeal had gone to government procurement agencies asking for release of war workers to vote and that such workers are largely pro-Roosevelt"; and finally, "a general belief exists that a large vote would benefit the Democratic ticket and for that reason the Association is pro-Democrat."[141]

Meanwhile, Raymond Feltus was advised to ask Governor Dewey for a get-out-the-vote appeal.[142] That was the last thing Dewey wanted. As

Isaiah Berlin noted, "Dewey is credited by some people with deliberate Machiavellianism in pitching his utterances in as low a key as possible to avoid stirring up new issues and so stimulate too high a turnout of voters, since he counts on apathy to work against Roosevelt."[143] Indeed, the association had beseeched both presidential and both vice presidential candidates to make such appeals. Dewey, backed into a corner by such a patriotic-sounding appeal, finally issued a statement in support of votes from "every qualified citizen."[144] The association also "secured statements endorsing its program from some twenty governors, Republican and Democrat."[145]

The association's national activities kicked off in New York City. Mayor Fiorello La Guardia appeared with Kaiser on the first day of voter registration in New York. The association arranged for a parade of horse-drawn carriages carrying Broadway show casts from Columbus Circle down Broadway to City Hall.[146] Kaiser and LaGuardia did a radio broadcast of New York's opening-day registration activities.[147] LaGuardia did not, however, participate in any of the association's other activities. Mayors of forty-three cities, including Detroit, Los Angeles, Chicago, San Francisco, and Pittsburgh, declared November 1–7 "Get-Out-the-Vote Week."[148]

The association managed to line up two hundred network radio shows to devote their entire program or part of it to the campaign to get out the vote. They also conducted a direct-mail campaign to mayors of all cities with populations larger than twenty-five thousand and placed announcements in national weekly magazines such as *Colliers, Harpers Bazaar*, the *Saturday Evening Post, Woman's Day*, and *Glamour*.[149] The climax of the association's push was a nationwide radio broadcast including Kaiser and mayors of Boston, Detroit, Los Angeles, and seven other major cities.[150]

If Kaiser's role as chairman were judged by levels of fund-raising, he failed. The association collected a mere $57,333, $15,000 of which came from Kaiser's enterprises (and another $5,000 of which came from Andrew Jackson Higgins).[151] If judged by the turnout in the 1944 election, the association succeeded: instead of the forty million Gallup had predicted, about forty-eight million—well over 50 percent of those registered—voted.[152] The result was the reelection of President Roosevelt by a wide margin. Of course, the CIO conducted a door-to-door campaign to get out the Democratic vote, and more servicemen and servicewomen voted than in 1942 so the impact of each effort is difficult to determine. *Newsweek*, for one, argued that Roosevelt would have lost without the CIO's efforts.[153] Turnout surpassed the threshold needed to win by eight million,

and of those, more than 70 percent (just as Gallup had predicted) went to Roosevelt.

Kaiser had attracted many critics for his performance as chairman of the association, and most were motivated by partisan concerns. One in particular had a different motive: jealousy. Andrew Jackson Higgins, the southern "Paul Bunyan," had headed the avowedly partisan Businessmen for Roosevelt, delivering numerous speeches during the last five weeks of the campaign. Afterward, he complained "[One] man who gripes me is Kaiser. He contributed to a nonpartisan outfit which was organized ostensibly for the purpose of getting out the vote." Then Higgins got to what really bothered him, the attention Kaiser received: "After he sat at the Teamsters dinner, when Roosevelt first spoke, Kaiser got exercised and was afraid he would hurt himself, so he wallowed his fat belly around, and tried to sit in at a Republican dinner, to prove how nonpartisan he was." Higgins then alluded to Kaiser's reputation as a tightwad: Kaiser "refused to give a dime, and there is no proof that he gave a dime to the Roosevelt campaign, but his press agents are now spouting off what great assistance he gave the president and his press agents also see that there is an announcement about once a week that he had a luncheon engagement with the president."[154]

Actually, Kaiser's people were doing just the opposite. His high-profile involvement in a cause that was of political interest to the White House risked making him a target of a postwar conservative backlash. Potential fallout from his involvement with the association, along with his reputation as Roosevelt's favorite businessman, led adviser Paul Cadman to caution Kaiser against involvement in too many liberal or Democratic causes: "As long as we refuse to affiliate with, sponsor, endorse, or donate to, or write articles and make statements for any and all of these organizations, we are on safe ground."[155]

And what about the commander in chief, whose urgent invitation to Hyde Park finally convinced Kaiser to head up the association? On January 10, ten days before his fourth inauguration, Roosevelt sent Kaiser a letter of thanks for his efforts on behalf of the association. Kaiser, who had so resisted the idea of becoming chairman, now planned to turn the Nonpartisan Association into a permanent body, an idea Roosevelt, not surprisingly, strongly supported.[156]

That never happened. The association was plagued from the beginning by an inability to raise sufficient funds. Fittingly, one of the last major pleas for money was made to the man who had helped create the Wendell Willkie phenomenon: Henry Luce. Luce had conditionally agreed to serve on the association's national committee, and he was included in the

list of committee members for distribution of information, but his name never appeared on the group's letterhead.[157] This may have been a form of payback to Kaiser, who had agreed the previous year to serve on the board of directors of Luce's pet project, United China Relief.[158] He did, however, submit a statement in support of "a big vote on November 7."[159] Feltus wrote Kaiser, "If you have the time, I am certain that Walt Disney, Harry Warner, and Henry Luce would make substantial contributions as a result of a telephone call from you. I have been trying to see Luce, but he is in Florida and will not return for another week or so. The long distance operator could trace him for you."[160] The association died the next month because of insufficient financial support.[161]

Kaiser suffered a far greater blow in April, when President Roosevelt died. Kaiser's relationship with the Roosevelt administration had evolved from an extension of administration policy in the days of antitrust to a symbol of the wartime arsenal of democracy to an answer to administration political concerns. As a symbol of opposition to big business, he had attracted the support of the administration in the late 1930s. As a symbol of opposition to bureaucratic bottlenecks, he had attracted bipartisan support during the war. Finally, as a visible supporter of the president, Kaiser would attract tremendous Republican criticism.

With the war over and Roosevelt gone, Kaiser lost access to the White House; he would never again have such a close relationship with a president. In late 1945, Kaiser sensed that Washington would not offer the entrepreneurial opportunities it once had: he had Chad Calhoun made arrangements to close the Washington office and return to Oakland.[162] For the moment, Mr. Kaiser had returned from Washington.

History, which seeks to overlook in her heroes the traits that irritate their contemporaries, may treat the Kaiser-government-money theme with great generosity.

Fortune, *1951*

EPILOGUE
A REVERSAL OF FORTUNE

Five years after generating enthusiasm for Henry Kaiser in general and his cargo plane proposal in particular, Time/Life ran its equivalent of a retraction. In a 1947 article about George Marshall, Robert Lovett, and the U.S. State Department, *Fortune* revealed that Kaiser's "absurd" idea "endangered" wartime production schedules. During the war, the army air force "Statistical Control" group investigated the plan's merit. They concluded that it would require 10,022 such planes and 120,765 aircrew members to transport the same cargo that required 44 ships manned by 3,200 sailors.[1] What Time/Life once referred to as a "runaround" from the government now was described as cool judgment.

By performing analyses such as this, the group of analysts—one of whom was Robert McNamara—earned the moniker the "Whiz Kids" and after the war resurrected the Ford Motor Company.

In the meantime, Kaiser had launched another new enterprise, this time in the same industry as the "Whiz Kids." In August 1945, he used his popularity as a springboard to plunge into consumer markets for the first time. He mounted what would become the stiffest challenge to Detroit automakers since that of *Time*'s 1929 Man of the Year, Walter Chrysler. Just as he had done in shipbuilding, Kaiser captured the American imagination with the Kaiser-Frazer Auto Company. Investors subscribed to more than $50 million worth of stock and consumers placed thousands of orders for a car not yet in production. Time/Life, of course, was on top of the story. Luce's publications gave Kaiser's enterprises—and especially Kaiser-Frazer—a helpful boost into the postwar world with abundant coverage.

Kaiser continued to receive considerable attention from Luce's publications, but they now reported bad news more frequently. Stories entitled "Trouble for Kaiser" and "Trouble for H.J." appeared in 1946 editions of *Time*. In 1947, *Time* reported layoffs at Kaiser-Frazer and suggested that its cars were overpriced.[2]

Kaiser complained bitterly after Time/Life's coverage of him became more balanced. Kaiser wrote to Luce: "I believe a crisis exists between *Time*, *Life*, and *Fortune* and the Kaiser-Frazer Corporation. The crisis has arisen out of the tremendous influence on public opinion which your publications have enjoyed through interesting and, until recently, factual reporting of the news." During the war, Kaiser learned what benefits accrued to those whom Time/Life praised in print. Now his letter to Luce expressed fears about the consequences of the dark side of media attention: "I am aware of the power of your publications. Whether use of that power indiscriminately can destroy Kaiser-Frazer Corporation is a matter of conjecture, but past events prove it can seriously impede and retard eventual success."[3]

Rising to Kaiser's defense was none other than Andrew Jackson Higgins, who wrote to Kaiser: "Is there no limit to how far the editors of [*Time*] dare go? For a long time they felt themselves free to belittle and ridicule any individual, but it would appear that they now feel exempt and free to use unethical methods to damage a man in his business. . . . I hope you sue the hell out of them."[4] Higgins was feeling the effects of abandonment by Time/Life once the war ended. Since the end of 1945, only

one story about him had appeared in Luce's magazines, entitled "More Trouble for Andy."[5]

Time/Life had been kinder to Kaiser. *Fortune* saw Kaiser-Frazer as a symbol that America was breaking free from the shackles of the New Deal, free from "worries over politics and taxes." Roosevelt and many of the New Dealers who had helped Kaiser so much were gone. With the war over, Time/Life described a businessman who could now turn his attention to the private sector, where the "almost magical appeal of [his] name" would provide instant credibility for his products. Kaiser-Frazer, suggested *Fortune*, would help usher in a time when "free enterprise seems freer than it has been for years."[6] Indeed, the new enterprise was begun at Kaiser's initiative, without overt government encouragement.[7] The Kaiser reality was at last approaching his Time/Life legend just as a shift in American attitudes occurred.

One of the telltale signs of a major shift in cultural attitudes is when the same behavior evokes utterly different responses than it once did. This is especially true during postwar periods. Henry Kaiser became the subject of an American postwar ritual: the investigation of government contractors. Wartime contractors, as Eliot Janeway put it, hope that "come I-day—Investigation Day—Congress would agree that the results at the time were worth the price."[8] In Kaiser's case, behavior that had endeared him to the public in wartime—breaking bureaucratic rules, spending public money freely to meet war demand—provided fodder for congressional scrutiny.

Kaiser faced stiff criticism from Congress as Republicans gained power. On April 17, 1946, New Hampshire senator Styles Bridges delivered a speech, which became a fourteen-page press release, criticizing Henry Kaiser and his relationship with the federal government.[9] Bridges called Kaiser, among other things, the "coddled darling of the New Deal."[10] Thus began a feud between Bridges and Kaiser that lasted into the next decade.

Kaiser had experienced public attacks before, but relatively infrequently. From 1942 through 1945, Kaiser was mentioned seventeen times on the floor of Congress, and only one reference was negative. The press had also been kind to Kaiser during the war. The most prolific chronicler of Kaiser's exploits—besides the reverential Time/Life—had been *Business Week*. Although *Business Week* published articles noting Kaiser's difficulties, it was careful not to attack this home front hero. One notable exception to Kaiser's remarkably positive wartime coverage had been syndicated columnist Westbrook Pegler. Pegler had criticized Kaiser during the war

for his dependence on government contracts and called him a "soft touch" for labor unions.[11] Pegler, however, had been a relatively lonely voice. The Bridges speech was different from a Pegler column because it signaled a change in the mood of both Congress and the public toward the New Deal and any individuals who had been identified with it.

What a difference a year made. Of the fourteen references to Kaiser in Congress in 1946, six were negative. Usually the subject was Kaiser's accumulation of loans from the RFC or criticism of how he performed on contracts. Kaiser's visibility during the war and the extent of his connection with the government made him an easy target for critics afterward. Congress investigated Kaiser's profits from shipbuilding and his loans from the RFC. Individual congressmen took turns attacking Kaiser; to them, the erstwhile extension of New Deal industrial policy now symbolized government waste. The election of a Republican Congress in November—the first since Roosevelt's election in 1932—was a harbinger of increased criticism of anyone associated with the New Deal. Roosevelt was dead and many New Dealers, including erstwhile Kaiser supporters Henry Morgenthau, Harold Ickes, Leon Henderson, and Sam Rosenman, were gone, so Kaiser made a good target.

The change in power on Capitol Hill was but one result of the upheaval and uncertainty of 1945–46 in the United States. No sooner had the Allies vanquished Germany and Japan than relations between the Soviet Union and the West began to deteriorate. At home, many believed that with the war over, economic depression would return. After the New Deal and the war had stimulated government involvement in the economy, the future relationship between business and government seemed uncertain.

With the end of the war and the transition to a new (albeit Democratic) administration, boundaries between Kaiser's enterprises and the government were becoming more formal and less permeable, as were relationships within Kaiser's organization. Relationships between the Kaiser organization and the federal government were no longer fluid. The principal difference is that Kaiser now paid for services in the private sector that he had once received free of charge from the federal government.

With his government-based guides gone, Kaiser sought to supplement Chad Calhoun's services with legal help from the private sector. Sam Rosenman stayed on as a speechwriter for Truman until February 1946, when he returned to private practice. Soon after, he was retained as one of Kaiser's Washington lawyers, and within two months of leaving government, he toured Kaiser's various West Coast facilities, including the Fontana steel plant.[12] Rosenman's transition from government attorney to

private practitioner reflected the new environment. One of his first assignments for Kaiser was to evaluate the "propriety" of Kaiser hiring another former government lawyer.[13] Rosenman worked for Kaiser until the summer of 1947.[14]

By then, Oscar Cox had become Kaiser's principal Washington attorney. When the Lend-Lease program ended in 1945 and Cox announced his intention to return to private practice in New York, Henry Kaiser contacted him.[15] Cox subsequently set up a private practice in Washington rather than New York, and Kaiser was one of his first clients. One of the services Cox offered was dealing with congressional investigations, whether that meant accompanying Kaiser to hearings or preparing rebuttals to attacks. Cox and his associate, Lloyd Cutler, also offered Kaiser advice on how to proceed in international matters—an increasingly important field for American business and one for which the experience in the Lend-Lease program prepared Cox and Cutler well. With their assistance, Kaiser engaged in major enterprises in India, Africa, South America, the Middle East, and elsewhere.

Another of the postwar changes in the organization involved the establishment of a large public relations department that would respond when Kaiser was attacked—particularly by politicians and the press. Such a department had not been necessary during the war, when nearly every reference to Kaiser recorded in the *Congressional Record* had been positive and America's press saw in Kaiser a much-needed heroic figure on the home front. In September 1946, Kaiser's public relations organization published and began distributing *Questions and Answers about Henry J. Kaiser*, a pamphlet that responded to increasingly hostile media questions and congressional attacks regarding Kaiser's wartime relations with the government.[16]

The appearance of Kaiser's public relations pamphlet signaled that he had completed many of the necessary organizational changes to respond to the new postwar environment. Chad Calhoun remained in Washington until the 1960s, Oscar Cox and Lloyd Cutler handled most government-related legal matters, and Kaiser's own public relations staff helped maintain his image. Functions that had once been performed for the company by government lawyers and the mass media were now performed within the Kaiser organization. Kaiser's lobbying strategy also changed. With industrial facilities in California, Washington, Pennsylvania, Michigan, and Louisiana, Kaiser now was poised to lobby individual members of Congress and to focus less on the executive branch.

The structure of Kaiser's organization changed, too, beginning to resemble America's other corporate giants. The empire's subsequent reorga-

nization heralded a more modern—and hierarchical—corporate structure. This was a calculated move. Kaiser's organization had once reflected the freewheeling, amorphous style of the Roosevelt administration. Taking on the appearance of more conventional companies improved Kaiser's chances of obtaining private financing when he turned to New York instead of Washington for loans. In 1949, formal organization charts first appeared throughout the Kaiser empire.[17] In 1952, Kaiser issued a press release listing the $440 million of private financing obtained by his various concerns in the past sixteen months.[18] As he had done during the New Deal, Kaiser had adopted an organizational appearance and style that was familiar to those whom he approached for financing.

Ironically, it was in this new environment that Kaiser—with government help—made his most successful move in industrial enterprise, one that Interior Secretary Harold Ickes had proposed five years earlier: entry into the aluminum business. In 1945, a U.S. circuit court had found aluminum giant Alcoa in violation of the Sherman Antitrust Act, opening the door to new industry entrants. In early 1946, when the War Assets Administration put government-owned plants up for sale or lease, Kaiser made the solidest bid. Negotiations concluded on April 1: Kaiser leased two plants in the state of Washington, with the option to buy later.[19] Kaiser's aluminum company was nearly an instant success and became the crown jewel of his industrial empire. Kaiser Aluminum was also the last major enterprise Kaiser would launch.

Kaiser's experiences as a government entrepreneur in the postwar era contrast sharply with those of Andrew Jackson Higgins and Howard Hughes. Kaiser's wartime exploits were most often compared—in the pages of *Time* and elsewhere—to those of Higgins. Indeed, John Morton Blum's history of the home front does so as well.[20] Yet Higgins was a genuine "war baby" who had only fifty employees in 1937 and more than twenty thousand—and plans to employ seventy-five to eighty thousand—during the war.[21] After the war, the market for merchant shipbuilding dried up, hurting both Kaiser and Higgins. Higgins disappeared; Kaiser did not. Higgins returned to building commercial craft and pleasure boats and dabbled in the production of housing materials. His enterprises, which had taken off as a consequence of increased government demand for boats, sank as quickly as they had risen.

Kaiser's organization, by contrast, experienced dramatic growth in the 1950s as it reaped the benefits of the other enterprises he began in the 1940s. By the time of the inaugural Fortune 500 in 1955, Kaiser's alu-

minum, steel, and auto companies, if combined, would have ranked among America's top fifty industrial concerns.[22]

Kaiser did experience setbacks, however, in the 1950s. Kaiser's strengths —in material handling and mass production—had been ideal for a "hot war" environment like World War II. The industry Kaiser entered that most embodied those characteristics—automobiles—posed insurmountable hurdles because of its demands in marketing. Kaiser had done best when marketing to a single customer: the government. Yet the Cold War environment offered opportunities to sell to that one large customer that Kaiser could not exploit. This is best seen by comparing Kaiser's experience to that of his onetime partner, Howard Hughes.

By the end of the "Spruce Goose" episode in 1947, Hughes seemed finished as a government contractor. Shortly after the war ended, many would have argued that might not be a bad thing because the defense budget was shrinking, not growing. The company had been working on a weapons control system that combined radar and computer, which could find and destroy enemy planes at any time of day and under any weather conditions. Late in 1948, with Cold War tensions building in Eastern Europe, the American military began frantically seeking an all-weather interceptor, and Hughes had the jump on bigger firms. A succession of contracts to install interceptors on planes and missiles followed. Then the Korean War broke out.[23]

Hughes became the sole-source supplier for the entire air force interceptor program. His research lab grew to more than one thousand scientists, becoming America's second largest corporate scientific and engineering organization (behind only Bell Labs), including more than four hundred Ph.D.'s. When the Korean War ended, the military did not shrink as it had after World War II, and Hughes Aircraft continued to grow. It became one of a handful of the largest defense contractors and one of the country's largest privately held companies. On the eve of the 1950s, Hughes Aircraft was a $2 million company; by the 1970s, it was a $2 billion giant.

Hughes was engaged in a growing industry that helped distinguish the West from the rest of the country but also kept the region's connection to the federal government alive. The 1950s aerospace industry was drawn to California by its aircraft roots and the technological capabilities of its major research universities. In turn, the industry's technological response to government needs created Silicon Valley and the other research centers in California. A survey performed by the Stanford Research Institute in

1958 showed that 84 percent of electronics firms in California—the cradle of the individualist entrepreneur—performed a majority of their business as either prime- or subcontractors for the federal government.[24] The computer industry, a boon both to California's economy and to its entrepreneurial mystique, was jump-started with funds from Washington.

In some respects, then, the 1942 Kaiser-Hughes partnership represented the present (Kaiser) teamed up with the near future (Hughes). Although Henry Kaiser was identified with regional economic growth in the West, after he completed work on the major western dams, Kaiser was less directly involved with the region's industrial future than Hughes was.

Kaiser was more wedded to the industries of the East. He challenged mature industries with high barriers to entry, from cement to magnesium to shipbuilding to steel to aluminum to automobiles, with mixed results. Kaiser-Frazer rose quickly to the position of America's fourth largest automaker but, like other independents, succumbed to the competition from Detroit's big three. In metals, Kaiser's principal impact came in aluminum rather than in magnesium. Kaiser Aluminum was successful and is still one of America's three biggest producers along with Alcoa and Reynolds. Kaiser also boasted a very successful cement company, and Kaiser Engineers—a continuation of Kaiser's original construction outfit—was one of the largest of its kind in the world. Kaiser never produced more than a fraction of America's steel output. Before going out of business in the 1980s, Kaiser Steel's principal impact on the industry was in the field of labor relations. In 1946, 1952, and 1959, Kaiser broke ranks with "solid steel" either to avert a strike or to settle before the larger eastern producers.

The performance of the various enterprises of Kaiser's industrial empire has been a mixed bag compared to the great expectations generated in the 1940s. Most insiders (and outsiders as well) attribute any decline of Kaiser's industrial enterprises to the impossibility of a successor filling the great man's shoes. Indeed, his son Edgar was not the visionary and charismatic doer his father had been. Yet an analysis of the company's "core competence" may provide a better explanation. From the outset, this organization combined impressive production skills with intimate government relations. Consequently, developing traditional marketing and distribution skills was less of a priority. As a result, when Kaiser tried consumer products (especially cars and aluminum foil), inadequate marketing and inadequate distribution systems would continually frustrate him.

Many other government contractors, such as Hughes, thrived after World War II without ever having to try to enter consumer markets. The big growth market for them would be in aircraft/aerospace. Henry Kaiser's

last major attempt at aircraft production came during the Korean War, when Kaiser-Frazer produced cargo planes. Kaiser was never a major factor in that market again.

Kaiser's marketing weakness was not sufficiently compensated with technical expertise. He did not accumulate a stable of similarly talented scientists and engineers, and he never succeeded in becoming a big player in aerospace or electronics. While "hot war" rewarded production geniuses who could take government designs and crank out as many as they could, the Cold War was about perpetual innovation and small-batch production. That rewarded research-based firms such as Hughes because an arms race requires developing state-of-the-art weapons systems.

By the time Henry Kaiser died in 1967, what would become his greatest legacy had not grown anywhere near its current size: the Kaiser Permanente health maintenance organization. Kaiser Permanente was, however, on its way to revolutionizing its industry, became the world's largest HMO, and remains squarely in the middle of many discussions of American health care reform.

A detailed post–World War II study of Kaiser's governmental relations and an analysis of the subsequent performance of the various components of his empire are grist for another study's mill. In the 1970s, *Fortune* reported the breakup of Kaiser Industries and explained the move as a measure to maximize shareholder value. It was, however, much more than that: it was the end of a distinctively American story. No one individual has ever created—from scratch—a more diversified empire than Henry J. Kaiser or one whose enterprises so thoroughly represented the fruits of government entrepreneurship.

CONCLUSION

Henry Kaiser's Washington story has significance for both its particular and general aspects. Kaiser's enterprises offer an important reminder of what was possible for government entrepreneurs at a time—the 1930s and 1940s—when barriers between the public and private sectors were becoming blurred. His rise also offers lessons and raises questions that are relevant to the twenty-first century.

As a government entrepreneur in Washington in the 1930s and 1940s, Henry Kaiser did not fit the contemporary stereotype of government contractors. They were portrayed as special-interest operators who lobbied the government to do things it would not otherwise do, something Kaiser had earlier done, both as a representative of the Six Companies and as the president of the Associated General Contractors of America. Yet Kaiser's efforts in primary industries were extensions of administration policy, not results of his attempts to change policy. Kaiser's cement, steel, magnesium, and aluminum enterprises all shared one characteristic: they were preceded by government expressions of interest in the establishment of a new entry into each of these industries.

Henry Kaiser's encounter with the federal government not only belies the most common explanation of government behavior—responses to the lobbying of special interests—but it calls for another look at New Deal relations with business. The language Roosevelt employed in the late 1930s ("economic royalists") combined with his support of antitrust activity to give him an antibusiness label. New Deal history has presented the administration's relations with business through the lens of established big business. Therefore, business-government relations during Roosevelt's second term are described almost entirely in acrimonious terms. Yet the Kaiser saga shows that on the eve of World War II, the president and the New Deal supported other businessmen who embodied administration principles.

The administration made its policy objectives—antitrust, labor relations, regional development—known and encouraged industry to follow. Not all the initiative, however, came from the government. Individual

companies such as Kaiser's were responsible for making specific proposals for new enterprise. Only when they had done so would the government assist them in seeking loans and contracts. New Deal government entrepreneurship, then, involved a symbiotic relationship with well-defined roles for government and business.

Our strong tradition of individualism obscures such relationships. America has embraced the myth of the individualistic, self-made entrepreneur. Similarly, Americans credit entrepreneurial efforts that occur at the cusp of the private and public sectors entirely to the imagination and initiative of the individual entrepreneur. There is little doubt that America owes much of its sustained economic growth to inspired individuals whose ingenuity, courage, resilience, and creativity have not only established companies but shaped entire industries. From automobiles to computers, it is routine—and appropriate—to identify individuals such as Henry Ford and Bill Gates with revolutionary change.

Yet Henry Kaiser's experiences in Washington provide a counterpoint to a long-standing American belief, aided and abetted by journalists and biographers, that entrepreneurs are shapers of their own world. Despite what America's television, radio, and print media—including Henry Luce's publications—have suggested, such virtuoso performances have not by themselves been sufficient to sustain our economy. Government entrepreneurship, which does not fit the myth of all-powerful, self-determining heroes, plays a greater and greater role in our everyday life.

Early research in computers was funded by the government, and many of America's high-tech developments resulted from government demands on the aerospace industry during the Cold War. Henry Ford's company was not government-funded, but the roads used by his customers, and those of his competitors, were. America's West Coast, haven for the modern myth of the self-made man, stands as one of the great economic success stories of the twentieth century, a story made possible by federal projects that provided the area with sufficient power and water for massive growth.

Roles for government and business are not always so well defined, but changes in policy invariably provide opportunities for government entrepreneurs. Recent examples include a host of environmental firms and minority contractors. We can see opportunities for government entrepreneurship both in times of government growth (as in the rise of the military-industrial complex) and in times of government retrenchment (when, for example, veterans of the military-industrial complex such as Lockheed stand in line to administer state welfare systems).

Since the rise of Henry Kaiser, government entrepreneurship has not only proliferated, but it has changed to reflect a new economy. Most notable has been America's gradual shift from an economy emphasizing the production of goods to one emphasizing the proffering of services. MCI, Charles Schwab, and Netscape Communications each depended on a government-created niche or on government protection from giant competition to launch their service-based enterprises.

Equally important is the fact that government's active support is not necessary to provide entrepreneurial opportunity. Government entrepreneurs avail themselves of opportunities from governmental inaction as well as action. No better example of the former exists than Kaiser's empire.

Whereas Kaiser's most prominent business enterprises were established with the active assistance of the government (receipt of loans, contracts, and favorable leases for ships, steel, autos, cement, and magnesium; breaking a monopoly for aluminum), Kaiser's greatest lasting accomplishment came about through government *inaction*. While various Western countries instituted national health care systems, the United States did not. Therefore, Kaiser's health maintenance organization, which he originally established to keep his workers healthy, became the form of medical insurance coverage used by a majority of Americans by the 1980s.

America's brand of mixed (private and public) capitalism has always featured a substantial role for government entrepreneurship and will likely continue to do so. American suspicions of government ownership or operation of enterprise have led to private ownership of everything from railroads to airlines, from telegraph to telephone. In addition to transportation and communications, government entrepreneurship has flourished whenever the private sector provides a public good: construction and agriculture are other examples, along with health care.

The experiences of government entrepreneurs offer historians ample opportunity to ask how well they pursued available opportunities and to examine the finer points of their strategy. With the extensive focus by business historians in recent years on the workings of the enterprise itself, government relations and responses loom as yet another entrant on the list of organizational capabilities. In the case of Henry Kaiser, an "internalist" approach would focus on Chad Calhoun as Henry Kaiser's agent in Washington and on how Kaiser elicited the assistance of government lawyers and the media to accomplish his goals.

Paying attention to the organization and its capabilities is necessary, but not sufficient, for the study of business enterprise. In this book, I have examined the motives and strategies of Kaiser's customer—the government

—as well. That is just a start, however. The study of government entrepreneurs allows us the opportunity to view the enterprises of Kaiser and others as agents of society. Because government policy or action (or inaction) made those enterprises possible, an assessment of the enterprises as agents of society is necessary to determine how enlightened the policies were.

Making such an assessment of Kaiser's World War II enterprises is rather straightforward on the surface: they helped win the war for the Allies. Yet Kaiser's establishment of shipyards on the West Coast had wider ramifications. He offered large-scale employment to women and African Americans and sparked a substantial migration of workers from the South, East, and Midwest to the West Coast.

What about the postwar impact of his enterprises? To what extent did the government-mandated breakup of Alcoa and Kaiser's entry into the aluminum industry benefit society? Kaiser Steel appears to have disappeared without a ripple, but did it influence the availability of steel in the West? Did Kaiser's approach to labor relations transform the industry in any way? Or was his legacy in that industry merely that of a newcomer garnering a small share of a shrinking pie? Such questions are beyond the scope of this particular study but are not beyond the scope of business history.

The behavior of government entrepreneurs is a window onto our society, and tracing changes in the opportunities they exploit can reveal much about the direction our society has taken. The study of government entrepreneurship can provide invaluable information for addressing the question, What kind of society do we want?

NOTES

ABBREVIATIONS

AISIP   Papers of the American Iron and Steel Institute, Hagley Library, Greenville, Del.

BRP   Bureau of Reclamation Papers, National Archives, Washington, D.C.

CRCCF   California Road Construction Contract File, California State Archives, Sacramento, Calif.

DNCP   Papers of the Democratic National Committee, Franklin D. Roosevelt Library, Hyde Park, N.Y.

DPP   Drew Pearson Papers, Lyndon B. Johnson Library, Austin, Tex.

EKP   Edgar Kaiser Papers, Bancroft Library, Berkeley, Calif.

ETP   Eugene Trefethen Papers, Bancroft Library, Berkeley, Calif.

FEAP   Papers of the Foreign Economic Administration, National Archives, Washington, D.C.

HHP   Herbert Hoover Papers, Hoover Institute, Stanford, Calif.

HJKP   Henry J. Kaiser Papers, Bancroft Library, Berkeley, Calif.

HLIP   Harold L. Ickes Papers, Library of Congress, Washington, D.C.

MLSP   Margaret L. Suckley Papers, Wilderstein Preservation, Rhinebeck, N.Y.

NAMP   Papers of the National Association of Manufacturers, Hagley Library, Greenville, Del.

OCP   Oscar Cox Papers, Franklin D. Roosevelt Library, Hyde Park, N.Y.

OF   Office Files, Franklin D. Roosevelt Papers, Franklin D. Roosevelt Library, Hyde Park, N.Y.

PPF   President's Personal File, Franklin D. Roosevelt Papers, Franklin D. Roosevelt Library, Hyde Park, N.Y.

RED   Records of the Election Division, California State Archives, Sacramento, Calif.

RG   Record Group

SIRP   Samuel I. Rosenman Papers, Franklin D. Roosevelt Library, Hyde Park, N.Y.

TCP   Thomas Corcoran Papers, Library of Congress, Washington, D.C.

TGP   Theodore Granik Papers, Library of Congress, Washington, D.C.

WCP   Wayne Coy Papers, Franklin D. Roosevelt Library, Hyde Park, N.Y.

CHAPTER ONE

1. See War Production Board, Planning Committee Minutes, meeting 1 (Feb. 20, 1942), 2; and meeting 2 (Feb. 23, 1942), 3–4. Courtesy of Robert R. Nathan.

2. Address of Henry J. Kaiser at the National Press Club, July 30, 1942, HJKP, carton 298.

3. Based on references in the *Reader's Guide to Periodical Literature* and *Industrial Arts Index*; Lewis, *Public Image of Henry Ford*, 413.

4. Schumpeter, *Theory of Economic Development*, 65–66; Schumpeter, *Capitalism, Socialism, and Democracy*, 83. Schumpeter refers to capitalism's process of continual internal revolution (in which the entrepreneur acts as the catalyst for change) as "Creative Destruction." Schumpeter's model includes five types of new combinations: introduction of a new good or service; introduction of a new method of production; opening a new market; achieving a new source of raw-material supply; and carrying out a new organization of an industry (such as creating or breaking up a monopoly). Entrepreneur Kaiser engaged in all five types of new combinations.

In a 1935 birthday salute to Kaiser, Leland W. Cutler described him as "respectfully destructive." See message of May 6, 1935, in HJKP, carton 347.

5. Jones with Angly, *Fifty Billion Dollars*, 5.

6. Jonathan Hughes and Harold Livesay offer good examples of this interpretation. See Hughes, *Vital Few*, and Livesay, *American Made*. Jameson Doig and Erwin Hargrove take a different approach, providing a series of profiles demonstrating entrepreneurial behavior in the ranks of government, with one peripheral account of a government contractor. See Doig and Hargrove, *Leadership and Innovation*.

7. Chandler, in seminal books in the 1960s, 1970s, and 1990s, showed that the organization's ability to outperform the market in certain functions led to the success of large, vertically integrated companies in certain industries. Chandler devotes little attention, however, to institutional relationships that influenced the success of Kaiser and many others: relationships with government, labor unions, and universities, to name a few. See Chandler, *Strategy and Structure*; Chandler, *Visible Hand*; Chandler, *Scale and Scope*.

8. As more "individual" success stories are told, we will gain a more accurate perspective on America's "self-made" image. A recent step in that direction is Dan Morgan's *Rising in the West*, which traces the rags-to-riches history of a family that left Oklahoma for California in 1934. Patriarch Oca Tatham realized the dream of self-employed entrepreneurship and became a millionaire by the 1960s. According to Morgan, Tatham's future was uncertain until "the [World War II] defense boom saved his neck." In addition, Morgan shows that the individual initiative of immigrants like Tatham was boosted by "the greatest infrastructure program ever undertaken by the federal government and probably by any government in the history of the world": the dam, power, and water projects begun in the 1930s (ibid., 134–38).

9. Blum, *V Was for Victory*, 115–16.

10. McQuaid, *Big Business and Presidential Power*, 16.

11. Kuznets, *Modern Economic Growth*, 236–37.

12. See Foner, *Free Soil*, 16–17; Smith, *Virgin Land*, 201–10. Although Frederick Jackson Turner's "Significance of the Frontier in American History" is most readily associated with the "safety-valve" idea, Smith shows that the intellectual roots of Turner's concept ran from Ben Franklin through George Washington and Thomas Jefferson and blossomed in the writings of Horace Greeley.

13. Even in the wake of the *Grapes of Wrath*-era migrations to the West Coast and the huge federally funded western public works projects of the 1930s, West Coast public opin-

ion at decade's end reflected suspicion of, rather than an embrace of, government's role. Among America's seven geographic regions, the Pacific Coast ranked a close second in percentage of people who believed a decrease in government spending would increase prosperity. Similarly, the Pacific Coast ranked second in percentage of those choosing "have government let business alone" as a means of increasing national prosperity (Elmo Roper, "Report on a Survey Prepared for the National Association of Manufacturers," Apr. 1939, NAMP, accession 1411, series 100-S, box 67, pp. 14, 20).

Such a regional attitude cries out for an accompanying narrative, and Roper's numbers come to life in Morgan's *Rising in the West*, which notes that Uncle Sam's programs had considerably more impact on a family's financial situation than on its worldview. Despite the abundant benefits the Tathams had derived from the government, they maintained an individualistic, "pull-yourself-up-by-your-bootstraps" mentality (Morgan, *Rising in the West*, 134–38).

14. In the 1990s, language from the 1930s returned. This time the target was not the private sector economic power of the East but that of the public sector. After California's 1994 gubernatorial election, in which control of illegal immigration was the key issue, Governor Pete Wilson said, "California is not simply a colony of the federal government to be taxed without limit to pay for the costs of federal failure" (*Washington Post*, Nov. 11, 1994).

15. Nash, *American West in the Twentieth Century*, 89.

16. Foster, "Giant of the West," 23.

17. "A. B. Ordway Comments," May 1, 1955, EKP, carton 225, folder 9.

18. It would be interesting to see how the "can-do" Kaiser would have been viewed during the post-Vietnam, post-Watergate era. Attitudes of students at the University of Michigan Business School in the early 1980s suggest the magnitude of the change that had occurred since the early 1960s. In 1981, Dow Chemical's CEO, Paul Orrefice, visited the school for a "brown-bag" lunch and was grilled at length about Dow's production of napalm for use in Vietnam. Orrefice's explanation, that Dow was simply providing what the government wanted, did not satisfy the students. By contrast, a 1961 poll conducted by the University of Michigan Graduate School of Business named Henry Kaiser one of the ten most admired businessmen—the same Kaiser whose Permanente Metals had produced incendiary materials used in the firebombing of Dresden and Tokyo during World War II ("These 10 Are Rated Greatest Living U.S. Businessmen," HJKP, carton 342).

19. Susman, *Culture as History*, 32.

20. Bellah et al., *Habits of the Heart*, 20–21, 43. Bellah and his colleagues refer to James Oliver Robertson's treatment of individualism and American business. Robertson concludes that big business is "distrusted *and* admired by Americans" and explains: "Admiration for the great mythical corporation grew because Americans assumed that at the center of the octopus was the single eye, the single controlling brain—the . . . independent, single American individual. In the mythology of corporations, every giant corporation has been *created* by a single individual—from Rockefeller to J. P. Morgan to Henry Ford to Henry Kaiser" (Robertson, *American Myth*, 177).

21. One version of this story involved the challenges met in the Bonneville Dam project. Edgar Kaiser recalled, "We really weren't mature enough to see why it couldn't be done, and maybe that's why it was done" (Kaiser Industries, *Kaiser Story*, 23).

22. "C. K. Prahalad Gives McInally Lecture in Hale," *Dividend*, Spring–Summer 1995, 30.

23. Interview, Lloyd Cutler, June 19, 1991.

24. Velie, "Truth about Henry Kaiser," 25.

25. Cadman, "Henry Kaiser," 131; Foster, *Henry J. Kaiser*, 59.

26. Interview, Lloyd Cutler, June 19, 1991.

27. Gerard Piel, letter to author, Jan. 2, 1991.

28. Taylor, "Builder No. 1," 10.

29. McQuaid, "Corporate Liberalism."

30. Lewis, *Public Image of Henry Ford*, 363, 471.

31. M. L. Suckley, Diary, May 22, 1944, MLSP, JD 184–85.

32. Mead, *And Keep Your Powder Dry*, 165.

33. Galbraith, *A Life in Our Times*, 125.

34. Interview, Robert R. Nathan, Oct. 17, 1991; interview, Robert Sandberg, Aug. 6, 1991; Foster, *Henry J. Kaiser*, 238.

35. Interview, Robert Nathan, Oct. 17, 1991; interview, Lincoln Gordon, Jan. 9, 1992.

36. Gerard Piel to author, July 29, 1992.

37. Freidel, *Franklin D. Roosevelt*, 295, 294.

CHAPTER TWO

1. Gunther, *Inside U.S.A.*, 69.

2. Foster, *Henry J. Kaiser*, 9; Heiner, *Henry J. Kaiser*, 9.

3. Foster, *Henry J. Kaiser*, 13–14, 16.

4. Ibid., 20.

5. Kaiser to E. E. Spring, Esq., Feb. 14, 1914, HJKP, carton 348.

6. Heiner, *Henry J. Kaiser*, 12.

7. See Foster, *Henry J. Kaiser*, 30.

8. Heiner, *Henry J. Kaiser*, 23.

9. Foster, *Henry J. Kaiser*, 30–31; *Warren Story*, 1.

10. U.S. Bureau of the Census, *Statistical History*, 8, 623, 668, 621.

11. See Mooney, *Builders for Progress*, 49; *Constructor*, Feb. 1928, 33; *Engineering World*, June 1922, 337; California Department of Public Works, *Report*, 9.

12. "Notes of Meeting of Henry J. Kaiser, Henry J. Kaiser, Jr., Chad Calhoun, and Mr. Murphy and Miss McEnany of *Fortune*," June 22, 1943, HJKP, carton 21, folder 26.

13. Morrison, *Those Were the Days*, 21–22.

14. Caro, *Path to Power*, 370.

15. *Western Construction News*, Jan. 10, 1926, 18. In 1923 the figure had fallen to 35 percent (but was 40 percent for highway and excavating contractors).

16. "Earth Movers I," 106.

17. Morrison, *Those Were the Days*, 25, 66.

18. Ingram, *A Builder*, 30, 29; *Constructor*, Nov. 1926, 44; "History of the Kaiser Companies" (ca. 1943), HJKP, carton 349; Northern California Contractors, *Monthly Letter*, Nov. 1925; *Fortune*, Aug. 1943, 106.

19. Donald Duffy to author, Jan. 5, 1993.

20. See Seeley, *Building the American Highway System*.

21. U.S. Bureau of the Census, *Fifteenth Census*, Construction Industry, 21, 23, 25; U.S. Bureau of the Census, *Fifteenth Census*, Abstract, 758–59.

22. Foster, *Henry J. Kaiser*, 32; Heiner, *Henry J. Kaiser*, 30, 409, 25.

23. Years after the fact, once Kaiser had become a household name, an engineer for Skagit County, Washington, commented on one of his early innovations: "[Henry Kaiser] has done several outstanding things, but the rubber tire for the wheelbarrow is a lot of glory for any one man" (quoted in Heiner, *Henry J. Kaiser*, 29).

24. American Public Works Association, *History of Public Works*, 99.

25. Seeley, *Building the American Highway System*, 73.

26. LeTourneau, *Mover of Men and Mountains*, 148.

27. Ibid., 144–45.

28. Heiner, *Henry J. Kaiser*, 21–22; Foster, *Henry J. Kaiser*, 35.

29. *Mount Shasta Herald*, Aug. 31, 1922, Dec. 23, 1923; Foster, *Henry J. Kaiser*, 36; Patch to Fletcher, Dec. 15, 1922, CRCCF, no. 350.

30. Cultural historian Warren Susman observed in 1920s America a "particular middle-class delight in what could be measured and counted," which he attributed to "the mounting effort to rationalize all aspects of men's activities" (*Culture as History*, 141).

31. This is part of Tom Price's account of the early days with Kaiser. See "History of the Kaiser Companies," 26, HJKP, carton 349.

32. U.S. Bureau of Public Roads, *Report of a Study*, 24; Cadman, "Henry Kaiser," 36; *Constructor*, July 1928, 22; *California Blue Book*, 147.

33. See *Sacramento Union*, Sept. 12, 13, 1911.

34. T. A. Bedford to A. B. Fletcher, July 18, 1921, CRCCF, no. 313.

35. H. F. Morton to Kaiser, Dec. 11, 1923, CRCCF, no. 431. Emphasis added.

36. Kaiser to Highway Commission, Dec. 5, 1923, CRCCF, no. 431.

37. Kaiser to Stanton, July 14, 1923, CRCCF, no. 314.

38. *Mount Shasta Herald*, May 24, July 12, 1923.

39. Morrison, *Those Were the Days*, 2–3.

40. Caro, *Path to Power*, 370.

41. Kaiser to the Board of Highway Commissioners and the State Highway Engineer, July 19, 1923, CRCCF, no. 314.

42. Wooden to Fletcher, June 27, 1922, Fletcher to Kaiser, Dec. 27, 1922, Stanton to Morton, Feb. 1, 1923, all in CRCCF, no. 368.

43. Kaiser to Morton, Feb. 22, 1923, CRCCF, no. 368.

44. *Engineering News-Record*, Sept. 16, 1926, 462.

45. *Constructor*, Dec. 1925, 27.

46. *Constructor*, June 1925, 26.

47. *Monthly Letter*, Sept. 1924.

48. Heiner, *Henry J. Kaiser*, 39.

49. *Constructor*, Dec. 1925, 27.

50. Mooney, *Builders for Progress*, 38.

51. *Monthly Letter*, Feb. 1928.

52. *Constructor*, Mar. 1929, 38.

53. *Constructor*, July 1931, 37.

54. *Monthly Letter*, May 1925, in HJKP, carton 296, folder 12.

55. State of California, Campaign Statements of Receipts and Expenditures, Sept. 18, 1926, report for Nov. 2, 1926 election, RED.

56. *Western Construction News*, Feb. 10, 1931, 86.

57. State of California, Campaign Statements of Receipts and Expenditures, particularly Sept. 18, 1926, report for Nov. 2, 1926 election, RED.

58. Interview, Lloyd Cutler, June 19, 1991.

59. Caro, *Means of Ascent*, 420.

60. Caro, *Path to Power*, xv–xvi, 469–75.

61. Donald Duffy to author, Jan. 5, 1993.

62. *Constructor*, Dec. 1923, 30.

63. Interview, Clay Bedford, Jan. 7, 1964, tape in possession of Alex Troffey.

64. White, *Earl Warren*, 28.

65. Hawley, "Herbert Hoover."

66. *Western Construction News*, Mar. 25, 1930, 153. After Warren concluded his investigation and prosecution, the *News* published a small item noting that in the wake of the paving scandals, Oakland had switched to the city manager form of government. Still boosting its own, it announced: "Here is another opportunity for some engineer to prove that an engineering training is the prerequisite to economic management" (*Western Construction News*, Nov. 10, 1930, 537).

67. Morton to U.S. Fidelity & Guaranty Co., June 24, 1924, CRCCF, no. 431.

68. Cadman, "Henry Kaiser," 56; *Engineering News-Record*, Jan. 5, 1928, 22.

69. *Constructor*, Apr. 1931, 38.

70. *Western Construction News*, Nov. 10, 1927; Foster, *Henry J. Kaiser*, 39; "History of the Kaiser Companies, Vol. I," 85, HJKP, carton 349; Cadman, "Henry Kaiser," 42.

CHAPTER THREE

1. Hofstadter, *Age of Reform*, 11–12.

2. One recent book that profiles those who pursued either political or pecuniary opportunity from the Roosevelt administration is Schwartz, *New Dealers*.

3. I have adapted the phases presented by Arthur Schlesinger Jr. and Richard Lauderbaugh. Schlesinger saw the "watershed" between the First and Second New Deals occurring in 1935, with the "fading out" of the NRA remnants and a change in personnel from the brain trusters to the Keynesians and Brandeisians. For government entrepreneurs, I see the first major change coming in 1936. The election year brought increased government spending and a campaign marked by antibusiness rhetoric. See Schlesinger, *Politics of Upheaval*, 385–99.

Lauderbaugh framed the "New Deal War" in the years 1939–41. Indeed, the New Deal was on its deathbed in 1939 and was rescued by the emergency posed by Hitler in Europe. For government entrepreneurs, the issue of industry newcomers moved from the purview of the Temporary National Economic Committee and the Justice Department to the National Defense Advisory Commission and the Office of Production Management. See Lauderbaugh, *American Steel Makers*, 13, 16, 31–59.

4. *Constructor*, July 1928, 21.

5. U.S. Bureau of the Census, *Statistical History*, 618–19.

6. Ibid., 623.

7. Leuchtenburg, *Franklin D. Roosevelt*, 70.

8. Ibid.

9. Waters, *Colorado*, 337.

10. *Christian Science Monitor*, Aug. 18, 1936.

11. Stevens, *Hoover Dam*, 27, 169.

12. Hawley, "Herbert Hoover," 116–40.

13. *Constructor*, Apr. 1931, 39.

14. Stevens, *Hoover Dam*, 47.

15. "Earth Movers I," 214; Foster, *Henry J. Kaiser*, 294 n. 9.

16. Stevens, *Hoover Dam*, 169.

17. U.S. Congress, House Committee on Appropriations, *Hearings, Second Deficiency Appropriations Bill*, May 6, 1932, 215–22.

18. Ray Lyman Wilbur to Hoover, May 23, 1932, HHP, carton 28.

19. U.S. Congress, House Committee on Labor, *Hearings, Wages*, 21.

20. *New York Times*, Aug. 2, 1932, 10, Aug. 25, 1932, 16.

21. Kaiser to Elwood Mead, Apr. 5, 1934, HJKP, carton 3.

22. Earl Lee Kelly to Kaiser, Jan. 10, 1934, ibid.

23. Interview, Jack Carlson, Aug. 27, 1992.

24. Hyman, *Marriner S. Eccles*, 77.

25. Mattox to McIntyre, Oct. 1, 1935; Roosevelt to Kaiser, Oct. 1, 1935, both in PPF 2924.

26. 1936 contributors list, Democratic National Committee, DNCP.

27. *Western Construction News*, Dec. 10, 1931, 635.

28. Vol. 155 (Scrapbook, 1932–34), HJKP.

29. *Oakland Tribune*, Aug. 25, 1967, 1.

30. Foster, *Henry J. Kaiser*, 53. Kaiser testified in 1932 that "my companies are open-shop" (U.S. Congress, House Committee on Labor, *Hearings, Wages*, 19).

31. Stevens, *Hoover Dam*, 48.

32. Foster, *Henry J. Kaiser*, 50–51; Stevens, *Hoover Dam*, 55, 60, 70–71.

33. Stevens, *Hoover Dam*, 71–72.

34. Ibid., 59, 83, 72.

35. Ibid., 101, 282.

36. Ibid., 252, 213–14; Foster, *Henry J. Kaiser*, 53.

37. Kaiser speech to National Press Club, Sept. 30, 1942, HJKP, carton 298.

38. U.S. Congress, House Committee on Labor, *Hearings, Wages*, 19, 25.

39. "Memorandum," Aug. 3, 1937, HJKP, carton 4.

40. Kaiser to Page, Jan. 3, 1939, BRP, Project Correspondence File 1930–45, Central Valley 011, box 98.

41. The official was John Frey of the metal trades. See Kaiser to Eccles, May 21, 1940, HJKP carton 6, folder 22.

42. Speech, July 30, 1942, HJKP, carton 298.

43. The first study of Kaiser's health maintenance organization is Hendricks, "Necessary Revolution." Details of the program's inception are on pages 80–125.

44. Amy Kesselman explores the experiences of women at Kaiser's shipyards in *Fleeting Opportunities*. Kesselman describes Kaiser's revolutionary day care centers on pages 74–89.

45. Foster, *Henry J. Kaiser*, 108–9.

46. Galambos, *Cooperation and Competition*, 293.

47. Schumpeter, *Theory of Economic Development*, 90–92. The "characteristic task" of an entrepreneur, writes Schumpeter, "consists precisely in breaking up old, and creating

new, tradition." He also notes that society is no less accepting of an entrepreneur in its midst who "moves about in society as an upstart, whose ways are readily laughed at."

48. Schlesinger, *Politics of Upheaval*, 395.

49. Kaiser to Pagel, May 4, 1939, HJKP, carton 4.

50. Kaiser to Cowell, Calaveras, Yosemite, Santa Cruz, and Pacific Portland Cement Companies, Feb. 17, 1933, HJKP, carton 3, folder 29.

51. Testimony of Frank Fetter, professor emeritus of economics, Princeton University, U.S. Congress, Senate Committee on Interstate Commerce, *Hearings on S. 4055*, 14.

52. U.S. Congress, Senate Committee on Interstate Commerce, *Hearings on S. 4055*, 8.

53. *Fortune*, Sept. 1948, 74.

54. Loescher, *Imperfect Collusion*, 84–85.

55. Roosevelt to Morgenthau, Mar. 28, 1938, OF 1012.

56. In 1924, after receiving a cease and desist order from the government, U.S. Steel agreed to refrain from using basing point pricing "insofar as it is practicable to do so." The 1933 NRA steel code legalized basing point practices until the expiration of the NRA act in 1935. From March to April 1936, the Senate Interstate Commerce Committee held hearings—focusing on cement and steel—on a bill designed to outlaw the basing point practice. The bill died in committee. See Berry to Roosevelt, June 20, 1936, OF 342.

57. "Report of Senator Herbert C. Jones on the Existence of a Reputed Cement Trust," May 15, 1929, Records of the Office of the Secretary of the Interior, E-766, box 1, National Archives.

58. U.S. Bureau of the Census, *Statistical History*, 630; Loescher, *Imperfect Collusion*, 619.

59. *New York Times*, May 6, 1933, 1.

60. Ibid.

61. Ickes, Diary, May 8, 1933, 84, HLIP.

62. George Gay to Kaiser, Feb. 21, 1933, HJKP, carton 3, folder 29.

63. Schlesinger, *Coming of the New Deal*, 100; Hawley, *New Deal and the Problem of Monopoly*, 94.

64. W. A. Ayres, chairman of Federal Trade Commission, to FDR, Dec. 23, 1937, OF 1012.

65. U.S. Congress, Senate Committee on Interstate Commerce, *Hearing on S. 4055*, 291. See also U.S. Temporary National Economic Committee, *Government Purchasing*, 36.

66. U.S. Congress, Senate Committee on Interstate Commerce, *Hearings on S. 4055*.

67. Foster, *Henry J. Kaiser*, 63, 65–69.

68. Ickes to Knox, n.d, HJKP, carton 6, folder 28.

69. Introductory comments, Kaiser Public Relations Conference, Apr. 30, 1955, EKP, carton 225, folder 9.

70. "Earth Movers II," 220.

71. "Comments of G. G. Sherwood on Cement Situation," Mar. 14, 1938, HJKP, carton 3, folder 29.

72. Blum, *Years of Crisis*, 409.

73. U.S. Temporary National Economic Committee, *Government Purchasing*, 316–17.

74. Blum, *Years of Crisis*, 414.

75. Freidel, *Franklin D. Roosevelt*, 210.

76. Wayne C. Taylor, assistant secretary of the treasury, to FDR, Mar. 29, 1938, OF 1012.

77. U.S. Temporary National Economic Committee, *Government Purchasing*, 36.

78. Ayres to Roosevelt, Dec. 23, 1937, OF 1012.

79. Price to Kaiser, Mar. 18, 1937, HJKP, carton 3.

80. Kaiser to Miss I. M. Cowell and Mr. S. H. Cowell, Feb. 21, 1938, HJKP, carton 3, folder 29.

81. Kaiser to Charles M. Cadman, Mar. 12, 1938, ibid.

82. H. F. Morton to Kaiser, Apr. 25, 1938, ibid.

83. Sherwood to Trefethen, Apr. 28, 1938, HJKP, carton 3, folder 39.

84. S. O. Harper to Construction Engineer, Sacramento, California, July 1, 1938, BRP, Project Correspondence File 1930-45, Central Valley 011, box 98.

85. "Plan for Entering Cement Field," May 7, 1938, HJKP, carton 3, folder 29.

86. John C. Page to Ickes, May 19, 1939, BRP, Project Correspondence File 1930-45, Central Valley 011, box 98.

87. Fred H. Brown to Morgenthau, June 2, 1939, ibid.

88. Kaiser to Edward Heller, Sept. 8, 1938, HJKP, carton 3, folder 29, Minutes of RFC Executive Board, 90:260 (July 7, 1939), 91:1012 (Aug. 18, 1939), 91:1647 (Aug. 29, 1939), 93:205 (Oct. 4, 1939), Records of the Reconstruction Finance Corporation, National Archives.

89. Loescher, *Imperfect Collusion*, 56.

90. *Constructor*, Aug. 1936, 1.

91. Schlesinger, *Politics of Upheaval*, 280, 387.

92. Lauderbaugh, *American Steel Makers*, 24.

93. Testimony of Ben Fairless, head of U.S. Steel, Nov. 7, 1939, U.S. Temporary National Economic Committee, *Iron and Steel*, 10536.

94. Opening statement by Leon Henderson, Dec. 3, 1938, U.S. Temporary National Economic Committee, *Economic Prologue*, 173.

95. Testimony of Professor M. G. de Chazeau, Nov. 6, 1939, U.S. Temporary National Economic Committee, *Iron and Steel*, 10473.

96. By March 1937, Lubin and Eccles were already calculating the difference between the recent steel industry wage increase and the industry's subsequent price increase. Eccles informed Roosevelt that "the rise in steel prices has been greatly in excess of the rise that would be sufficient to compensate for the wage advance" (Eccles to Roosevelt, Mar. 12, 1937, OF 342). A few weeks later, Lubin produced statistical data demonstrating that "prices of steel had increased twice the amount paid by the industry in higher wages" (Early to Roosevelt, Apr. 3, 1937, OF 342).

97. Lauderbaugh, *American Steel Makers*, 27.

98. Ibid., 29.

99. Currie, Henderson, and Lubin were Eccles's "unshaken allies" (Hyman, *Marriner S. Eccles*, 237). Ickes met regularly with Cohen, Corcoran, and Jackson in 1939 and 1940 (Ickes, Diary, 4215, HLIP; Ickes, *Lowering Clouds*, 5, Sept. 16, 1939).

100. Hawley, *New Deal and the Problem of Monopoly*, 406-7.

101. Lauderbaugh, *American Steel Makers*, 29. Nearly a year before, Eccles had shown how the ideas of the Keynesians and Brandeisians could complement each other when

dealing with the issue of prices: "The price rises to which I refer are the result primarily of . . . factors including . . . monopolistic practices by certain groups in both industry and organized labor. . . . The remedy for a price inflation when the country has unused manpower, natural resources, and capital is through more, not less production" (Eccles, *Beckoning Frontiers*, 298).

102. Eccles, *Beckoning Frontiers*, 311.

103. U.S. Temporary National Economic Committee, *Economic Prologue*, Dec. 3, 1938, 157–83.

104. Lauderbaugh, *American Steel Makers*, 40–41.

105. U.S. Temporary National Economic Committee, *Economic Prologue* (Dec. 3, 1938), 175.

106. Kaiser, *Management Looks at the Postwar World*, 10.

107. McQuaid, *Big Business and Presidential Power*, 15.

108. Roosevelt, *Press Conferences*, 14:269.

109. Roosevelt to Delano, Nov. 15, 1939, OF 342, box 1.

110. Roosevelt to Kennedy, June 11, 1935, ibid.

111. Roosevelt, *Press Conferences*, 14:269; Freidel, *Franklin D. Roosevelt*, 210.

112. Roosevelt, *Public Papers*, 1:742–56.

113. Schlesinger, *Coming of the New Deal*, 323.

114. Roosevelt, *Roosevelt and Conservation*, 405–6.

115. U.S. Civilian Production Administration, *Program and Administration*, 10.

116. Currie to FDR, Sept. 19, 1939, OF 342, box 1. Currie's explanation of the 1937 recession had focused on the steel industry's price increases. He noted that those increases—supposedly to compensate for increased labor costs—resulted in U.S. Steel's break-even point moving from 50 percent of capacity to 43 percent (Lauderbaugh, *American Steel Makers*, 206–7).

117. Lauderbaugh, *American Steel Makers*, 46.

118. Currie to Roosevelt, Oct. 16, 1939, OF 342, box 1.

119. *Wall Street Journal*, Oct. 16, 1939, 1.

120. W. C. Mendenhall, director of USGS, and Jon W. Finch, director of Bureau of Mines, to Ickes, Nov. 3, 1939, OF 342, box 1.

121. Roosevelt to Delano, Nov. 15, 1939, ibid.

122. *Iron Age*, Nov. 30, 1939, 54.

123. "Possibilities of Expanding Steel Production in the Pacific Coast Region," n.d., 12, OF 342, box 1.

124. "The Feasibility of a Steel Plant in the Lower Columbia River Area," June 28, 1938, ibid.

125. Roosevelt to Ickes, Dec. 21, 1939 in Roosevelt, *Roosevelt and Conservation*, 405–6.

126. Lauderbaugh, *American Steel Makers*, 50.

127. Early to Ickes, Sept. 13, 1940, OF 342.

128. Ickes to Early, Sept. 24, 1940, ibid.

CHAPTER FOUR

1. Calhoun to Kaiser, May 1, 24, 1940, HJKP, carton 5.

2. Sherwood, *Roosevelt and Hopkins*, 3.

3. Somers, *Presidential Agency*, 10; Connery, *Navy and Industrial Mobilization*, 79.

4. Calhoun to Kaiser, July 4, May 24, 1940, HJKP, carton 5.

5. Chad Calhoun, Magnesium Confidential, July 2, 1941, HJKP, carton 318, folder 9.

6. Calhoun to George Havas, Oct. 16, 1940, HJKP, carton 316, folder 15. Emphasis added.

7. U.S. Civilian Production Administration, *Program and Administration*, 19–20.

8. Nash, *American West Transformed*, 7.

9. Havas to Kaiser, June 7, 1940, HJKP, carton 5, folder 1.

10. James and James, *Biography of a Bank*, 460–61.

11. Gerard Piel to author, Jan. 2, 1991.

12. *Fortune*, Apr. 1966, 135.

13. Interview, George Meader, Oct. 24, 1990; interview, Robert Nathan, Oct. 3, 1991.

14. *Western Construction News*, Aug. 10, 1929, 421; *Western Construction News*, July 10, 1930, 340; *Engineering News-Record*, Apr. 11, 1929, 611; *Engineering News-Record*, June 5, 1930, 950.

15. See, for instance, Ober to Kaiser, Mar. 27, 1937, HJKP, carton 3; Ober to Kaiser, Feb. 9, 1940, HJKP, carton 4.

16. Ober to Sherwood, Jan. 17, 1938, HJKP, carton 3.

17. Edgar Kaiser to Ober, Jan. 5, 1939, ibid.

18. Ordway to Kaiser, Feb. 6, 1967, HJKP, carton 321.

19. Every now and then Ober would go beyond listing information and provide an opinion. See, for instance, Ober to Kaiser, Jan. 25, 1940, HJKP, carton 4.

20. The papers of Henry J. Kaiser and his administrative genius, Eugene E. Trefethen Jr., at the University of California, Berkeley's Bancroft Library are full of Calhoun's letters from Washington. Boxes 127 and 316 of the Kaiser papers provide an excellent glimpse of Calhoun's 1940-41 Washington activities, and boxes 47-51 of the Trefethen papers show Calhoun's Washington activities from 1942 to the mid-1950s.

21. *Fortune*, Apr. 1966, 135. For reasons unknown to his old colleagues in the Kaiser organization, Calhoun later became squeamish about his paper trail. In his will he requested that his widow destroy his papers, and she complied (interview, Robert Sandberg, Jan. 18, 1991).

22. Galbraith, *A Life in Our Times*, 325.

23. *Fortune*, Apr. 1966, 135.

24. Calhoun to Kaiser, Aug. 21, 1940, HJKP, carton 5, folder 1.

25. Calhoun to Kaiser, July 22, 1940, HJKP, carton 127, folder 11.

26. Calhoun to Kaiser, Dec. 5, 1940, HJKP, carton 316, folder 15.

27. Velie, "Truth about Henry Kaiser," 26; interview, Gerard Piel, Apr. 9, 1991. Kaiser, for instance, exhibited a westerner's suspicion of concentration of economic power, but Calhoun's sensitivity to the issue far surpassed Kaiser's. In July 1940, when it appeared all defense-related airplane manufacturing would go to the existing airplane companies, Calhoun wrote, "Sounds like monopoly or its second cousin" (Calhoun to Kaiser, July 23, 1940, HJKP, carton 127, folder 11).

28. Calhoun to Kaiser, Sept. 7, 1940, HJKP, carton 316, folder 15.

29. Smith to Granik, May 2, 1941, TGP, box 72, "Misc. Correspondence—1941."

30. Interview, Fred Drewes, Sept. 2, 1992.

31. Telegram, Calhoun to Johnson, May 21, 1940, HJKP, carton 127, folder 11.

32. Hyman, *Marriner S. Eccles*, 160.

33. Eccles to Kaiser, Oct. 29, 1940, HJKP, carton 128, folder 6.

34. Biographical note on Theodore Granik, n.d., TGP, finder's aid.

35. Utah Construction's stake in the Columbia Construction Company ranged from 22.5 percent in early 1940 to 11.25 percent in December. Utah Construction also owned 10 percent of Kaiser's Permanente Cement Company and would become a 6 percent owner in Kaiser's shipbuilding venture in December 1940. See Lackey to Sherwood, Feb. 26, 1940, HJKP, carton 5, folder 11; Sherwood to Lackey, Dec. 17, 1940, HJKP, carton 5, folder 12; "History of the Kaiser Companies, Vol. II," 200B, 255A, HJKP, carton 298.

36. Hyman, *Marriner S. Eccles*, 272.

37. Calhoun to Kaiser, July 9, 1940, HJKP, carton 5.

38. Calhoun, Magnesium Confidential, Sept. 1940, HJKP, carton 318, folder 9.

39. Eccles to Kaiser, Oct. 29, 1940, HJKP, carton 128, folder 6. Despite a career of loyalty to Eccles, including seven years in Washington, Clayton was so impressed by Kaiser that he offered his services to the industrialist in August 1942. He wrote: "Several times during the past year I have had an urge to write you. More recently, the urge has become too strong to suppress in view of the electrifying plans you are now working on. . . . Your plans for cargo planes would now require the rapid building of an organization. . . . You might have need of a financial man who knows the ropes not only from commercial banking experience but from the Government end also. . . . Should you feel that I could be useful to you in your new organization as a financial officer, I would welcome a discussion with you. While I am presently in a most interesting spot, I have been in the Government service nearly eight years and would welcome a return to private business. . . . Should I hear nothing from you, I would assume that you have your personnel problems already solved and we will just forget that I ever wrote this letter" (Clayton to Kaiser, Aug. 26, 1942, HJKP, carton 15).

40. Hyman, *Marriner S. Eccles*, 40–41, 170.

41. Lash, *Dealers and Dreamers*, 318-19.

42. Hyman, *Marriner S. Eccles*, 237.

43. Calhoun to Kaiser, July 4, May 24, 1940, HJKP, carton 5.

44. Calhoun to Kaiser, Aug. 21, Sept. 17, 1940, HJKP, carton 5.

45. U.S. Civilian Production Administration, *Program and Administration*, 47.

46. Calhoun to Kaiser, Sept. 7, 1940, HJKP, carton 127, folder 11.

47. Calhoun to Kaiser, Dec. 19, 1940, ibid.

48. U.S. Civilian Production Administration, *Program and Administration*, 49.

49. Calhoun to Kaiser, Dec. 19, 1940, HJKP, carton 127, folder 11.

50. Calhoun to Kaiser, July 22, 1940, HJKP, carton 162, folder 5.

51. Calhoun to Kaiser, Aug. 21, 29, 1940, HJKP, carton 316, folder 15.

52. Calhoun to Kaiser, Sept. 3, 1940, ibid.

53. Lauderbaugh, *American Steel Makers*, 51, 52.

54. Calhoun to Kaiser, Sept. 3, 1940, HJKP, carton 316, folder 15. Congress had approved the fund on June 28 for "direct financing of army and navy facilities" (Connery, *Navy and Industrial Mobilization*, 471). For reaction inside the Kaiser organization to the establishment of the fund, see Calhoun to Kaiser, Sept. 6, 1940, HJKP, carton 127, folder 11.

55. Calhoun to File, Dec. 21, 1940, 1, HJKP, carton 316, folder 15.

56. Calhoun to File, Sept. 4, 1940, ibid.

57. Ketchum, *Borrowed Years*, 148.

58. Lauderbaugh, *American Steel Makers*, 43.

59. Roosevelt, *Press Conferences*, 15:487–88.

60. Calhoun to File, Sept. 4, 1940, HJKP, carton 316, folder 15.

61. Calhoun to Kaiser, Sept. 3, 1940, ibid.

62. Watkins, *Righteous Pilgrim*, 396, 663–75, 681.

63. Calhoun to File, Sept. 19, 1940, HJKP, carton 316, folder 15.

64. Ibid.

65. Ickes, Diary, Dec. 1, 1938, 2523, HLIP.

66. Calhoun to Kaiser, Oct. 1, 1940, HJKP, carton 316, folder 15.

67. Kaiser to Reilly, Oct. 4, 1940, ibid.

68. Calhoun, Magnesium Confidential, Sept. 1940, Calhoun, Magnesium Confidential, Oct. 3, 1940, HJKP, carton 318, folder 9.

69. Lauderbaugh, *American Steel Makers*, 33.

70. Roosevelt, *Public Papers*, 9:237.

71. Kaiser to Ickes, Oct. 4, 1940, HJKP, carton 128, folder 6.

72. Kaiser to Eccles, Oct. 14, 1940, ibid. Kaiser had met with Marion Folsom of the NDAC on September 19, but to no avail; Folsom was convinced Dow Chemical could produce enough magnesium (Calhoun to File, Sept. 19, 1940, HJKP, carton 318, folder 9).

73. Calhoun to Kaiser, Oct. 16, 1940, HJKP, carton 316, folder 15.

74. Calhoun to Havas, Oct. 17, 1940, ibid. Robert Nathan argues that whereas many organizations were content to make their presence known, Kaiser was the most dogged about following up (interview, Oct. 17, 1991).

75. Eccles to Kaiser, Oct. 29, 1940, HJKP, carton 128, folder 6. Emphasis added.

76. Wattis to Sherwood, Jan. 15, 1941, Harris to Kaiser Co., Feb. 12, 1941, Wattis to Sherwood, June 15, 1941, Wattis to Kaiser, June 7, 1941, all in HJKP, carton 11, folder 15.

77. Roosevelt, *Public Papers*, 9:544–45.

78. Calhoun to File, Dec. 11, 1940, HJKP, carton 316, folder 15.

79. *Washington Post*, Dec. 9, 1940.

80. Lindley speech at National Press Club, July 30, 1942, HJKP, carton 298.

81. Lauchlin Currie, unpublished memoir, ca. 1952, 175.

82. Calhoun to File, Dec. 11, 1940, HJKP, carton 316, folder 15.

83. Currie memoir, 175–76.

84. Sandilands, *Lauchlin Currie*, 99.

85. Calhoun to File, Dec. 11, 1940, HJKP, carton 316, folder 15.

86. Galbraith, *A Life in Our Times*, 108.

87. The principal concern Girdler expressed in their December 5 meeting involved the question of potential demand for steel. He believed the government's economists were overstating future needs. Kaiser and Calhoun pointed out that regardless of their accuracy, such extreme estimates were likely to help them obtain a government contract. Girdler agreed (Calhoun to Kaiser, Dec. 5, 1940, HJKP, carton 316, folder 15).

88. Calhoun to Kaiser, Dec. 12, 1940, ibid.

89. Calhoun to Kaiser, Dec. 13, 1940, HJKP, carton 127, folder 11.

90. Calhoun to Kaiser, Dec. 17, 1940, HJKP, carton 316, folder 15.

91. Calhoun to Kaiser, Dec. 12, Dec. 6, 1940, ibid.

92. Calhoun to Kaiser, Dec. 17, 1940, ibid.

93. Ibid.

94. Calhoun to Kaiser, Dec. 18, 1940, ibid.

95. Calhoun to Kaiser, Dec. 21, 1940, ibid.

96. Calhoun to File (re: Henderson), Dec. 24, 1940, Calhoun to File (re: Currie), Dec. 24, 1940, ibid.

97. Henry J. Kaiser Jr. to Girdler, Jan. 27, 1941, HJKP, carton 10.

98. "Memo re Conversation with Tom Girdler and HJK, Aug. 5, 1942," HJKP, carton 14, folder 42.

99. Calhoun to Kaiser, Dec. 18, 1940, HJKP, carton 316, folder 15. Currie described the procedure as "tying the proposed project in with other companies and applying for a certificate of necessity to permit the utilization of their profits in a rapid writing off of the steel plant" (memoir, 175).

100. Calhoun to Kaiser, Dec. 19, 1940, HJKP, carton 127, folder 11.

101. Calhoun to File, Dec. 24, 1940, HJKP, carton 316, folder 15.

102. Calhoun to File, Dec. 24, 1940, ibid.

103. Bain, *Barriers to New Competition*, 169–70.

104. In a monopoly or near-monopoly situation, cooperative pricing can prevent entry even if the newcomer has the wherewithal to achieve necessary economies of scale. This is because when entry is made on a large scale, prices will go down. So "even when new entrants are physically able to operate *just as efficiently as existing firms* [a real challenge for nascent industrialist Kaiser], the interaction between price and large-scale entry can be a significant deterrent to new entry" (Scherer, *Industrial Market Structure*, 225–33. Emphasis added).

105. Calhoun to Kaiser, Dec. 21, 1940, HJKP, carton 162, folder 5.

106. Lauderbaugh, *American Steel Makers*, 33.

107. In May 1939, Treasury Secretary Morgenthau wrote that Harry Hopkins "says today the president listens to Bob Jackson, Leon Henderson, Eccles, and he said the economists he has confidence in are Henderson, Currie, and Lubin" (Blum, *Years of Urgency*, 26).

108. U.S. Civilian Production Administration, *Program and Administration*, 93.

109. Mitchell, *Every Kind of Shipwork*, 127.

CHAPTER FIVE

1. HJKP, carton 32, folder 22.

2. Jeffrey L. Meikle notes the outside contracting for industrial design, particularly in the 1930s, in *Twentieth Century Limited*. For comment on advertising expertise, see Marchand, *Advertising the American Dream*. JoAnne Yates discusses the corporate use of efficiency experts in *Control through Communication*.

3. Interview, Robert Sandberg, Apr. 6, 1991.

4. Foster, *Henry J. Kaiser*, 234.

5. Louchheim, *Making of the New Deal*, 229; Goulden, *Super-Lawyers*, 27.

6. Kiplinger, *Washington Is Like That*, 312.

7. Irons, *New Deal Lawyers*, 300.

8. Cutler quoted in Goulden, *Super-Lawyers*, 8. Chad Calhoun used this wording, too. Years before John F. Kennedy's address to the 1960 Democratic convention, Calhoun said: "Pioneering in Washington, D.C. is not out of place because this is a 'frontier' town. . . . Everywhere there are new frontiers. New worlds, new opportunities are limited only by the

willingness of the mind to conceive them" (Speech to public relations conference, Apr. 30, 1955, EKP, carton 225, folder 9). See also Schlesinger, *A Thousand Days*, 60, 66.

9. Corcoran's work for the New Deal has been well chronicled by Schlesinger, Joseph Lash, and a host of insiders, including Harold Ickes. See Lash, *Dealers and Dreamers*; Schlesinger, *Coming of the New Deal*; Schlesinger, *Politics of Upheaval*. Corcoran's private practice, however, has been more the subject of speculation. He discussed it in interviews with Studs Terkel and Katie Louchheim. See Terkel, *"Good War,"* 318–21; and Louchheim, *Making of the New Deal*. Besides such oral histories, the best sources on his practice are Goulden, *Super-Lawyers*, and the FBI's wiretaps of Corcoran's phone from 1945 to 1947. These sources agree with Corcoran's own accounts in one main respect: his chief service was providing "know-who" and the ability to bring a deal together, rather than "know-how," special legal knowledge. For an analysis of what the FBI phone taps reveal, see Lichting, "Tommy the Cork," 42.

10. Kaiser wrote to an associate in late 1944 that "I have not endorsed legislation of any type" (Kaiser to Morton, Dec. 22, 1944, HJKP, carton 26, folder 25).

11. Goulden, *Super-Lawyers*, 145.

12. Louchheim, *Making of the New Deal*, 117.

13. Goulden, *Super-Lawyers*, 148.

14. U.S. Congress, Senate Special Committee Investigating National Defense Program, *Hearings* (1941), 3907.

15. Goulden, *Super-Lawyers*, 154.

16. Horsky, *Washington Lawyer*.

17. Murphy, *Brandeis/Frankfurter Connection*, 7.

18. Corcoran was with the RFC from 1932 until 1940, and before becoming a presidential adviser, one of his first tasks with the RFC had been to help Henry Kaiser secure funds for the construction of the San Francisco–Oakland Bay Bridge. See Corcoran, "Rendezvous with Democracy," TCP, box 586A, section 3, 20–21.

19. Schlesinger, *Politics of Upheaval*, 228–29.

20. Robert Stern, Frank Watson, Milton Katz, Henry Fowler, Telford Taylor, Thomas Emerson, Joseph Rauh, Frank Thornton Greene, and many others were "placed" by Corcoran. See Louchheim, *Making of the New Deal*, 56, 63, 79, 107, 120, 145, 206, 228, 240.

21. Irons, *New Deal Lawyers*, 298.

22. Corcoran, "Rendezvous with Democracy," TCP, box 586A, section 2, 13.

23. Janeway, *Struggle for Survival*, 169.

24. Corcoran, "Rendezvous with Democracy," TCP, box 586A, section 2, 24.

25. Even in his first federal government job, as assistant secretary of the navy, Roosevelt was adept at cultivating the image of a man who "boldly slashed red tape" (Burns, *Roosevelt: The Lion and the Fox*, 61). On matters of naval procurement, Roosevelt arranged to be approached directly by representatives of the Bureau of Supplies and Accounts, rather than going through the normal chain of command.

26. Tom Corcoran came to symbolize the New Deal's antibureaucratic style, and to administration critics he personified its excesses. Impatient with lines of authority and bureaucratic channels, he found ways to expedite important matters. David Reisman, a New Deal lawyer before becoming an eminent sociologist, was critical of the antibureaucratic and extrajurisdictional nature of the New Deal. He saw it as undemocratic and as showing "contempt for ordinary Americans" (Louchheim, *Making of the New Deal*, 75). David

Lilienthal, head of the Tennessee Valley Authority, agreed, and focused his criticism on one individual: Thomas Corcoran. He decried Corcoran's practice of "trying to slip things through, without adequate consideration and discussion" (Anderson, *Presidents' Men*, 50).

27. Blum, *Years of Urgency*, 186.

28. Calhoun to File, Dec. 24, 1940, HJKP, carton 316, folder 15.

29. Murphy, *Brandeis/Frankfurter Connection*, 209.

30. Blum, *Years of Urgency*, 100–103.

31. Steel, *Walter Lippmann*, 389.

32. Mitchell, *Every Kind of Shipwork*, 121–23; Foster, *Henry J. Kaiser*, 69.

33. Mitchell, *Every Kind of Shipwork*, 127.

34. U.S. Civilian Production Administration, *Program and Administration*, 26–27.

35. Interviews, David Ginsburg, Nov. 25, Dec. 10, 1992, May 3, 1993.

36. Burns, *Roosevelt*, 83; Herzstein, *Henry R. Luce*, 202–3.

37. Emerson, *Young Lawyer*, 144; Burns, *Roosevelt*, 116.

38. When a businessman is confronted with a change in his environment, he may choose between adaptive or creative responses. Creative responses characterize the entrepreneur (Aitken, *Explorations in Enterprise*, 24).

39. U.S. Congress, Senate Special Committee Investigating National Defense Program, *Hearings* (1941), 3871.

40. Corcoran, "Rendezvous with Democracy," TCP, box 586A, "Setting the Table for War," 2.

41. Corcoran, "Rendezvous with Democracy," TCP, box 586A, "The New York Connection," 11.

42. Durr, *Early History*, 8.

43. Schwartz, *New Dealers*, 94, 314. In addition to a chapter on Jesse Jones, Schwartz devotes separate chapters to Tom Corcoran and Henry Kaiser. He does not, however, explore the Corcoran-Kaiser relationship.

44. Ickes, Diary, Feb. 16, 1941, 5224, HLIP.

45. Jones was later able to derail Kaiser's attempts to obtain RFC loans for both the production of synthetic rubber and the construction of airplanes (Jones with Angly, *Fifty Billion Dollars*, 331).

46. Ickes, Diary, 5224, HLIP.

47. Horsky, *Washington Lawyer*, 131.

48. Taylor, "Builder No. 1," 9.

49. "Magnesium, Lesson in Speed," 67.

50. "Master Builder," 28; "Kaiser's Steel," 26.

51. *Fortune*, July 1941, 126.

52. Smith to Granik, May 21, 1941, TGP, carton 72, "Misc. Correspondence—1941."

53. Vatter, *U.S. Economy*, 61, 60.

54. U.S. Civilian Production Administration, Industrial Statistics Division, *War Industrial Facilities*.

55. Ickes, *Lowering Clouds*, 436.

56. Calhoun to Kaiser, Feb. 18, 1941, HJKP, carton 7.

57. Ickes, *Lowering Clouds*, 421.

58. Ickes to Knox, n.d., HJKP, carton 7.

59. Ickes, Diary, 438, 445, HLIP.

60. Cuneo to Corcoran, Apr. 3, 1941, TCP, box 496, folder 1.

61. U.S. Congress, Senate Special Committee Investigating National Defense Program, *Hearings* (1947), 23625.

62. Corcoran to Tully, Oct. 9, 1941, PPF 6721.

63. Janeway to author, Mar. 11, 1992.

64. U.S. Congress, Senate Special Committee Investigating National Defense Program, *Hearings* (1941), 3899.

65. *Newsweek*, Dec. 8, 1941, 49.

66. U.S. Congress, Senate Special Committee Investigating National Defense Program, *Hearings* (1941), 3911.

67. Foster, *Henry J. Kaiser*, 99, 303 n. 29.

68. U.S. Congress, Senate Special Committee Investigating National Defense Program, *Hearings* (1941), 3923, 3925.

69. Foster, *Henry J. Kaiser*, 91.

70. Kaiser to Roosevelt, June 9, 1941, OF 342, box 1.

71. "The Origins of Kaiser Steel," 9, HJKP, carton 162, folder 5.

72. Currie to Roosevelt, May 23, 1941, OF 342.

73. Roosevelt to OPM, May 26, 1941, OF 342; Foster, *Henry J. Kaiser*, 93. Gano Dunn, sensing the implications of Roosevelt's change of tactics, resigned within a few weeks (ibid., 92).

74. Roosevelt, *Press Conferences*, Dec. 28, 1943, 22:246–51.

75. Foster, *Henry J. Kaiser*, 94–95. Ironically, although the Geneva plant was authorized nearly a full year before Kaiser's Fontana plant, U.S. Steel geared it up for full production nearly a year *after* Kaiser's plant was up and running. See Broadcast, John B. Hughes, Oct. 7, 1942, HJKP, carton 13, "Hughes, John B. 1942."

CHAPTER SIX

1. Lubin to Roosevelt, Mar. 23, 1945, PPF 2924.

2. Needham, Louis, and Broiley, Inc. Advertising Agency (Chicago), "Check on Attitude toward Henry J. Kaiser, April 1943," HJKP, carton 18, folder 25.

3. At the end of 1944, Earl Reynolds was arguing in favor of expanding the organization's public relations capabilities: "We are definitely in 'Big Business' and the history of Big Business during the past several years has proven the soundness of firstly having good policies and secondly properly interpreting these policies to the public" (Reynolds to Carl Olson, Dec. 12, 1944, HJKP, carton 148, folder 21). Reynolds became Kaiser's public relations man in southern California (Ordway to Elliott, Aug. 26, 1966, HJKP, carton 257).

4. U.S. Congress, Senate Special Committee Investigating National Defense Program, *Hearings* (1947), 23638.

5. Foster, *Henry J. Kaiser*, 60.

6. Kaiser to Bechtel, Apr. 9, 1941, HJKP carton 316, folder 18.

7. Interview, Jack Carlson, Aug. 27, 1992.

8. Henry Luce and Time, Inc., have been the subjects of prominent and provocative studies since Luce's death. Halberstam's *Powers That Be*, Swanberg's *Luce and His Empire*, and Herzstein's *Henry R. Luce* focus—often critically—on the way Luce wielded power through his publications. Elson's *Time, Inc.* and *World of Time, Inc.*, and Baugham's

Henry R. Luce portray Luce less as a power broker and more as "minister of information" for policy makers.

The Kaiser story was such a consistent feature in *Time*, *Life*, and *Fortune* during the war that Kaiser's absence from these books is surprising. One possible explanation is in the sources used, which ranged from Halberstam's extensive interviews with Luce's associates and contemporaries, to Herzstein's use of the papers of Luce and Time, Inc., to Elson's access to Luce himself. Because the primary goal in these books was to ascertain Luce's attitudes and behavior, his letters and the various interviews are the principal sources. When the magazines themselves are used as documents, it is either to demonstrate the distinct *Time* style, to focus on editorial battles, or to highlight pieces Luce personally wrote or edited (such as the "American Century" editorial in 1941).

Kaiser and Luce rarely met or corresponded, however, so the Luce-Kaiser story can be found mainly on the pages of *Time*, *Life*, and *Fortune* and in the widespread imitation of the language and themes of the articles.

9. The primary vehicles were *Time*, with a weekly circulation of 1.16 million, *Life*, with 4 million, and the Radio March of Time, with 18 million weekly listeners (Swanberg, *Luce and His Empire*, 214).

10. Twenty-seven of the sixty-eight Kaiser articles listed from 1941 to 1943 were from *Time*, *Life*, or *Fortune*. The *Reader's Guide* list, however, is by no means complete. Twice, three Kaiser stories appeared in one issue of *Time*, and one issue of *Business Week* had three, but each of those issues warranted only a single listing in the *Reader's Guide*.

11. Baugham, *Henry R. Luce*, 59.

12. Halberstam, *Powers That Be*, 46.

13. *Fortune*, Dec. 1941, 93.

14. *Time*, Aug. 10, 1942, 20–21.

15. Halberstam, *Powers That Be*, 45.

16. Swanberg, *Luce and His Empire*, 174–75.

17. Baugham, *Henry R. Luce*, 119.

18. Elson, *Time, Inc.*, 460–63.

19. Elson, *World of Time, Inc.*, 5.

20. Herzstein, *Henry R. Luce*, 219.

21. Winkler, *Politics of Propaganda*, 12.

22. "Tugwell Upped," 10.

23. *Fortune*, Feb. 1940, 20.

24. Swanberg, *Luce and His Empire*, 53.

25. "Henry Kaiser's Dream," 82.

26. Kaiser to Luce, Mar. 14, 1945, HJKP, carton 177.

27. Eliot Janeway to author, Mar. 11, 1992; Gerard Piel to author, July 29, 1992.

28. *Time* first popularized the word "tycoon" in the 1920s (Elson, *Time, Inc.*, 86).

29. "Who Can't?," 13. In mid-1942, Kaiser's magnesium operation was still not making money because it had not attained sufficient economies of scale, which required additional government approval (G. G. Sherwood to Trefethen, May 28, 1942, HJKP, carton 15, "E. E. Trefethen, Jr., 1942").

30. "Permanente Squeaks Through," 77–78. Just before publication of that story, *Life* reporter Gerard Piel offered to get Kaiser's magnesium story published in a positive light: "Can get Permanente story repaired with another story in *Time* if you will airmail to me

immediately detailed review history of plant. Including originally projected capacity and completion date, production rate for present and immediate future, description of process, and story on accidents" (Piel to Kaiser, Jan. 26, 1943, HJKP, carton 21, folder 26). Kaiser responded that he could not provide the necessary information without permission from the Office of War Information and Office of War Production. Kaiser intended instead to "publish a small booklet in the nature of advertising. Until that time I am afraid we will have to be content to accept the unjust criticism which is not due us" (Kaiser to Piel, Feb. 2, 1943, ibid.).

31. Herzstein, *Henry R. Luce*, 88–89.

32. Halberstam, *Powers That Be*, 51.

33. "Notes Taken 6/22/43 of Meeting between Henry J. Kaiser, Sr., Jr., and Chad F. Calhoun and Mr. Murphy and Miss McEneny of *Fortune*," HJKP, carton 21, folder 26.

34. Calhoun to H. F. Morton, Feb. 14, 1942, HJKP, carton 12, folder 3.

35. Piel to author, July 29, 1992.

36. Piel to Kaiser, Mar. 20, 1942, HJKP, vol. 157.

37. Piel, "No. 1 Shipbuilder."

38. Foster, *Henry J. Kaiser*, 83–84.

39. Vickery to Kaiser, Dec. 24, 1942, HJKP, carton 15, "U.S. Government—Vickery, Admiral H. L., 1942." A few days after receiving Vickery's letter, Kaiser referred the admiral to a *Time* article about Liberty Ship designer William Francis Gibbs. *Time* credited Gibbs's "radical, straight-from-the-hip methods" with the "technological revolution which made four-day Liberty Ships possible." Kaiser good-naturedly wrote, "Your letter must have been misdirected; however, both you and I would be interested in just one tiny little thing—how long it took them to build the prefabricated ship outlined in the photographs" (Kaiser to Vickery, Dec. 24, 1942, ibid.).

40. "News and Views of John B. Hughes," Mutual Broadcasting System, Apr. 18, 1942, HJKP, carton 13, "Hughes, John B., 1942."

41. Lane, *Ships for Victory*, 175–76.

42. Kaiser to Hoyt, Aug. 28, 1942, HJKP, carton 13, "Hoyt, Palmer, *The Oregonian*, 1942."

43. *New York Times*, Sept. 24, 1942, 1; Nov. 13, 1942, 15.

44. Lane, *Ships For Victory*, 210.

45. *New York Times*, Nov. 18, 1942, 16.

46. "Kaiser's Problems," 24; "Kaiser Plan Fails," 18; "Wonder Man Hit," 30; "Winner: Kaiser," 15; "Who Can't?," 12; "Kaiser's Circus: Production Miracle," 98.

47. "Kaiser Plans a Steel Plant," 77.

48. *Fortune*, July 1941, 128.

49. Duffield, "Officials Wince as Fabulous Mr. Kaiser Heads for Washington"; Kihm, "Kaiser Enterprises Organized in Seven Key Corporations."

50. "Henry J. Kaiser," *Current Biography* (1942), 431.

51. "Chrysler Motors," 37.

52. "Omen for Kaiser," 89.

53. Piel, "No. 1 Shipbuilder," 84.

54. Arthur Northwood Jr. to Kaiser, Sept. 16, 1942, HJKP, carton 14, folder 51.

55. Neil Shauer to Kaiser, Oct. 28, 1942, Kaiser to Shauer, Oct. 31, 1942, ibid.

56. E. Harvey to *Fortune*, Sept. 11, 1942, HJKP, carton 13, "F–Fg Miscellaneous, 1942."

57. "Master Builder," 28; "Kaiser's Steel," 24; Taylor, "Builder No. 1," 10.

58. Gerard Piel to Kaiser, Dec. 30, 1942, HJKP, carton 21, folder 26.

59. *New York Times*, May 20, 1942, 1.

60. *Time Capsule/1942*, 186.

61. Lewis, *Public Image of Henry Ford*, 347–52, 354–55.

62. Piel, "No. 1 Shipbuilder," 81.

63. Lane, *Ships for Victory*, 469–70.

64. Herzstein, *Henry R. Luce*, 111.

65. Kaiser to Mrs. Arthur H. Sulzberger, June 24, 1944, HJKP, carton 24, folder 4.

66. Kaiser to Marvin McIntyre, Oct. 5, 1942, OF 5101 "Henry J. Kaiser."

67. Trefethen to F. A. Albright, Aug. 13, 1942, HJKP, carton 11, folder 27.

68. Hughes to Trefethen, Oct. 26, 1942, Trefethen to Kaiser, Oct. 28, 1942, carton 13, "Hughes, John B., 1942."

69. "Boss," 214.

70. Strahan, *Andrew Jackson Higgins*, 51–53.

71. Kaiser's and Higgins's competitors on the East Coast had been predominantly organized by the AFL's rival, the CIO (Lane, *Ships for Victory*, 196, 252).

72. "Boss," 216.

73. Ibid., 1, 101.

74. Ross and Wren, "Andrew Jackson Higgins' Dream," 18.

75. Deutsch, "Shipyard Bunyan," 22.

76. "Boss," 216. The following month, *Life* did a pictorial entitled "Mr. Higgins and His Wonderful Boats."

77. Baugham, *Henry R. Luce*, 106.

78. Saunders, *Pioneers!*, 64–73, 116–29.

79. Lane, *Ships for Victory*, 184.

80. Ibid., 144.

81. Ibid., 186–87; Strahan, *Andrew Jackson Higgins*, 99.

82. Foster, *Henry J. Kaiser*, 180.

83. F. H. Hogue Jr. to Robert Nathan, May 22, 1942, FEAP, RG 169, entry 22, box 242 "Cargo Planes."

84. Roosevelt to E. R. Stettinius Jr., July 11, 1942, Stettinius to Oscar Cox, July 13, 1942, FEAP, RG 169, entry 23, box 246 "Air Transport"; William Wasserman and George W. Ball to Oscar Cox, Aug. 7, 1942, FEAP, RG 169, entry 23, box 247 "Cargo Submarines and Cargo Planes."

85. F. H. Hogue Jr. to Robert R. Nathan, May 22, 1942, WCP, box 7, "Phil Graham" folder.

86. *New York Times*, Jan. 30, 1942, 28; Mar. 22, 1942, sec. 4, 8.

87. "Grover Loening Address to Foreign Commerce Club, May 20, 1942," HJKP, carton 127, folder 10.

88. F. H. Hogue Jr. to Robert R. Nathan, May 22, 1942, FEAP, RG 169, entry 22, box 242 "Cargo Planes."

89. *New York Times*, June 2, 1942, 11.

90. "Cargo Planes (chronology)," n.d, HJKP, carton 127, folder 18.

91. W. H. Penaat to Kaiser, June 18, 1942, HJKP, carton 127, folder 9.

92. Trefethen to H. V. Lindbergh, June 25, 1942, Calhoun to Kaiser, July 2, 1942, HJKP, carton 127, folder 18.

93. Kaiser to McIntyre, July 9, 1942, HJKP, carton 127, folder 18.

94. Lane, *Ships for Victory*, 184, 193.

95. *New York Times*, July 19, 1942, 1.

96. Deutsch, "Shipyard Bunyan," 22.

97. "Crepe Hung in Louisiana," 74.

CHAPTER SEVEN

1. That week, in Richmond, Kaiser delivered his thirtieth merchant ship to the British Purchasing Commission, the final vessel on his original shipbuilding contract of December 1940. Kaiser completed the ships well ahead of the delivery schedule. See William Francis Gibbs to Kaiser and Clay Bedford, July 22, 1942, HJKP, carton 13, "Gi-Gq—Miscellaneous, 1942."

2. "Five Thousand-Plane Fleet Is Suggested," HJKP, carton 262.

3. Ibid.

4. Foster, "Prosperity's Prophet," 165. Two subsequent examples of Kaiser's optimism are his December 1942 speech to the National Association of Manufacturers and his March 1944 speech at the *New York Times*'s Hall program. See Kaiser, *Management Looks at the Postwar World*; Kaiser, "Conversion without Depression," Mar. 16, 1944, HJKP, carton 262.

5. Henry Kaiser had, however, thought out how the process in Washington would work regarding cargo planes in some detail: "The first decision that must be made in Washington is: Are they going to build cargo planes? I am satisfied that they will make that decision. Then when that decision is made they will have to decide what department. Will it be the War, the Navy, or the Maritime. Now, it naturally should follow that it would fall to the Maritime to build cargo ships because it is within its jurisdiction, they are handling cargo and have the shipping administration of it. Very definite differences between Military and commercial—not so much fussing, stewing, etc. Like the difference in a cargo vessel or in a truck as against a fine automobile. Therefore, I am satisfied that eventually it will drift into the Maritime Commission" ("Excerpts of Telephone Conversation between Mr. Lewis at Washington and Mr. Kaiser, July 24, 1942," HJKP, carton 13, "Lewis, Fulton, Jr., 1942").

6. Interview, Rep. George Meader, Oct. 24, 1990.

7. "Excerpts of Telephone Conversation between Mr. Lewis at Washington and Mr. Kaiser, July 24, 1942," HJKP, carton 13, "Lewis, Fulton, Jr., 1942."

8. Foster, *Henry J. Kaiser*, 86.

9. "Notes on Telephone Conversation with Higgins, July 19, 1942," HJKP, carton 13, "H—Miscellaneous, 1942." Kaiser sent Higgins a copy of the speech the next day (Kaiser to Higgins, July 20, 1942, HJKP, carton 127, folder 19).

10. Roosevelt, *Press Conferences*, 20:23.

11. U.S. Congress, Senate Special Committee Investigating National Defense Program, *Higgins Contracts*, July 28, 1942, 5710.

12. *New York Times*, Aug. 3, 1942, 1.

13. "Excerpts from Telephone Conversation with Mr. Parrish of *Oregonian*, July 24, 1942," HJKP, carton 127, folder 28.

14. Edgar Kaiser wrote to Hoyt, thanking him for his public relations efforts: "Certainly, you have done an excellent job of coverage, and regardless of the outcome, it is causing so much comment that something stimulative and beneficial to all is certain to result" (E. Kaiser to Hoyt, July 29, 1942, HJKP, carton 13, folder "Hoyt, Palmer, 1942").

15. Foster, *Henry J. Kaiser*, 114. Hoyt telephoned radio broadcaster John B. Hughes on Saturday night, for instance, and Hughes was able to mention Kaiser's proposal in a Sunday night broadcast (Hughes to Kaiser, July 20, 1942, HJKP, carton 13, "Hughes, John B., 1942").

16. Lundy, "Kaiser," 221. Parrish would continue to help with Kaiser speeches (Parrish to Kaiser, Sept. 30, 1942, HJKP, carton 13, "Parrish, Philip—*The Oregonian*, 1942"). Parrish later wrote to Kaiser, "It is one of the things of which I shall always be proud—and shall tell my grandchildren—that when you were whipping American industry into the mood to win this war, I was able to give a little help" (Parrish to Kaiser, n.d., HJKP, carton 19, folder 47).

17. Kaiser's relations with Meyer had been helped considerably by an article by Alfred Friendly that appeared in the *Washington Post* in May. Chad Calhoun wrote to Meyer that it was "one of the finest presentations yet made of Mr. Kaiser and his shipbuilding accomplishments" (Calhoun to Meyer, May 20, 1942, HJKP, carton 15, "*Washington Post*, Eugene Meyer, 1942"). Calhoun also wrote to Friendly, "All I could directly say to you would be superlative" (Calhoun to Friendly, May 20, 1942, ibid.).

18. Hoyt to Kaiser, July 29, 1942, HJKP, carton 13, "Hoyt, Palmer—*The Oregonian*, 1942."

19. Telegram, Kaiser to Hoyt, July 30(?), 1942, ibid. Hoyt wrote back: "Congratulations. This is at least an opening wedge. If I can be of further service please advise" (Hoyt to Kaiser, Aug. 7, 1942, ibid.).

20. Steel, *Walter Lippmann*, xv.

21. Lippmann, "Miracles and Muddles."

22. Berlin, *Washington Despatches*, 60.

23. Anne F[errereira] to Trefethen, Aug. 28, 1942, HJKP, carton 13, "Fa–fk—Miscellaneous, 1942."

24. Telegram, Kaiser to Hoyt, July 30(?), 1942, HJKP, carton 13, "Hoyt, Palmer—*The Oregonian*, 1942."

25. Janeway to Kaiser, July 15, 1942, HJKP, carton 13, folder 35.

26. Kaiser to Janeway, July 16, 1942, ibid.

27. Kaiser speech, July 23, 1942, HJKP, carton 262, "Henry J. Kaiser Speeches—*March of Time* Broadcast, 1942."

28. Janeway to Kaiser, July 24, 1942, HJKP, carton 13, "Janeway, Eliot, 1942."

29. Luce to Henry J. Kaiser Jr., Sept. 21, 1942, HJKP, carton 14, folder 51.

30. "Kaiser Takes to the Air," 71.

31. Janeway, "Trials and Errors," 184.

32. Cohn to H. F. Morton, July 13, 1942, HJKP, carton 13, "Motion Pictures, 1942." Like a Hollywood star, Kaiser began to receive fan mail—so much that his associates learned to send to his lieutenants any material they wanted Kaiser to see (Paul Cadman to Eugene Trefethen, Sept. 16, 1942, HJKP, carton 12, folder 1).

33. Edward Finney to Kaiser, Sept. 9, 1942, Jason Joy to Kaiser, Sept. 28, 1942, Bud Albright to L. L. Behrens, Dec. 1, 1942, all in HJKP, carton 13, "Motion Pictures, 1942."

34. Republic Pictures sent out announcements of "our motion picture tribute to the

shipbuilding industry. . . . 'Man from Frisco' will be shown in Loewes Theaters in New York City and at the Strand Theater in Brooklyn" (Republic Pictures form letter, June 21, 1944, HJKP, carton 24, folder 2).

35. "Excerpts of Telephone Conversation between Mr. Lewis at Washington and Mr. Kaiser, July 24, 1942," HJKP, carton 13, "Lewis, Fulton, Jr., 1942."

36. Martin F. Smith to Kaiser, July 24, 1942, HJKP, carton 127, folder 16.

37. Murdock to Kaiser, Aug. 21, 1942, HJKP, carton 13, "M—Miscellaneous, 1942."

38. "Ship Purge," 7; *Time*, May 18, 1942, 16; "Services Critical of Civilian Job," 5; Lundy, "Kaiser," 223; Loriana H. Francis to Kaiser, Oct. 26, 1942, HJKP, carton 13, "F—Miscellaneous, 1942."

39. Donald Nelson to Kaiser, Aug. 10, 1942, HJKP, carton 127, folder 18.

40. "Telephone Conversation between Mr. H. Kaiser and Mr. Glenn L. Martin—Aug. 10, 1942," HJKP, carton 14, folder 42.

41. Ibid.

42. Ibid.

43. Girdler complained that he had waited for a year while the army, navy, and WPB sat on his proposal for cargo planes. Now that Kaiser's name was never far from any cargo plan idea, Girdler had agreed to discuss further the idea of working together ("Memo re Conversation with Tom Girdler & HJK, 8/5/42," HJKP, carton 14, folder 42).

44. Kaiser to Vance Breese, Aug. 18, 1942, HJKP, carton 127, folder 18.

45. Telegram, Kaiser to Loening, Aug. 18, 1942, Telegram, Loening to Kaiser, Aug. 19, 1942, HJKP, carton 127, folder 18.

46. Barlett and Steele, *Empire*, 107.

47. Chad Calhoun notes, n.d., HJKP, carton 127, folder 18. Kaiser was interested but cautious. He wired Clay Bedford, head of his Richmond shipyards: "Do not employ any men from other aircraft companies until my return [from Washington], and at that time do not employ any without my specific approval. In the event we desire at that time to accept any applications we will not do so without written release from the corporation employing the individual involved" (Kaiser to Bedford, Aug. 13, 1942, ibid.

48. *New York Times*, Aug. 7, 1942, 1; "Telephone Conversation with Howard Hughes, Aug. 21, 1942," HJKP, carton 127, folder 18.

49. Roosevelt had expressed interest in cargo planes even before Kaiser's July 19 speech. On July 11, he had directed Lend-Lease administrator Edward Stettinius Jr. to investigate the possibilities of lighter-than-air metal cargo airships aimed at supplying Russia and the Chinese mainland. Roosevelt wrote that the idea "shows promise of giving the United Nations a great advantage over the Axis in long-range air transport" (Roosevelt to Stettinius, July 11, 1942, FEAP, RG 169, entry 23, box 246, "Air Transport").

50. "Telephone Conversation with Howard Hughes, Aug. 21, 1942," HJKP, carton 127, folder 18.

51. Ibid.

52. Ibid. In mid- to late 1942, Kaiser was intent on shrinking the space between the drawing board and production. His steel plant in Fontana was being built using drawings finished the day before or even the same day (Foster, *Henry J. Kaiser*, 95).

53. Hendricks, "Necessary Revolution," 144; "Telephone Conversation with Howard Hughes, Aug. 21, 1942," HJKP, carton 127, folder 18.

54. Foster, *Henry J. Kaiser*, 320 n. 15.

55. "Telephone Conversation with Howard Hughes, Aug. 21, 1942," HJKP, carton 127, folder 18.

56. "Fabulous Team," 20.

57. Foster, *Henry J. Kaiser*, 180–83.

58. Quoted in "Who Can't?," 13.

59. Kaiser to Hoyt, Aug. 28, 1942, HJKP, carton 13, "Hoyt, Palmer—*The Oregonian*, 1942."

60. "International News Service," n.d., HJKP, carton 12.

61. U.S. Congress, Senate Special Committee Investigating the National Defense Program, *Part 14*, 5695, 5699, 5710–11.

62. "Phoned by International News Service," [Aug. 27, 1942], HJKP, carton 13.

63. Arnold, *Voltaire and the Cowboy*, 184.

64. Ickes, *Lowering Clouds*, 431.

65. Notes on telephone conversation, Arnold and Kaiser, Aug. 28, 1942, HJKP, carton 12, folder 13.

66. Edgar Kaiser to Henry Kaiser Jr., May 25, 1942, Hughes to Kaiser, Aug. 27, 1942, HJKP, carton 13, "Hughes, John B.—Radio Commentator, 1942."

67. "News and Views by John B. Hughes, Aug. 27, 1942," ibid.

68. Less than a month earlier, Henderson had invited Kaiser to join an advisory committee on cement prices (Henderson to Kaiser, July 31, 1942, HJKP, carton 13, "Office of Price Administration, 1942"). Kaiser declined (Kaiser to Henderson, Aug. 11, 1942, ibid.).

69. Inch to International News Service, Aug. 27, 1942, HJKP, carton 12.

70. Kaiser to Hoyt, Aug. 28, 1942, HJKP, carton 13, "Hoyt, Palmer—*The Oregonian*, 1942."

71. Kaiser to Henderson, Aug. 29, 1942, HJKP, carton 13, "H—Miscellaneous, 1942."

72. Russell Birdwell to Kaiser, Aug. 29, 1942, HJKP, carton 11, folder 48.

73. Leon Henderson press release, Sept. 2, 1942, HJKP, carton 12.

74. It is a grand old American tradition vicariously to enjoy the exploits of those who do not follow the "rules of the game." It is no coincidence, for instance, that the cowboy has played a role in American consciousness far larger than his actual contributions to society. Sociologists such as Seymour Martin Lipset explain this phenomenon as an outgrowth of an egalitarian society. Where deference to elites is not the norm, there is a "greater propensity to redefine the rules or ignore them" (Lipset, *Revolution and Counterrevolution*, 49).

75. "Magnesium, Lesson in Speed," 67.

76. *Washington Post*, Dec. 18, 1995.

77. Janeway, *Struggle for Survival*, 251.

78. Calhoun to Kaiser, Aug. 28, 1942, ETP, box 47.

79. "Omen for Kaiser," 89.

80. "Kaiser and the Bureaucrats," 268.

81. Pearson, *Diaries*, xiii.

82. Berlin, *Washington Despatches*, 611.

83. Notes, Drew Pearson, Aug. 3, 1942, DPP, container G237, 1 of 3.

84. "Washington Merry-Go-Round," Apr. 9, 1942, HJKP, vol. 157; Pearson, "Miracle Man Kaiser."

85. The head of WPB planning, a Kaiser admirer, thought Kaiser was able to contrib-

ute more to the war effort as a gadfly to various agencies—and prolific producer—than he would have done as an administrator (Interview, Robert Nathan, Oct. 3, 1991). Pearson and Kaiser became close friends. Pearson asked Kaiser to host his radio show in addition to writing his newspaper column when Pearson was on vacation. They even explored the possibility of investing together in broadcasting ("Memorandum in re Organization of Corporation to Acquire Don Lee Broadcasting System," n.d., DPP, "Henry Kaiser," container G237, 1 of 3).

86. Calhoun to Kaiser, Sept. 2, 1942, ETP, box 47.

87. U.S. Congress, House Committee on the Merchant Marine and Fisheries, *Higgins Contracts*, 73.

88. "Excerpts from Conversation between Kaiser and Mr. Gimmick, July 23, 1942," HJKP, carton 15, "United Seaman's Service, 1942."

89. Land to Kaiser, Aug. 21, 1942, ibid.

90. Kaiser to Land, Aug. 31, 1942, HJKP, carton 15, "U.S. Government—Land, E. S.—War Shipping Administration, 1942."

91. Calhoun to Kaiser, Sept. 2, 1942, ETP, box 47. The day before, Meyer had written Kaiser offering advice on how to deal with Reese Taylor's replacement as head of the steel branch of the WPB (Meyer to Kaiser, Sept. 1, 1942, HJKP, carton 15, "*Washington Post*, 1942").

92. Calhoun to Kaiser, Sept. 2, 1942, ETP, box 47.

93. Calhoun to Kaiser, Sept. 12, 1942, HJKP, carton 13, "Nelson, Donald—War Production Board, 1942." Nelson and Pearson exchanged more letters on the subject. See Nelson to Pearson, Sept. 15, 1942, HJKP, carton 13, "Nelson, Donald—War Production Board, 1942."

94. Donald Nelson to Sen. Truman, Feb. 11, 1944, HJKP, carton 309, folder 9; Foster, *Henry J. Kaiser*, 183.

95. H. E. Talbott to Jesse Jones, Sept. 15, 1942, HJKP, carton 13, "J—Miscellaneous, 1942." Emphasis added.

96. Lane, *Ships for Victory*, 338.

97. *Time Capsule/1942*, 194.

98. Ibid., 194, 188.

99. Strahan, *Andrew Jackson Higgins*, 182, 230.

100. Barlett and Steele, *Empire*, 117.

101. Trefethen to Kaiser, Sept. 21, 1942, HJKP, carton 127, folder 19.

102. Leonard J. Strong to Kaiser, Oct. 7, 1942, ibid.

103. Kaiser to Hughes, Apr. 10, 1943, HJKP, carton 309, folder 9.

104. Nelson to Truman, Feb. 11, 1944, ibid.

105. Donald Nelson to Jesse Jones, Feb. 11, 1944, ibid.

106. Foster, *Henry J. Kaiser*, 179.

107. Nelson to Truman, Feb. 11, 1944, HJKP, carton 309, folder 9.

108. Kaiser to Grafton, Aug. 27, 1942, HJKP, carton 13, "G—Miscellaneous, 1942."

109. Calhoun to Kaiser, Feb. 8, 1943, HJKP, carton 21, folder 7.

110. Foster, *Henry J. Kaiser*, 320 n. 14.

CHAPTER EIGHT

1. Cox to Hopkins, May 10, 1943, OCP, box 147, "Diaries, May–June 1943."

2. Kaiser had addressed some of these issues—albeit not as forcefully—in November on the *Herald Tribune*'s radio program, *Forum of the Air* (*New York Times*, Nov. 17, 1944).

3. Foster, *Henry J. Kaiser*, 128; Kaiser, *Management Looks at the Postwar World*.

4. Berlin, *Washington Despatches*, 121.

5. Kaiser, *Management Looks at the Postwar World*, 10.

6. Kaiser to Eugene Meyer, Dec. 1, 1942, HJKP, carton 13, "National Association of Manufacturers, 1942."

7. Kaiser to Meyer, Jan. 1, 1943, HJKP, carton 15, "*Washington Post*, 1942."

8. Kaiser, *Management Looks at the Postwar World*, 16.

9. Foster, *Henry J. Kaiser*, 142.

10. Cadman to Kaiser, Dec. 11, 1942, HJKP, carton 12, folder 1.

11. Kaiser's political associations with the Luce household had more to do with Luce's wife, Clare Booth Luce, but were still minor. Kaiser sent her a congratulatory letter after she won a congressional seat in November 1942 (Clare Booth Luce to Kaiser, Nov. 5, 1942, HJKP, carton 13, folder 50).

12. In 1950, responding to a complaint from Kaiser, Luce wrote, "It saddens me to think that the only time you write me . . . is when you're mad at me" (Foster, *Henry J. Kaiser*, 125).

13. Kaiser had just done a favor for Luce: he found him some Pullman railroad tickets, not the simplest task in wartime (Corinne Thrasher to Kaiser, June 25, 1943, HJKP, carton 21, folder 26).

14. Questions about his veracity would have the greatest ramifications if Kaiser expected to enter the political arena. Nonetheless, even years after his political possibilities disappeared, such questions prompted greater eruptions than anything else. See "Notes Taken 6/22/43 of Meeting between Henry J. Kaiser, Sr., Jr., and Chad F. Calhoun, and Mr. Murphy and Miss McEneny of *Fortune*," HJKP, carton 21, folder 26.

15. Taylor, "Builder No. 1," 10; Piel, "No. 1 Shipbuilder," 89.

16. Berlin, *Washington Despatches*, 458–59.

17. According to William Tuttle, Eleanor Roosevelt had suggested that Kaiser begin a program of day care centers at his shipyards. Kaiser's innovation, decades ahead of its time, attracted more attention than anybody else's day care centers (Foster, *Henry J. Kaiser*, 77, 298 n. 31).

18. Cox to Hopkins, May 10, 1943, OCP, box 147, "Diaries, May–June 1943."

19. Portland Oregonian, Dec. 31, 1944.

20. Foster, *Henry J. Kaiser*, 105.

21. Calhoun to Kaiser, Jan. 11, 1946, ETP, carton 47.

22. Lewis, *Public Image of Henry Ford*, 363.

23. Kaiser had an embarrassed Paul Cadman sing this song about him to some newsmen in 1944 (Foster, *Henry J. Kaiser*, 243).

24. As Washington lawyer Clifford Durr later put it: "Policy is made throughout the whole governmental structure. . . . Within the federal government one of the levels significant as a focus for the initiation of new policies is the level immediately below that of the chief departmental executive. Persons at this level are close enough to the top so that

they can seize opportunities to make suggestions or to influence their chiefs" (Durr, *Early History*, v).

25. Cox devised an ingenious way to provide the French with airplanes while staying within the legal confines of the Neutrality Act. An aircraft carrier waited at a Quebec harbor for loading of planes transferred from both the army and the navy. Cox's plan called for transfer of the planes to the Curtiss Company, which "sold" them to DuPont in exchange for explosives, which Curtiss used to "pay" the army and navy. DuPont would then sell the planes to the French. The French would get their planes but without directly paying the U.S. government for them. France fell, however, before the planes arrived (Nelson, *Arsenal of Democracy*, 74–75).

26. For details of the framing of the act, see Kimball, *Most Unsordid Act*, 130–40.

27. By late 1942, Cox knew Kaiser; he had invited a friend to a luncheon with Kaiser (V. S. Makaroff to Cox, Nov. 3, 1942, HJKP, carton 13, "M—Miscellaneous, 1942").

28. Hand, *Counsel and Advise*, 175.

29. Sherwood, *Roosevelt and Hopkins*, 184.

30. Murphy, *Brandeis/Frankfurter Connection*, 118, 130, 194, 195.

31. Anderson, *Presidents' Men*, 50.

32. A good example was Kaiser's proposal for manpower reconversion in 1944. Rosenman offered advice after Calhoun told him the basics of the plan, then Rosenman read—and offered a few revisions—to a formal letter of proposal (Calhoun to file, Mar. 19, 1944, HJKP, carton 24).

33. Interview, Fred Drewes, Sept. 2, 1992.

34. Roosevelt, *Public Papers*, Jan. 6, 1941, 10:672. Kaiser speech, "Production—The Fifth Freedom," Nov. 16, 1942, HJKP, carton 262.

35. Critics of Kaiser's wartime profits would have been surprised to learn that Kaiser's solution to the manpower hoarding problem in shipbuilding and other industries was to eliminate cost-plus contracts, returning to the practice of competitive bidding (Roosevelt to Rosenman, Mar. 5, 1943, OF 172; Kaiser to Roosevelt, Mar. 17, 1944, OF 5101; Calhoun to file, Mar. 19, 1944, HJKP, carton 24).

36. Lane, *Ships for Victory*, 196.

37. Strahan, *Andrew Jackson Higgins*, 165.

38. U.S. Congress, Senate Special Committee Investigating the National Defense Program, *Hearings*, Mar. 9, 1943, 7009.

39. U.S. Congress, House Committee on Naval Affairs, *Investigation of the War Effort*, 2600.

40. Foster, *Henry J. Kaiser*, 185; Calhoun to Kaiser, Nov. 24, 1943, HJKP, carton 262, folder 17.

41. Cox to Kaiser, Mar. 17, 1943, OCP, box 89.

42. Foster, *Henry J. Kaiser*, 186.

43. According to Michael Beschloss, Kaiser replaced Joseph Kennedy in that role (*Kennedy and Roosevelt*, 257).

44. *New York Times*, Apr. 29, 1944, 1.

45. Cox to Rosenman, May 3, 1944, OCP, box 147, "Diary—May 1944."

46. Ibid.

47. Strahan, *Andrew Jackson Higgins*, 216–17; Hassett, *Off the Record*, 243.

48. Ward, *Closest Companion*, 301–2.

49. Kaiser had met with Roosevelt on May 18 to discuss postwar economic reconversion (Hassett, *Off the Record*, 244).

50. In 1940, when contemplating a third term, he had given many signals about possible successors, from Harry Hopkins to James Farley to James Byrnes (Goodwin, *No Ordinary Time*, 106–7).

51. *Oakland Post Enquirer*, Apr. 21, 1944.

52. Velie, "Truth about Henry Kaiser," 65.

53. Equally damaging to Kaiser's attractiveness to labor was his "leaden appearance" before the United Steelworkers in May 1944. Instead of discussing the challenge labor policies at his Fontana steel plant presented to the rest of the industry, Kaiser chose this venue to unveil an ill-fated proposal. He presented a plan to build three to five thousand airports and one million personal aircraft in the postwar years. Kaiser bragged that "some day I expect [the plan] to be an historic document" (Gerard Piel to author, Apr. 30, 1991; Kaiser speech, May 9, 1944, HJKP, carton 262).

54. Velie, "Truth about Henry Kaiser," 65.

55. Rosenman to Roosevelt, June 30, 1944, OF 140.

56. Herzstein, *Henry R. Luce*, 45, 81.

57. Strahan, *Andrew Jackson Higgins*, 166.

58. Foster, *Henry J. Kaiser*, 118–19.

59. Velie, "Truth about Henry Kaiser," 65.

60. Barnard, *Wendell Willkie*, 464.

61. "Government by Default," *Time*, May 29, 1944, 19–20.

62. *New York Times*, Nov. 22, 1943, 11, Sept. 6, 1943, 19.

63. *New York Times*, Dec. 5, 1943, 48, Dec. 27, 1943, 12.

64. *New York Times*, Jan. 20, 1944, 36.

65. *New York Times*, Jan. 12, 1944, 1; Jan. 27, 1944, 1, Apr. 1, 1944, 1.

66. Macauley to Baldwin, June 15, 1944, HJKP, carton 163, folder 64.

67. Graham et al. to Kaiser, June 8, 1944, HJKP, carton 151.

68. "Excerpts from Conversation between HJK and Mr. Gimmick, July 23, 1942," HJKP, carton 15, "United Seaman's Service, 1942."

69. Kaiser to Mrs. Edward Macauley, June 10, 1944, HJKP, carton 151.

70. Macauley to Kaiser, June 14, 1944, ibid.

71. Feltus to Kaiser, June 16, 1944, Kaiser to Feltus, June 19, 1944, ibid.

72. Feltus to Hoyt, June 16, 1944, HJKP, carton 163, folder 45.

73. *New York Times*, Jan. 4, 1944; Hoyt to Kaiser, June 27, 1944, HJKP, carton 151.

74. Hoyt to Macauley, July 7, 1944, HJKP, carton 163, folder 62.

75. Kaiser to Hoyt, June 29, 1944; Calhoun to Kaiser, June 30, 1944, HJKP, carton 151.

76. Calhoun to Kaiser, June 30, 1944, ibid.

77. Feltus to Macauley, July 11, 1944, HJKP, carton 163, folder 64.

78. Feltus to Swope, June 27, 1944, HJKP, carton 164, folder 30.

79. Feltus to Mack, June 22, 1944, HJKP, carton 163, folder 62.

80. Ibid.

81. Feltus to Henderson, July 5, 1944, HJKP, carton 163, folder 44.

82. Feltus to Dr. Frank P. Graham, July 1, 1944, HJKP, carton 163, folder 41.

83. "Gallup Vote Total 1944 Predictions and Deductions," Apr. 10, 1944, HJKP, carton 163, folder 65.

84. Ibid.

85. Ibid.

86. Feltus to LaFollette, July 10, 1944, HJKP, carton 163, folder 57.

87. "Gallup Vote" memo, Apr. 10, 1944, HJKP, carton 163, folder 65.

88. Ibid.

89. Ibid.

90. Ibid.

91. Feltus to Randolph Paul, July 14, 1944, HJKP, carton 164, folder 13.

92. Macauley to Rep. Joseph Clark Baldwin, June 15, 1944, HJKP, carton 163, folder 64.

93. Feltus to Paul, July 14, 1944, HJKP, carton 164, folder 13.

94. Rosenman, *Working with Roosevelt*, 463.

95. Ibid., 467–68.

96. Blum, *Years of War*, 283.

97. Feltus to Paul, July 14, 1944, HJKP, carton 164, folder 13.

98. Macauley to Feltus, July 22, 1944, HJKP, carton 163, folder 64.

99. Chairman to John Doe, July 31, 1944, HJKP, carton 164. Swing ended up supporting Roosevelt, helping to write a key speech for the president (Rosenman, *Working with Roosevelt*, 480).

100. Strahan, *Andrew Jackson Higgins*, 232–33.

101. Feltus to Macauley, Aug. 8, 1944, HJKP, carton 163, folder 64.

102. Ibid. Roosevelt's critics sometimes referred to him as the "Great White Father." See Blum, *V Was for Victory*, 5.

103. Hassett, *Off the Record*, 266.

104. Oscar Cox, Diary, Aug. 20, 1944, OCP, box 49.

105. Somers, *Presidential Agency*, 84.

106. Rosenman, *Working with Roosevelt*, 455–62.

107. Kaiser to Rosenman, Aug. 10, 1944, HJKP, carton 24, folder 2.

108. Hassett, *Off the Record*, 266.

109. Ibid.

110. Kaiser to Mrs. Eleanor Roosevelt, Aug. 22, 1944, HJKP, carton 23, folder 17.

111. "Anecdotes and Notes by Rosenman re FDR," SIRP, container 5.

112. Kaiser to Harold Ryan, Aug. 25, 1944, HJKP, carton 151; *New York Times*, Aug. 27, 1944, 29.

113. TCP, carton 247, "Campaign File—National Committee for Independent Voters 1940."

114. Feltus to Corcoran, Sept. 18, 1944, TCP, carton 59, "F Miscellany—Fe-Fi."

115. Land to FDR, Sept. 23, 1944, PPF 4402.

116. Roosevelt, *F.D.R.*, 374–75; FDR to Macauley, Feb. 5, 1942, PPF 4402.

117. Presidential Memorandum for Hon. Jim Rowe, Sept. 16, 1940, PPF 4402.

118. Calhoun to John Doe, n.d., HJKP, carton 163, folder 57.

119. Minutes of Oct. 3 meeting, HJKP, carton 164, folder 1.

120. Skadden to Feltus, Sept. 23, 1944; minutes of Oct. 3 meeting, ibid.

121. *New York Times*, Sept. 21, 1944, 26.

122. Kaiser to Roosevelt, Sept. 20, 1944, HJKP, carton 151.

123. Cox to Kaiser, Sept. 23, 1944, ibid.

124. Mrs. Ogden Reid to Kaiser, Sept. 14, 1944, ibid. Mrs. Reid and Kaiser had become acquainted when Kaiser participated in the *Herald Tribune*'s *Forum of the Air* in November 1942. She had provided Kaiser with speechwriting assistance. See Kaiser to Cadman, Nov. 4, 1942, HJKP, carton 12; Mrs. Reid to Kaiser, Nov. 25, Dec. 1, 3, 1942, HJKP, carton 13, "*New York Herald Tribune*, 1942"; Kaiser to Mrs. Reid, Nov. 28, 1942, HJKP, carton 13, "National Association of Manufacturers, 1942."

125. Feltus to Mrs. Ogden Reid, Sept. 19, 1944, HJKP, carton 164, folder 19.

126. Lasker to "Friend," Aug. 29, 1944, HJKP, carton 163, folder 3; Barnard, *Wendell Willkie*, 261, 594.

127. "Meeting, National Committee, Oct. 1944," HJKP, carton 164, folder 1; Barnard, *Wendell Willkie*, 160.

128. Barnard, *Wendell Willkie*, 238, 442; Feltus to Luce, Dec. 13, 1944, HJKP, carton 164, folder 4.

129. Feltus to list, Dec. 13, 1944, HJKP, carton 164, folder 4.

130. Rosenman, *Working with Roosevelt*, 471–79.

131. Roosevelt, *Public Papers*, 13:285, 290.

132. Berlin, *Washington Despatches*, 428.

133. Rosenman, *Working with Roosevelt*, 486.

134. Roosevelt, *Public Papers*, 13:287; *New York Times*, Sept. 24, 1944, 1.

135. Reinsch, *Getting Elected*, 17.

136. Hassett, *Off the Record*, 268.

137. Mrs. Irving Gates to Kaiser, Oct. 7, 1944, HJKP, carton 163, folder 41.

138. Maverick to Kaiser, Sept. 26, 1944, HJKP, carton 23, folder 17.

139. Hoyt to Kaiser, Sept. 30, 1944, HJKP, carton 151.

140. Kaiser to Hoyt, Oct. 3, 1944, ibid.

141. Minutes, Oct. meeting, HJKP, carton 164, folder 1.

142. William H. Allen, director of Institute for Public Service, to Feltus, Sept. 28, 1944, HJKP, carton 163, folder 1.

143. Berlin, *Washington Despatches*, 425.

144. Paul E. Lockwood to Kaiser, Oct. 11, 1944, HJKP, carton 164, folder 2.

145. Memorandum, n.d., HJKP, carton 164, folder 1.

146. William H. Allen to Feltus, Oct. 3, 1944, HJKP, carton 163, folder 1; Feltus to La-Guardia, Oct. 4, 7, 1944, HJKP, carton 163, folder 57.

147. *New York Times*, Oct. 10, 1944.

148. "Citizenship Week—Nov. 1–7," HJKP, carton 163, folder 10; Memorandum, n.d., HJKP, carton 164, folder 1.

149. Memorandum, n.d., HJKP, carton 164, folder 1.

150. "Script for Telephone Discussion," Nov. 3, 1944, HJKP, carton 24, folder 12.

151. Report, Aaron Fuchs & Company, Nov. 14, 1944, HJKP, carton 164, folder 5. Three of Kaiser's enterprises each gave the legal $5,000 limit, as did Higgins, to the Nonpartisan Association.

152. The turnout fell short of the goal of fifty million envisioned by both Kaiser and Roosevelt (Rosenman, *Working with Roosevelt*, 506).

153. In 1943, CIO head Sidney Hillman had created the nation's first political action

committee, a principal goal of which was to rally the labor movement behind the president. See Fraser, *Labor Will Rule*, 503, 535; *New York Times*, Dec. 28, 1944, 13.

154. Strahan, *Andrew Jackson Higgins*, 239–40.

155. Foster, *Henry J. Kaiser*, 122.

156. Roosevelt to Kaiser, Jan. 10, 1945, HJKP, carton 151, "White House, 1945"; Feltus to Kaiser, Jan. 31, 1945, HJKP, carton 164, folder 4.

157. Luce to Kaiser, Oct. 7, 1944, HJKP, carton 163, folder 2; Feltus to Luce, Dec. 13, 1944, HJKP, carton 164, folder 4.

158. B. A. Garside to Kaiser, Oct. 25, 1943; Garside to Kaiser, Dec. 29, 1943, HJKP, carton 153, folder 8.

159. "Statement from Henry Luce," n.d., HJKP, carton 163, folder 54.

160. Feltus to Kaiser, Dec. 27, 1944, HJKP, carton 163, folder 54.

161. Feltus to Kaiser, Jan. 31, 1945, HJKP, carton 164, folder 4; Feltus to Macauley, Jan. 31, 1945, HJKP, carton 163, folder 64; Kaiser to Robert H. Ellis, Feb. 23, 1945, HJKP, carton 151.

162. Calhoun to Kaiser, Feb. 19, 1946, HJKP, carton 157, folder 19.

EPILOGUE

1. *Fortune*, Dec. 1947, 85, 217; Byrne, *Whiz Kids*, 35–36, 40–41.

2. "Drive Them Off the Floor," 83–84.

3. Kaiser to Luce, Apr. 1, 1947, HJKP box 32, folder 23.

4. For Higgins letter, see Edgar Kaiser to Henry Kaiser, Mar. 18, 1947, HJKP box 32, folder 23.

5. "More Trouble for Andy," 83.

6. "Adventures of Henry and Joe," 97–98.

7. Kaiser did, however, receive a favorable lease from the Reconstruction Finance Corporation for his Willow Run plant. The plant, at which Henry Ford produced bombers during the war, cost the government $100 million to build. Kaiser's lease called for payments averaging $1 million per year (Langworth, *Kaiser-Frazer*, 38).

8. Janeway, *Struggle for Survival*, 251.

9. "Address of Senator Styles Bridges," AISIP, box 31.

10. Ibid., 1.

11. Foster, *Henry J. Kaiser*, 80, 116–17.

12. Calhoun to Rosenman, Apr. 4, 1946, ETP, box 47.

13. Calhoun to Kaiser, July 30, 1946, ETP, box 47. When Rosenman began to write his memoirs, Felix Frankfurter prevailed on him to leave out references to his political involvement with the White House. Rosenman complied (Hand, *Counsel and Advise*, 194, 303, 422). Rosenman's memoirs, published in 1952, also excluded any reference to his relationship with Kaiser. That omission, also, may have constituted a favor to a friend. By the early 1950s, Kaiser's connections with the New Deal made him the target of many critics, of whom Styles Bridges was the most persistent. See Rosenman, *Working with Roosevelt*.

14. Their chief mission, to improve the terms of Kaiser's steel loan, failed. Kaiser paid one hundred cents on the dollar when he repaid the loan in 1950 (Foster, *Henry J. Kaiser*, 104).

15. Cox responded: "I can't tell you how much I appreciate your perfectly swell note of

August 23rd about my going into private practice. . . . It was good of you to suggest that when you are next in Washington or New York you will be willing to talk to me about the situation. I would like to take you up on that generous offer" (Cox to Kaiser, Sept. 5, 1945, OCP, box 89, "Henry J. Kaiser, 1944-45").

16. Foster, *Henry J. Kaiser*, 124.

17. See "Organization Charts—1949," HJKP, carton 277, folder 6.

18. "Expansion—Various Kaiser Companies," Sept. 23, 1952, HJKP, carton 76.

19. Foster, *Henry J. Kaiser*, 200.

20. Blum, *V Was for Victory*, 110-15.

21. Strahan, *Andrew Jackson Higgins*, 51; U.S. Congress, Senate Special Committee Investigating National Defense Program, *Higgins Contracts*, July 28, 1942, 5695.

22. "Fortune Directory," *Fortune*, July 1955.

23. Barlett and Steele, *Empire*, 170-72.

24. Stanford Research Institute, *California Economy*, 450.

BIBLIOGRAPHY

ARCHIVAL SOURCES

Austin, Texas
Lyndon B. Johnson Library
   Lyndon Baines Johnson Papers—Chronology
   Drew Pearson Papers

Berkeley, California
Bancroft Library, University of California
   Edgar Kaiser Papers
   Henry J. Kaiser Papers
   William Knowland Papers
   Papers of the Six Companies
   Eugene Trefethen Papers

Boston, Massachusetts
Baker Library, Harvard Business School
   Case Studies

College Park, Maryland
National Archives
   Papers of the Foreign Economic Administration

Detroit, Michigan
Walter Reuther Library, Wayne State University
   Walter Reuther Papers
   R. J. Thomas Papers

Fontana, California
San Bernardino Public Library
   Local History Collection

Greenville, Delaware
Hagley Library
   Papers of the American Iron and Steel Institute
   Papers of the National Association of Manufacturers

Hyde Park, New York
Franklin D. Roosevelt Library, National Archives
   Oscar Cox Papers
   Wayne Coy Papers

Papers of the Democratic National Committee
Papers of the National Defense Advisory Commission
Franklin D. Roosevelt Papers
Samuel I. Rosenman Papers

Oakland, California
Oakland Public Library
  Local History Collection

Rhinebeck, New York
Wilderstein Preservation
  Margaret L. Suckley Papers

Sacramento, California
California State Archives
  California Road Construction Contract File
  Papers of Earl Warren
  Records of the Election Division
California State Highway Commission
California State Library

San Francisco, California
Bank of America Archives

Stanford, California
Hoover Institute, Stanford University
  Herbert Hoover Papers
  Ray Lyman Wilbur Papers

Washington, D.C.
Federal Bureau of Investigation
  Henry J. Kaiser File
Library of Congress
  Thomas Corcoran Papers
  John P. Frey Papers
  Theodore Granik Papers
  W. Averell Harriman Papers
  Harold L. Ickes Papers
  Raymond Gram Swing Papers
National Archives
  Bureau of Reclamation Papers
  Records of the British Purchasing Mission
  Records of the Department of the Treasury
  Records of the National Recovery Administration
  Records of the National Resources Planning Board
  Records of the Office of Price Administration
  Records of the Reconstruction Finance Corporation
  Records of the Secretary of the Interior

Records of the Temporary National Economic Committee
Records of the War Production Board

BOOKS, ARTICLES, AND THESES

"Adventures of Henry and Joe in Autoland." *Fortune*, July 1946, 101–7, 240.

Aitken, Hugh G. J., ed. *Explorations in Enterprise*. Cambridge, Mass.: Harvard University Press, 1965.

Alford, Theodore C. "New Genius Rises." *Washington Star*, Mar. 2, 1941.

American Public Works Association. *History of Public Works in the United States, 1776–1976*. Edited by Ellis L. Armstrong. Chicago: American Public Works Association, 1976.

Anderson, Patrick. *The Presidents' Men: White House Assistants of Franklin D. Roosevelt, Harry S. Truman, Dwight D. Eisenhower, John F. Kennedy, and Lyndon B. Johnson*. Garden City, N.Y.: Doubleday, 1968.

Arnold, Thurman. *Voltaire and the Cowboy: The Letters of Thurman Arnold*. Edited by Gene M Gressley. Boulder: Colorado Associated University Press, 1977.

Bain, Joe Staten. *Barriers to New Competition: Their Character and Consequences in Manufacturing Industries*. Cambridge, Mass.: Harvard University Press, 1956.

Barlett, Donald L., and James B. Steele. *Empire: The Life, Legend, and Madness of Howard Hughes*. New York: Norton, 1979.

Barnard, Ellsworth. *Wendell Willkie: Fighter for Freedom*. Marquette: Northern Michigan University Press, 1966.

Baugham, James L. *Henry R. Luce and the Rise of the American News Media*. Boston: Twayne, 1987.

Beamis, George W. "A History of California Highway Finance." M.A. thesis, University of California, Los Angeles, 1931.

Bellah, Robert N., Richard Madsen, William M. Sullivan, Ann Swindler, and Steven M. Tipton. *Habits of the Heart: Individualism and Commitment in American Life*. New York: Harper & Row, 1985.

Berlin, Isaiah. *Washington Despatches, 1941–1945: Weekly Political Reports from the British Embassy*. Edited by H. G. Nicholas. Chicago: University of Chicago Press, 1981.

Beschloss, Michael R. *Kennedy and Roosevelt: The Uneasy Alliance*. New York: Norton, 1980.

Blum, John Morton. *V Was for Victory: Politics and American Culture during World War II*. New York: Harcourt Brace Jovanovich, 1976.

———. *Years of Crisis, 1928–1938*. Vol. 1 of *From the Morgenthau Diaries*. Boston: Houghton Mifflin, 1959.

———. *Years of Urgency, 1938–1941*. Vol. 2 of *From the Morgenthau Diaries*. Boston: Houghton Mifflin, 1965.

———. *Years of War, 1941–1945*. Vol. 3 of *From the Morgenthau Diaries*. Boston: Houghton Mifflin, 1967.

"The Boss." *Fortune*, July 1943, 101–2, 210–16.

Brubaker, Sterling. "The Impact of Federal Government Activities on California's Economic Growth, 1930–1956." Ph.D. diss., University of California, Berkeley, 1959.

Burke, Robert E. *Olson's New Deal for California*. Berkeley: University of California Press, 1953.

Burns, James McGregor. *Roosevelt: The Lion and the Fox*. New York: Harcourt, Brace, 1956.

———. *Roosevelt: The Soldier of Freedom*. New York: Harcourt Brace Jovanovich, 1970.

Byrne, John A. *The Whiz Kids: The Founding Fathers of American Business—And the Legacy They Left Us*. New York: Doubleday, 1993.

Cadman, Paul. "Henry Kaiser: The Man." Manuscript, Kaiser Permanente Health Plan, ca. 1944.

California Blue Book. Sacramento: California State Printing Office, 1928.

California Department of Public Works. *Report of the California Highway Commission, Part II*. Sacramento: California State Printing Office, 1922.

Caro, Robert A. *Means of Ascent*. Vol. 2 of *The Years of Lyndon Johnson*. New York: Knopf, 1990.

———. *The Path to Power*. Vol. 1 of *The Years of Lyndon Johnson*. New York: Knopf, 1982.

Chandler, Alfred D., Jr. *Scale and Scope: The Dynamics of Industrial Capitalism*. Cambridge, Mass.: Belknap Press, 1990.

———. *Strategy and Structure: Chapters in the History of the Industrial Enterprise*. Cambridge, Mass.: MIT Press, 1962.

———. *The Visible Hand: The Managerial Revolution in American Business*. Cambridge, Mass.: Belknap Press, 1977.

"Chrysler Motors." *Time*, Jan. 7, 1929, 37.

Connery, Robert H. *The Navy and the Industrial Mobilization in World War II*. Princeton: Princeton University Press, 1951.

"Crepe Hung in Louisiana." *Time*, July 27, 1942, 74.

Deutsch, H. B. "Shipyard Bunyan." *Saturday Evening Post*, July 1942, 22–23, 60–62.

Doig, Jameson W., and Erwin C. Hargrove, eds. *Leadership and Innovation: A Biographical Perspective on Entrepreneurs in Government*. Baltimore: Johns Hopkins University Press, 1987.

"Drive Them Off the Floor." *Time*, Mar. 10, 1947, 83.

Duffield, Eugene S. "Officials Wince as Fabulous Mr. Kaiser Heads for Washington." *Wall Street Journal*, Sept. 5, 1942, 1.

Durr, Clifford. *Early History of the Defense Plant Corporation*. Washington, D.C.: Committee on Public Administration Cases, 1950.

"The Earth Movers I." *Fortune*, Aug. 1943, 99–107, 210–14.

"The Earth Movers II." *Fortune*, Sept. 1943, 119–22, 219–26.

"The Earth Movers III." *Fortune*, Oct. 1943, 139–44, 193–99.

Eccles, Marriner. *Beckoning Frontiers*. New York: Knopf, 1951.

Elson, Robert T. *Time, Inc.: The Intimate History of a Publishing Enterprise, 1923–1941*. New York: Atheneum, 1968.

———. *The World of Time, Inc.: The Intimate History of a Publishing Enterprise, 1941–1960*. New York: Atheneum, 1973.

Emerson, Thomas I. *Young Lawyer for the New Deal: An Insider's Memoir of the Roosevelt Years*. Edited by Joan P. Emerson. Savage, Md.: Rowman & Littlefield, 1991.

"Fabulous Team: Kaiser and Hughes." *Time*, Aug. 31, 1942, 19.

Foner, Eric. *Free Soil, Free Labor, Free Men*. New York: Oxford University Press, 1970.

Foster, Mark S. "Giant of the West: Henry J. Kaiser and Regional Industrialization, 1930–1950." *Business History Review* 59 (spring 1985): 1–23.

———. *Henry J. Kaiser: Builder in the Modern American West.* Austin: University of Texas Press, 1989.

———. "Prosperity's Prophet: Henry J. Kaiser and the Consumer/Suburban Culture, 1930–1950." *Western Historical Quarterly* 17 (Apr. 1986): 165–84.

Fraser, Steve. *Labor Will Rule: Sidney Hillman and the Rise of American Labor.* New York: Free Press, 1991.

Freidel, Frank. *Franklin D. Roosevelt: The Apprenticeship.* Boston: Little, Brown, 1952.

Galambos, Louis. *Cooperation and Competition: The Emergence of a National Trade Association.* Baltimore: Johns Hopkins University Press, 1966.

Galbraith, John Kenneth. *A Life in Our Times: Memoirs.* Boston: Houghton Mifflin, 1981.

Goodwin, Doris Kearns. *No Ordinary Time: Franklin and Eleanor Roosevelt; The Home Front in World War II.* New York: Simon & Schuster, 1994.

Goulden, Joseph C. *The Super-Lawyers: The Small and Powerful World of the Great Washington Law Firms.* New York: Weybright & Talley, 1972.

Gunther, John. *Inside U.S.A.* New York: Harper & Bros., 1947.

Halberstam, David. *The Best and the Brightest.* New York: Random House, 1972.

———. *The Powers That Be.* New York: Knopf, 1979.

Hand, Samuel B. *Counsel and Advise: A Political Biography of Samuel I. Rosenman.* New York: Garland, 1979.

Hassett, William D. *Off the Record with FDR.* New Brunswick: Rutgers University Press, 1958.

Hawley, Ellis W. "Herbert Hoover, the Commerce Secretariat, and the Vision of an 'Associative State,' 1921–1928." *Journal of American History* 61 (1974): 116–40.

———. *The New Deal and the Problem of Monopoly: A Study in Economic Ambivalence.* Princeton: Princeton University Press, 1966.

Heiner, Albert P. *Henry J. Kaiser, American Empire Builder: An Insider's View.* New York: P. Lang, 1989.

Hendricks, Rickey Lynn. "A Necessary Revolution: The Origins of the Kaiser Permanente Medical Care Program." Ph.D. diss., University of Denver, 1987.

"Henry J. Kaiser." *Current Biography*, 1942, 431–35.

"Henry Kaiser's Dream." *Time*, May 25, 1942, 81–82.

Herzstein, Robert E. *Henry R. Luce: A Political Portrait of the Man Who Created the American Century.* New York: Scribner's, 1994.

Hofstadter, Richard. *The Age of Reform: From Bryan to F.D.R.* New York: Knopf, 1955.

Horsky, Charles A. *The Washington Lawyer.* Boston: Little, Brown, 1952.

Hughes, Jonathan. *The Vital Few: American Economic Progress and Its Protagonists.* New York: Oxford University Press, 1973.

Hyman, Sidney. *Marriner S. Eccles: Private Entrepreneur and Public Servant.* Stanford, Calif.: Graduate School of Business, 1976.

Ickes, Harold. *The Lowering Clouds, 1939–1941.* Vol. 3 of *The Secret Diary of Harold Ickes.* New York: Simon & Schuster, 1954.

Ingram, Robert L. *A Builder and His Family.* San Francisco: Privately printed, 1961.

Irons, Peter H. *The New Deal Lawyers.* Princeton: Princeton University Press, 1982.

James, Marquis, and Bessie Rowland James. *The Biography of a Bank: The Story of Bank of America N.T. & S.A.* New York: Harper & Row, 1954.

Janeway, Eliot. *The Struggle for Survival.* New York: Weybright & Talley, 1968.

———. "Trials and Errors." *Fortune,* Sept. 1942, 184.

Jones, Jesse H., with Edward Angly. *Fifty Billion Dollars: My Thirteen Years with the RFC (1932–1945).* New York: Macmillan, 1951.

"Kaiser and the Bureaucrats." *New Republic,* Sept. 7, 1942, 268.

Kaiser, Henry J. *Management Looks at the Postwar World.* New York: Newcomen Society, 1943.

Kaiser Industries. *The Kaiser Story.* Oakland: Kaiser Industries Corporation, 1968.

"Kaiser Plan Fails." *Business Week,* Oct. 24, 1942, 18.

"Kaiser Plans a Steel Plant." *Time,* Apr. 28, 1941, 77.

"Kaiser's Circus: Production Miracle." *Time,* Nov. 23, 1942, 98.

"Kaiser's Problems." *Business Week,* Oct. 10, 1942, 24–25.

"Kaiser's Steel." *Business Week,* May 3, 1941, 25–27.

"Kaiser Takes to the Air." *Time,* July 27, 1942, 71.

Kesselman, Amy. *Fleeting Opportunities: Women Shipyard Workers in Portland and Vancouver during World War II and Reconversion.* Albany: State University of New York Press, 1990.

Ketchum, Richard M. *The Borrowed Years, 1938–1941: America on the Way to War.* New York: Random House, 1989.

Kihm, Frank. "Kaiser Enterprises Organized in Seven Key Corporations." *Wall Street Journal,* Sept. 15, 1942, 1.

Kimball, Warren F. *The Most Unsordid Act: Lend-Lease, 1939–1941.* Baltimore: Johns Hopkins University Press, 1969.

Kiplinger, W. M. *Washington Is Like That.* New York: Harper, 1942.

Kuznets, Simon. *Modern Economic Growth: Rate, Structure, and Spread.* New Haven: Yale University Press, 1972.

Lane, Frederic C. *Ships for Victory.* Baltimore: Johns Hopkins University Press, 1951.

Langworth, Richard M. *Kaiser-Frazer, the Last Onslaught on Detroit: An Intimate Behind-the-Scenes Study of the Postwar American Car Industry.* Princeton: Princeton Publishing, 1975.

Lash, Joseph P. *Dealers and Dreamers: A New Look at the New Deal.* New York: Doubleday, 1988.

Lauderbaugh, Richard A. *American Steel Makers and the Coming of the Second World War.* Ann Arbor: UMI Research Press, 1980.

LeTourneau, Robert G. *Mover of Men and Mountains: The Autobiography of R. G. LeTourneau.* Englewood Cliffs, N.J.: Prentice-Hall, 1960.

Leuchtenburg, William E. *Franklin D. Roosevelt and the New Deal, 1932–1940.* New York: Harper & Row, 1963.

Lewis, David L. *The Public Image of Henry Ford: An American Folk Hero and His Company.* Detroit: Wayne State University Press, 1976.

Lichting, Allan J. "Tommy the Cork: The Secret World of Washington's First Modern Lobbyist." *Washington,* Feb. 1987, 41–49.

Limerick, Patricia Nelson. *Legacy of Conquest: The Unbroken Past of the American West.* New York: Norton, 1987.

Lippmann, Walter. "Miracles and Muddles in War Production." *Oakland Tribune*, July 21, 1942.

Lipset, Seymour Martin. *Revolution and Counterrevolution: Change and Persistence in Social Structures*. New Brunswick, N.J.: Transaction Books, 1988.

Littell, Norman M. *My Roosevelt Years*. Edited by Jonathan Dembo. Seattle: University of Washington Press, 1987.

Livesay, Harold C. *American Made: Men Who Shaped the American Economy*. Boston: Little, Brown, 1979.

Loescher, Samuel. *Imperfect Collusion in the Cement Industry*. Cambridge, Mass.: Harvard University Press, 1959.

Louchheim, Katie, ed. *The Making of the New Deal: The Insiders Speak*. Cambridge, Mass.: Harvard University Press, 1983.

Lowitt, Richard. *The New Deal and the West*. Bloomington: Indiana University Press, 1984.

Lundy, Herbert. "Kaiser: Master Builder." *New Republic*, Aug. 24, 1942, 221–23.

"Magnesium, Lesson in Speed." *Time*, Mar. 3, 1941, 67–68.

Marchand, Roland. *Advertising the American Dream: Making Way for Modernity, 1920–1940*. Berkeley: University of California Press, 1985.

"Master Builder." *Business Week*, Mar. 1, 1941, 28.

McCartney, Laton. *Friends in High Places: The Bechtel Story—The Most Secret Corporation and How It Engineered the World*. New York: Simon & Schuster, 1989.

McCullough, David. *Truman*. New York: Simon & Schuster, 1992.

McQuaid, Kim. *Big Business and Presidential Power: From FDR to Reagan*. New York: Morrow, 1982.

———. "Corporate Liberalism in the American Business Community, 1920–1940." *Business History Review* 52 (Autumn 1978): 345–57.

Mead, Margaret. *And Keep Your Powder Dry: An Anthropologist Looks at America*. Freeport, N.Y.: Books for Libraries Press, 1971.

Meikle, Jeffrey L. *Twentieth Century Limited: Industrial Design in America, 1925–1939*. Philadelphia: Temple University Press, 1979.

Mitchell, C. Bradford. *Every Kind of Shipwork: A History of Todd Shipyards Corporation, 1916–1981*. New York: Todd Shipyards Corporation, 1981.

Mooney, Booth. *Builders for Progress*. New York: McGraw-Hill, 1965.

"More Trouble for Andy." *Time*, Feb. 18, 1946, 83.

Morgan, Dan. *Rising in the West: The True Story of an "Okie" Family from the Great Depression through the Reagan Years*. New York: Knopf, 1992.

Morrison, Ann. *Those Were the Days*. Boise: Em-Kayan Press, 1951.

"Mr. Higgins and His Wonderful Boats." *Life*, Aug. 16, 1943, 100–112.

Murphy, Bruce Allen. *The Brandeis/Frankfurter Connection: The Secret Political Activities of Two Supreme Court Justices*. New York: Oxford University Press, 1982.

Nash, Gerald. *The American West in the Twentieth Century: A Short History of an Urban Oasis*. Albuquerque: University of New Mexico Press, 1977.

———. *The American West Transformed: The Impact of the Second World War*. Bloomington: Indiana University Press, 1985.

———. *Creating the West: Historical Interpretations*. Albuquerque: University of New Mexico Press, 1991.

Nelson, Donald. *Arsenal of Democracy: The Story of American War Production*. New York: Harcourt, Brace, 1946.

"Omen for Kaiser." *Time*, Sept. 7, 1942, 89.

Pearson, Drew. *Diaries, 1949–1959*. Edited by Tyler Abell. New York: Holt, Rinehart & Winston, 1974.

———. "Miracle Man Kaiser May Make the WPB Swallow Its Big 'If' on Those Cargo Planes." *San Francisco Chronicle*, Aug. 18, 1942.

"Permanente Squeaks Through." *Time*, Feb. 8, 1943.

Piel, Gerard. "No. 1 Shipbuilder." *Life*, June 29, 1942, 81–89.

Reinsch, J. Leonard. *Getting Elected*. New York: Hippocrene, 1988.

Robertson, James Oliver. *American Myth, American Reality*. New York: Hill & Wang, 1980.

Roosevelt, Franklin D. *Complete Presidential Press Conferences of Franklin D. Roosevelt*. 25 vols. New York: Da Capo Press, 1972.

———. *F.D.R.: His Personal Letters, 1905–1928*. Edited by Elliott Roosevelt. New York: Duell, Sloan & Pearce, 1948.

———. *Franklin D. Roosevelt and Conservation, 1911–1945*. Compiled and edited by Edgar B. Nixon. Hyde Park, N.Y.: General Services Administration, National Archives and Records Service, No. 962, 1957.

———. *Public Papers and Addresses of President Franklin D. Roosevelt*. Compiled by Samuel I. Rosenman. 13 vols. New York: Russell and Russell, 1969.

Rosenman, Samuel I. *Working with Roosevelt*. New York: Harper, 1952.

Ross, Stanley, and Paul C. Wren. "Andrew Jackson Higgins' Dream." *Liberty*, Feb. 13, 1943, 18–19, 67–68.

Rostow, W. W. *The Stages of Economic Growth: A Non-Communist Manifesto*. Cambridge, Eng.: Cambridge University Press, 1960.

Sandilands, Roger J. *The Life and Political Economy of Lauchlin Currie: New Dealer, Presidential Adviser, and Development Economist*. Durham, N.C.: Duke University Press, 1990.

Saunders, Hilary St. George. *Pioneers! O Pioneers!* New York: Macmillan, 1944.

Scherer, F. M. *Industrial Market Structure and Economic Performance*. Chicago: Rand McNally, 1970.

Schlesinger, Arthur M. Jr. *The Coming of the New Deal*. Vol. 2 of *The Age of Roosevelt*. Boston: Houghton Mifflin, 1958.

———. *The Politics of Upheaval*. Vol. 3 of *The Age of Roosevelt*. Boston: Houghton Mifflin, 1960.

———. *A Thousand Days: John F. Kennedy in the White House*. Boston: Houghton Mifflin, 1965.

Schumpeter, Joseph. *Capitalism, Socialism, and Democracy*. New York: Harper & Row, 1975.

———. *The Theory of Economic Development*. New York: Oxford University Press, 1974.

Schwartz, Jordan A. *The New Dealers: Power Politics in the Age of Roosevelt*. New York: Knopf, 1993.

Seeley, Bruce E. *Building the American Highway System: Engineers as Policy Makers*. Philadelphia: Temple University Press, 1987.

"Services Critical of Civilian Job." *Business Week*, Aug. 22, 1942, 5.

Sherwood, Robert E. *Roosevelt and Hopkins: An Intimate History*. New York: Harper, 1948.

"Ship Purge." *Business Week*, May 16, 1942, 7.

Smith, Henry Nash. *Virgin Land: The American West as Symbol and Myth*. Cambridge, Mass.: Harvard University Press, 1971.

Somers, Herman Miles. *Presidential Agency: OWMR, the Office of War Mobilization and Reconversion*. Cambridge, Mass.: Harvard University Press, 1950.

Stanford Research Institute. *The California Economy, 1947–1980*. Menlo Park, Calif.: Stanford Research Institute, 1961.

Steel, Ronald. *Walter Lippmann and the American Century*. New York: Vintage Books, 1981.

Stevens, Joseph E. *Hoover Dam: An American Adventure*. Norman: University of Oklahoma Press, 1988.

Strahan, Jerry E. *Andrew Jackson Higgins and the Boats That Won World War II*. Baton Rouge: Louisiana State University Press, 1994.

Susman, Warren I. *Culture as History: The Transformation of American Society in the Twentieth Century*. New York: Pantheon Books, 1984.

Swanberg, W. A. *Luce and His Empire*. New York: Scribner's, 1972.

Taylor, Frank J. "Builder No. 1." *Saturday Evening Post*, June 7, 1941, 9–11, 120–24.

Terkel, Studs. *"The Good War": An Oral History of World War Two*. New York: Pantheon Books, 1984.

Time Capsule/1942. New York: Time-Life Books, 1968.

"Trouble for H. J." *Time*, June 10, 1946, 83.

"Trouble for Kaiser." *Time*, Mar. 4, 1946, 79.

"Tugwell Upped." *Time*, June 25, 1934, 10.

Turner, Frederick Jackson. "Significance of the Frontier in American History." In *The Frontier in American History*, 3–43. New York: Henry Holt, 1920.

U.S. Bureau of the Census. *Fifteenth Census of the U.S.: 1930*. Washington, D.C.: U.S. Government Printing Office, 1933.

———. *The Statistical History of the United States from Colonial Times to the Present*. New York: Basic Books, 1976.

U.S. Bureau of Public Roads. *Report of a Study of the California Highway System to the California Highway Commission and Highway Engineer*. Washington, D.C.: U.S. Government Printing Office, 1920.

U.S. Civilian Production Administration. *Program and Administration*. Vol. 1 of *Industrial Mobilization for War: History of the War Production Board and Predecessor Agencies, 1940–1945*. Washington, D.C.: U.S. Government Printing Office, 1947.

U.S. Civilian Production Administration. Industrial Statistics Division. *War Industrial Facilities Authorized July 1940–August 1945*. Washington, D.C.: U.S. Government Printing Office, 1946.

U.S. Congress, House Committee on Appropriations. *Hearings, Second Deficiency Appropriations Bill*, 72d Cong., 2d sess., 1932. Washington, D.C.: U.S. Government Printing Office, 1932.

U.S. Congress, House Committee on Labor. *Hearings, Regulations of Wages Paid to Employees by Contractors Awarded Government Building Contracts*, 72d Cong., 2d sess., 1932. Washington, D.C.: U.S. Government Printing Office, 1932.

U.S. House Committee on the Merchant Marine and Fisheries. *Higgins Contracts*, 77th Cong., 2d sess., 1942. Washington, D.C.: U.S. Government Printing Office, 1942.

U.S. House Committee on Naval Affairs. *Investigation of the Progress of the War Effort*, 78th Cong., 1st sess., 1943. Washington, D.C.: U.S. Government Printing Office, 1943.

U.S. Congress, Senate Committee on Interstate Commerce. *Hearings on S. 4055, Uniform Delivered Prices*. 74th Cong., 2d sess., 1936. Washington, D.C.: U.S. Government Printing Office, 1936.

U.S. Senate Special Committee Investigating National Defense Program. *Hearings*. 77th Cong., 1st sess., 1941. Washington, D.C.: U.S. Government Printing Office, 1941.

———. *Hearings*. 78th Cong., 1st sess., 1943. Washington, D.C.: U.S. Government Printing Office, 1943.

———. *Hearings*. 80th Cong., 1st sess., 1947. Washington, D.C.: U.S. Government Printing Office, 1947.

———. *Higgins Contracts*. 77th Cong., 2d sess, 1942. Washington, D.C.: U.S. Government Printing Office, 1942.

———. *Part 14*. 77th Cong., 2d sess., 1942. Washington, D.C.: U.S. Government Printing Office, 1942.

U.S. Temporary National Economic Committee. *Economic Prologue*. Part 1 of *Hearings, Concentration of Economic Power*. Washington, D.C.: U.S. Government Printing Office, 1938.

———. *Government Purchasing—An Economic Commentary*. Monograph No. 19 of *Investigation of Concentration of Economic Power*. Washington, D.C.: U.S. Government Printing Office, 1940.

———. *Iron and Steel*. Part 19 of *Hearings, Concentration of Economic Power*. Washington, D.C.: U.S. Government Printing Office, 1939.

Vatter, Harold G. *The U.S. Economy in World War II*. New York: Columbia University Press, 1985.

Velie, Lester. "The Truth about Henry Kaiser." *Collier's*, July 27, 1946, 11–12, 65–66; Aug. 3, 1946, 24–26, 71; Aug. 10, 1946, 23, 63–65.

Wallace, Henry Agard. *The Price of Vision: The Diary of Henry A. Wallace, 1942–1946*. Edited by John Morton Blum. Boston: Houghton Mifflin, 1973.

Ward, Geoffrey C., ed. *Closest Companion: The Unknown Story of the Intimate Friendship between Franklin Roosevelt and Margaret Suckley*. Boston: Houghton Mifflin, 1995.

The Warren Story. Birmingham, Ala.: N.p., 1969.

Waters, Frank. *The Colorado*. New York: Rinehart, 1946.

Watkins, T. H. *Righteous Pilgrim: The Life and Times of Harold L. Ickes, 1874–1952*. New York: H. Holt, 1990.

White, G. Edward. *Earl Warren: A Public Life*. New York: Oxford University Press, 1982.

"Who Can't?" *Time*, Aug. 24, 1942, 12–13.

Winkler, Allan M. *The Politics of Propaganda: The Office of War Information, 1942–1945*. New Haven: Yale University Press, 1978.

"Winner: Kaiser." *Time*, Aug. 17, 1942, 15–16.

"Wonder Man Hit." *Business Week*, Mar. 27, 1943, 30–32.

Yates, JoAnne. *Control through Communication: The Rise of System in American Management*. Baltimore: Johns Hopkins University Press, 1989.

INDEX

(CIO), 75, 83, 155, 170, 206 (n. 71); political action committee, 160, 216–17 (n. 153). *See also* AFL-CIO

Consolidated Vultee Aircraft Company, 84, 130

Construction industry: Roosevelt and, 14, 29–30; Kaiser and, 15, 17, 19–20, 21–22, 26–27; mechanization of, 15, 20; difficulties of succeeding in, 17–18, 19, 22; working conditions in, 18, 42; day labor in, 22, 25, 26; Hoover and, 25–26; public works projects and, 26–27; political lobbying, 27–28

Constructor, 27, 34–35

Contractors Indemnity Exchange, 19

Coolidge, Calvin, 27

Coolidge administration, 36

Corcoran, Thomas: on Kaiser, 8, 137–38; as Washington lawyer/lobbyist, 12–13, 88, 92–94, 104–5; retained by Kaiser, 13, 24, 88, 90, 98; on LBJ, 29; as New Deal antitruster, 54, 55–56; in RFC, 93, 94, 98, 201 (n. 18); and Roosevelt, 94, 98, 165; as antibureaucratic New Dealer, 94, 201–2 (n. 26); and Kaiser's magnesium venture, 98–99, 100, 101, 102–4, 105; and rumors about Kaiser, 154

Corporate liberalism, 8–9

Corporations, 88, 97–98, 110, 189 (n. 20)

Corrigan, Douglas, 136

Council of Economic Advisors, 80

Covington and Burling, 90–91

Cowles, Gardner, Jr., 166–67

Cox, Oscar: as lawyer for Kaiser, 24, 90, 177, 217–18 (n. 15); in Roosevelt administration, 145, 146, 147, 148–50, 151–52; and arming of Allies, 149–50, 213 (n. 25); and Kaiser's chairmanship of Nonpartisan Association, 163–64, 166

Crum, Bartley, 167

Cuba: road construction in, 31, 32, 36

Cuneo, Ernest, 103

Current Biography, 115

Currie, Lauchlin: as economic adviser to Roosevelt, 54, 59, 80, 85; and Keynesian government spending, 55, 71; and 1937

recession, 55–56, 196 (n. 116); and Kaiser's West Coast steel plant, 57, 80–81, 82–83, 84, 85, 88, 89, 106; and Kaiser's magnesium venture, 96; as presidential emissary to China, 97

Curtiss Company, 213 (n. 25)

Cutler, Lloyd, 13, 24, 87, 92, 177

Davenport, Russell, 167

Day care, 43, 212 (n. 17)

Day labor, 22, 26, 27

Defense Plant Corporation, 141

Defense spending, 35, 179

Delano, Frederick, 57, 60

Democracy: "arsenal of," 1, 101; voter turnout and, 156, 157, 158

Democratic National Committee, 158, 160

Democratic Party, 27, 156, 159, 167

Dennison, Harry S., 9

Dewey, Thomas E., 155, 159, 161, 162, 166, 169–70

Dietrich, Noah, 141

Disney, Walt, 120, 172

Doolittle, James H., 117

Douglas, Donald W., 130

Douglas, William O., 157

Dow Chemical Company, 97; magnesium monopoly, 77, 84, 86, 103; napalm production, 189 (n. 18)

Dulles, John Foster, 90

Dunn, Gano, 105

DuPont Company, 213 (n. 25)

Durr, Clifford, 98, 212–13 (n. 24)

Eccles, Marriner, 57; as president of Utah Construction, 38, 70, 79; as chairman of Federal Reserve Board, 54, 56, 70, 85; and New Deal economic policy, 55–56, 195–96 (n. 101); and steel industry, 56, 195 (n. 96); support of Kaiser's ventures, 70, 71, 85, 89; and defense mobilization, 70–71, 95; and Kaiser's magnesium venture, 77, 78, 79, 84; and Kaiser's West Coast steel plant, 82–83, 84

Economist, 35

Eisenhower, Dwight D., 9, 107

Kaiser for steel plant, 65, 92; and
defense mobilization, 70–71; Corcoran
and, 93, 94, 98, 201 (n. 18); loan to
Kaiser for magnesium plant, 96, 97,
98–99, 100–101; wartime loans to
Kaiser, 101, 176

Reed, Stanley, 93

Regional development, 36

Reid, Mrs. Ogden, 159–60, 166, 167, 216
(n. 124)

Reilly, John D., 77, 95, 98

Reisman, David, 201–2 (n. 26)

Republican Party, 27; Willkie and, 68, 162;
Roosevelt's Teamsters speech and, 167;
capture of Congress in 1946, 176

Republic Pictures, 128, 208–9 (n. 34)

Republic Steel: proposed partnership with
Kaiser, 69, 73, 76, 77, 80–81, 83–84, 85

Reynolds, Earl, 203 (n. 3)

Reynolds Metals Company, 180

Richmond Field Hospital, 132

Road construction: in California, 17, 28;
Kaiser and, 19, 20, 21, 23–25, 31; federal
funding of, 19, 183; Kaiser's superhighway plan, 63, 71

Robert E. Peary, U.S.S., 115

Robertson, James Oliver, 6, 189 (n. 20)

Robinson, Samuel, 121–22

Rock, Sand, and Gravel Producers Association of Northern California, 42

Rogers, Ginger, 142

Rogers, Will, 3

Roosevelt, Anna, 118

Roosevelt, Eleanor, 64, 164–65, 212 (n. 17)

Roosevelt, Franklin D.: relations with
Kaiser, 9, 10, 39, 64, 85, 105; proposal of
political future for Kaiser, 9–10, 152–54;
as assistant navy secretary, 11, 50, 201
(n. 25); disregard for bureaucratic organization and jurisdiction, 11, 89, 94–95,
201 (n. 25); and construction industry,
14, 29–30; and antitrust campaign, 30,
182; and cement industry pricing, 47,
50–51; business hostility toward, 53, 55,
182; and economic policy, 55, 56, 85–86;
promotion of western steelmaking,

57–62, 73–74, 105, 106; and support of
Allies, 59, 95, 149–50; and war mobilization, 62, 64, 76, 77, 86, 106; and Kaiser's
steel venture, 74, 83, 85; antipathy for
Girdler, 75, 79–80; and growth of federal government, 90; relations with
Brandeis and Frankfurter, 93, 150; and
loan to Kaiser for magnesium plant,
99; and Luce, 110–11, 113, 154; and civil
rights, 113; and Kaiser's shipbuilding
venture, 120, 124–25, 139; and Kaiser's
cargo plane proposal, 139, 140; in 1944
election, 148, 152–53, 156, 158, 159,
160–61, 167, 170–71; negotiations with
Willkie, 162; and Kaiser's Nonpartisan
Association chairmanship, 163, 164,
165–66, 167, 168, 171; Teamsters union
speech, 167–69; death of, 172, 176

Roosevelt administration: assistance for
Kaiser's new ventures, 30, 56–57; and
cement industry pricing, 47, 50; and
1937–38 recession, 53–54, 55; Girdler's
hostility toward, 74, 75, 76, 77, 81, 82;
and government entrepreneurship,
78–79, 182–83; Time/Life publications
and, 109–10; and automobile industry,
147. *See also* New Deal

Roosevelt and Hopkins (Sherwood), 64

Root, Clark, Buckner and Ballantine, 166

Rosenman, Sam, 90, 217 (n. 13); work for
Roosevelt, 149, 150, 151, 168; promotion
of political career for Kaiser, 152, 153,
154–55; negotiations with Willkie, 162;
and Kaiser's recruitment by Nonpartisan
Association, 164, 165; retained as lawyer
by Kaiser, 176–77

Rosten, Leo, 109

San Francisco–Oakland Bay Bridge, 201
(n. 18)

San Jose Cement Company, 48

Sarnoff, David, 4

Saturday Evening Post, 113, 122

Saunders, Hilary St. George, 120

Schlesinger, Arthur, Jr., 44, 192 (n. 3)

Schram, Emil, 99

DATE DUE
